ALSO BY JOE POSNANSKI

The Soul of Baseball

The Machine

PATERNO

JOE POSNANSKI

SIMON & SCHUSTER

New York London Toronto Sydney New Delhi

SIMON & SCHUSTER
1230 Avenue of the Americas
New York, NY 10020

Copyright © 2012 by Joe Posnanski

All rights reserved, including the right to reproduce this book
or portions thereof in any form whatsoever. For information,
address Simon & Schuster Subsidiary Rights Department,
1230 Avenue of the Americas, New York, NY 10020.

First Simon & Schuster hardcover edition August 2012

SIMON & SCHUSTER and colophon are registered trademarks of
Simon & Schuster, Inc.

For information about special discounts for bulk purchases, please
contact Simon & Schuster Special Sales at 1-866-506-1949 or
business@simonandschuster.com.

The Simon & Schuster Speakers Bureau can bring authors to your live
event. For more information or to book an event, contact the Simon
& Schuster Speakers Bureau at 1-866-248-3049 or visit our website at
www.simonspeakers.com.

Designed by Joy O'Meara

Manufactured in the United States of America

1   3   5   7   9   10   8   6   4   2

Library of Congress Cataloging-in-Publication Data is available.

ISBN: 978-1-4516-5749-4
ISBN: 978-1-4516-5751-7 (ebook)

Endpaper photo credits: Jason Sipes/Altoona Mirror (front);
Patrick Waksmunski/Altoona Mirror (back)

For Margo, Elizabeth, and Katherine

Contents

ACT III: SUCCESS

ACT IV: WHAT COMES AFTER

THE FINAL ACT

We have difficulty as a nation—this is American, and it relates to our particular time—we have difficulty admiring people. We take such pride in our skepticism. But the natural antithesis of skepticism, the celebration and virtue of accomplishment, is wandering lost somewhere. It is the age of the antihero.

—BILL JAMES

PATERNO

Joe Paterno runs through the smoke and onto the field before the 2006
Orange Bowl (*Jason Sipes/Altoona Mirror*)

{ *Aria* }

Joe Paterno
speech to high school coaches
February 5, 1993, Hershey, Pennsylvania

What is a coach? We are teachers. Educators. We have the same obligations as all teachers, except we probably have more influence over young people than anybody but their families. And, in a lot of cases, more than their families.

To teach an academic subject is certainly not easy, but compared to coaching, it is. We can say two plus two is four to every kid and be sure that we are right. But in coaching, we have to literally get to the soul of the people we are dealing with.

We have to work with emotion, commitment, discipline, loyalty, pride.

The things that make the difference in a person's life.

They look to us for examples. A boy wants to be a man. But he doesn't know what a man is. They look to us for poise. Everybody doesn't get a fair shake in life. They look to us for values. You must relate athletic experiences to life. You are role models.

They look to us for consistency. We have to realize a kid will love us one day and hate us the next. That cannot change who we are and what we are about. We are there to help them reach for excellence . . . and not just win games.

We have to be understanding but tough. Firm. Real firmness is always helpful. Bill Clinton said, "I feel for you." Vince Lombardi said, "The pain is in your head."

Tom Boswell of the Washington Post *wrote about the difference beween excellence and success. He wrote:*

"Many people, particularly in sports, believe that success and excellence are the same. They are not. No distinction in the realm of games is more important. Success is tricky, perishable, and often outside our control. On the other hand, excellence is dependable, lasting, and largely within our control. Let me emphasize at once that nobody is all one way or another. The desire for success and love of excellence coexist in all of us. The question is: Where does the balance lie? In a pinch, what guides us?"

I think we all have to ask ourselves that question. In a pinch, what guides us—success or excellence? Which will give us shelter when the storm clouds gather?

{ *Overture* }

This is the story of a man named Joe Paterno, who in his long life was called moral and immoral, decent and scheming, omniscient and a figurehead, hero and fraud, Saint Joe and the devil. A life, of course, cannot be reduced to a single word, but Joe Paterno had something bold and soaring in his personality that attracted extremes. That boldness compelled him to do remarkable and unprecedented things. That boldness also led people to say that, at the end, his failures destroyed whatever good he had done.

THE OLD MAN SAT AT the kitchen table and stared at the pages scattered in front of him. He did not want to read them. He told his sons and daughters that he already knew what was written there, understood it well enough. He did not need to waste any more time on it. The old man had never been patient about such things. Digest and move on. Win or lose and then plan for the next game. "Continue to advance until you run out of ammunition," General George S. Patton had commanded. The old man admired Patton.

"Time is our enemy" is how the old man said it, and also "Put no effort into anything that isn't helpful." There was too much to do. There was no time to linger. But this was different. His sons and daughters insisted that he read every terrible word, that he stop for a moment, just stop, and let those words shock and suffocate him the way they shocked and suffocated millions. "Dad," they told him, "you have to know what you are up against."

Behind him—through the living room, past the front door, beyond the lawn—three dozen television cameras pointed at the house. Men and women, many of them young, held notepads and microphones and sandwiches. They drank soda pop through straws poking out of cardboard cups, and they talked to each other, mostly about the lack of hotel accommodations to be found anywhere near this small Pennsylvania town. They stared every now and again at the corner house on McKee Street to see if anything had changed. Did the door crack open? Was a window shade pulled up? They told each other gruesome jokes to pass the time.

To the old man's right was a window, and through it he could see television satellite trucks in the parking lot by the small park next door. The old man had never spent much time reminiscing— nostalgia too slowed life's advance—but lately he had found himself looking out this window and thinking about when his children played tag in that park, threw footballs to each other, spun in circles in the bright sunlight until they fell onto the grass. Those children were grown now, and they moved around him slowly, moons revolving in his gravity, and every now and again they peered in and tried to read the expression on his face. The park outside was called Sunset Park.

The old man tried to concentrate on the pages in front of him, but the words jumped up and stung him. *Penetration. Erection. Genitals. Oral.* What did these words have to do with him? His life? Even as a boy, when he played quarterback on his high school football team back in Brooklyn, he would lecture his teammates in his high-pitched squeal when one of them unleashed a swear word. "Aw gee, come on, guys, let's keep it clean!" They thought him a prude even then. He had lived a sheltered life—not by accident but by choice. The Paternos never even watched any television except *The Wonderful*

World of Disney on Sunday nights. The old man knew many things. He knew Latin. He knew why Aeneas pressed on. He knew where to find good ice cream, the words of the Boy Scout oath, the difference between Johannes Bach and Johann Sebastian Bach. He knew why Hemingway was greater than Fitzgerald and never hesitated to illuminate doubters. He knew the power of opera and spent much of his life working with overtures and intermezzos and arias playing in the background. Most of all, he knew how to turn young men into football players and football players into a football team and football teams into winners. The old man stared at the papers in front of him and asked his children questions about sex that embarrassed everyone, and he wondered if he knew anything at all.

THE TABLE IN JOE AND Sue Paterno's kitchen was large and round, as if pulled from Camelot. It was sixty-two inches in diameter, made of light brown oak, and stood thirty-one inches from the floor. The table was built by August Pohland, an architect who lived in Latrobe, Pennsylvania. Everyone called him Augie. He was one of those men who instinctively knew how to fix things, make things, solve problems. "My father," said Sue Pohland Paterno, "my father could do anything."

Pohland built his first round kitchen table many years before, after he returned from World War II. He made it for his own large family. This table was an inch-by-inch copy of that first one. This table fit neatly into the Paterno kitchen, but only after the kitchen was expanded and renovated, after Joe Paterno had become famous and, to his enduring and vocal embarrassment, wealthy. A thirty-inch lazy Susan stood in the middle, and it turned on a ball bearing discarded from one of the factories in Latrobe.

"Take 'em all," the factory foreman told Augie. "What are you going to do with old ball bearings?"

"I have an idea," Augie told him. He was a man of ideas.

When the house and children were small, when Joe was scraping by as the low-paid football coach of a cow college in the middle of nowhere, the table overwhelmed the room. It was pushed close to a corner, and any child seated on the wrong side of it at mealtime had no means of escape. A simple bathroom request would require a reverse game of dominoes, with every family member to the right standing in succession to allow the child to pass. When the table was used for family games of hearts, a card dealt weakly would settle in the middle and a child would have to stand on her chair and stretch simply to reach it.

Everyone told a slightly different story about how the Paternos got the table. One day the Pohland and Paterno families were gathered together and for reasons forgotten were talking about wishes—for Christmas gifts, family heirlooms, wedding presents, nobody really remembers. After this talk swirled around for a while, Joe spoke up: "You can keep all that stuff. All I want is the kitchen table." That was why Augie Pohland built this table, exactly like the one in his own home. He built it because it was Joe's only wish. "I don't know what I was thinking exactly," Joe said. "I guess I saw that table and just wanted a family that grew up around it."

DON ABBEY LIMPED FROM ROOM to room in his mansion on top of a mountain overlooking Pasadena. He pointed at a bear rug and the photograph nearby of him killing that very bear. "One shot," he said. He pointed at an enormous painting of his parents. He pointed at an award given to him for being the best blocker in America back in college. There was a time, not so long ago, when he was an athletic oddity, a speedy 240-pound Penn State fullback when some offensive linemen did not weigh that much. "I could block anybody. I didn't fear anybody." He paused. "I didn't even fear Joe. I hated him. But I didn't fear him."

The award for best blocker was given to him in 1969, twelve knee operations and a lifetime ago, and until recently he did not allow himself to think about it. His football years at Penn State pained him. Joe Paterno was the reason. "Penn State turned me into a functioning alcoholic," he explained. "Penn State gave me so much hate and so much depression in a way that it just took me a lot of living to get to the point to handle that and put it aside. . . . I didn't like Joe. He damn near killed me. He damn near destroyed me."

When Abbey had sunk to his lowest point, he pushed off the bottom and rushed back toward the surface. He pumped his fury into a real estate business. He never settled down. He never started a family. He worked relentlessly and made himself a billionaire. "I would always, in the early years, have two management criteria. One: Would my parents be proud of my decision? And: What would Joe do? Because I'm going to do the opposite."

Strange, then, that as he got older he found himself thinking about Joe Paterno. His feelings were not about forgiveness, not exactly. Even all these years later, as he walked by a photograph of an old Penn State coach named Bob Higgins, he stopped. "There's a real football coach," he said, pointing. "I mean no disrespect, but that's the kind of person I think of as a great football coach and a great man. . . . Joe had a shitty management style. Plain and simple."

No, his feelings were not about forgiveness because he was not certain that he had forgiven Paterno. His feelings were about something deeper than that, something he saw in himself. He thought about the way Paterno planned practices and games. Abbey planned like that. He thought about the way Paterno held his players to high standards—go to class, wear a tie, look people in the eye—and would not allow anyone around him to live a lazy life. Abbey did not want lazy people around him either. After more than two decades of silence, Abbey and Paterno began to talk again. And Abbey found the strangest thing: the man he had hated for much of his life, well, they shared common ground.

"You know, the guy worked his ass off," Abbey said. "He was a brilliant strategist, he out-prepared everybody, he had great fundamentals of what's right and wrong—as he defined what's right and wrong. And he actualized it. He set the goals. They were his goals. I didn't agree with them a lot of the time, but, boy, he ran things based on his goals."

Abbey smiled. The city was three miles below. Under the house was a shooting gallery where Hollywood stars, Tom Cruise among them, practiced for their movies. He liked hearing the sound of gunfire cracking from below. The walls were covered with paintings and photographs of family and friends and the place where he grew up. And heroes. George Patton was there. Vince Lombardi was there. Joe Paterno was there too.

"The key is to unravel the myth and explain his greatness. Because Joe had greatness. But the myth is not his greatness. Joe, for all his human fallacies that I love to talk about because I have a bunch too, had something else—something much harder to find."

PEOPLE WANDERED UP TO THE statue of Joe Paterno that stands by Beaver Stadium. Paterno disliked this statue. Not because of the craftsmanship or the dimensions or anything like that. The statue and the stone wall behind it and the words carved into the stone, it all felt like a celebration of self, a mausoleum. But even these were not the reasons for Paterno's distaste. The reason was a single finger, the index finger, that the statue of Joe Paterno raised to the heavens. We're No. 1. That's what that finger said. To Paterno, that finger was proof that they never got him, never really understood what drove him.

The people gathered at the statue now were not thinking about such subtleties. To them, the statue was something holy, the first place they thought of coming to when Paterno's name crossed their mind. This was the night that Penn State fired Joe Paterno. The night air chilled, and boyfriends wrapped their arms around girlfriends, fraternity brothers stood shoulder to shoulder, a father walked up in a Penn State sweatshirt that had shrunk, or perhaps the father had grown.

They stood in complete silence. This was not the conventional silence of, say, the moment before a show or the beginning of a class. This silence weighed down the air, made it heavy and stifling, the quiet you might feel at the Vietnam Memorial. Tears slid down cheeks, but no one cried out loud. Breath turned to steam, but no one breathed too loudly. A boy briefly tried to start a chant—*Joe Pa! Joe Pa!*—but no one followed and his words drowned in the dense autumn air. Silence returned with a vengeance.

Young men and women sat on the stone wall behind the statue and their feet dangled over the side. Nobody kicked, and nobody moved. They seemed like statues themselves, a part of the scenery. A boy of maybe eighteen kneeled in front of the statue as if in prayer. A girl of twenty or so felt her phone vibrate but did not answer it.

What would they say about Joe Paterno? That they grew up admiring him? That they came to Penn State because he coached there? That some of their greatest memories were of sitting here at Beaver Stadium, which towers behind Paterno's statue, watching the teams he coached? They would say that he was a man of principle, a man of education, a teacher first, a role model, a decent man above all. They would repeat some of his favorite sayings. "Go to the ball." "Be on time." "Good things happen when you hustle." They would recount his most famous victories—over Missouri in '70, over Louisiana State in '74, over Miami in '87, over Michigan in '94, over Ohio State in '05—and they would list a few of his best players. They would fill the dead spaces with trivia or plaudits or singular memories that, when spoken out loud, do not sound like very much.

He had his players wear plain uniforms!

He turned down millions of dollars to stay in State College!

He built Penn State, often with his own money!

What would they say? Joe Paterno taught life lessons. He graduated his players. He treated black and white with respect and with expectation. He stood for things—for discipline, for teamwork, for effort, focus, charity, triumph. That's what they would say. Yes, he won. The fans would only reluctantly admit that Paterno's long parade of victories mattered because the cynics, the angry ones, believed that they loved him only for those victories. But damn it, he did win! He made them feel like winners!

What would they say?

Across campus, students marched. Some threw rocks. Some turned over a television truck. Across America, people saw those rioting students, and they wept for America's youth, for those misguided young people whose priorities needed adjusting and who could not understand what really mattered in the world.

Here at the statue Joe Paterno never liked, they did not move, and they said nothing at all.

ON JUNE 22, 2012, JERRY Sandusky was convicted of forty-five counts of sexual abuse of young boys. Seven months earlier, two Penn State officials, Athletic Director Tim Curley and a university vice president, Gary Schultz, were charged with perjury and failure to report the incident that Mike McQueary and Joe Paterno had told them about in 2001.

This book is not a defense of Joe Paterno. It was not my intention to write such a book, and it was also not Paterno's expectation for me to write such a book. The only thing he ever asked of me was to write the truth as I found it. To help, he and Sue Paterno lent me many of his personal files and asked their family and friends and former players to be open with me. Paterno took the time to try to answer any question I asked. He intended to keep this open conversation going until the book was finished.

He died before the book was done.

I include this interlude to explain that what follows is the story of Joe Paterno's life. It is about a childhood in Brooklyn, a time at war, a college life at Brown University, and sixty-one years of coaching at Penn State. It is also about the ending, how Paterno was swept away by the scandal that led to his dismissal and the ten cancer-wracked weeks he lived after that. It is how he felt about it all and how the people around him responded. This is not a story about Jerry Sandusky. It is not a story about Penn State. It is not a detective story about a small community overrun by a media blitzkrieg. And it is also not the story of what might be true or assumptions or theories made in the dark. At the time of this writing, Sandusky is in jail serving what is essentially a life sentence, Tim Curley's and Gary Schultz's trials are also approaching, and an investigation by former FBI director Louis Freeh concluded that Penn State officials, Paterno among them, failed to protect a child against a child predator and "exhibited a striking lack of empathy for Sandusky's victims."

But Joe Paterno's life is over. I am aware that opinions have calcified so that many people have grown deaf to other viewpoints; with such horrible crimes being committed and alleged, it could not be any other way. But I have tried to be guided by the words in Walter Van Tilburg Clark's *The Ox-Bow Incident*: "We desire justice. And justice has never been obtained in haste and strong feeling."

"I GOT A QUESTION FOR you," Guido D'Elia said.

"Shoot."

He sat across the table, a pained look on his face. There had to be a record. That's what D'Elia believed. He had been a Penn State marketing man for a few years. He was Joe Paterno's man for much longer. The first time he met Paterno, he was a long-haired kid from Altoona who had some vague notion about becoming a big-shot television producer. That sounded better to him than working on the railroad, which is more or less what everyone else in Altoona did. They first met at a Penn State football game at West Virginia, where D'Elia was coordinating the television coverage. Someone said to him, "It's about time you met Coach Paterno." They were at a Holiday Inn whose room doors opened to the outside, and they walked down a long hall, door after door, and at the end they pulled one open. There was Joe Paterno sitting on one of the beds. Two players were sitting on the other bed, a third player sitting on the floor. They were all looking at the small television screen; Jimmy Carter and Gerald Ford were debating each other in their bid for the presidency.

What D'Elia remembered—and what he also never forgot, which is a little bit different—was the way Paterno was pressing the young men.

"Hey, what did you think of that argument?"

"Why do you think he said that?"

"How do you think that will play with the audience?"

"Who do you believe more?"

How long ago was that? Thirty years ago? Forty? The whole world had changed. But to D'Elia there was a part of Joe Paterno that never changed, a part of him that remained in that room, educating, challenging, questioning, making those players think. Oh, D'Elia was no lamb. Over the years he came to know Paterno in ways that few others would. He worked for Joe, he was Joe's circus barker, his hatchet man, his crisis manager, his tackling dummy, and the friend who told the old man things he did not want to hear. D'Elia often found himself on the sharp edge of some cutting Paterno fury. In all his life, right up to the end, Paterno never once told D'Elia that he was sorry, and he never told him "Thank you." They did not need those words. D'Elia understood that Paterno was no saint. He knew it better than anybody else.

But he also knew that Joe Paterno was real. The whole thing was real. That's what made it worthwhile. Paterno did not cheat in recruiting. He used every measure of threats and testing and pressure to prevent his players from using steroids. He did not sacrifice education for football victories. He did not use players and discard them. He did not lie to players. This was what made it all worthwhile, this was why D'Elia loved the man—not like a son looking through unfocused eyes but like a skeptic who had finally found one thing he could believe in.

"Why?" D'Elia asked me.

"Why what?"

"Why didn't he follow up? Why?"

He asked this in the most furious moment, when the scandal had reached its highest pitch, when people openly charged Joe Paterno with unspeakable evil. Madness circled. Fury hovered. Nobody could hear anything but the roar. But D'Elia knew all that was just white noise. "We don't want heroes," he had said time and again. "We don't want to believe anyone can be better than ourselves."

But now he looked at me and asked the real question, the one that pounded at him, the question that glowed red beneath all the bluster and lies and absurdities. "Why didn't he follow up?" he asked again.

I looked at him.

"Find the answer to that," he said, "and you have the story."

JOEY PATERNO, THE GRANDSON, COULD do a dead-perfect impression of his grandfather's walk. They were built the same way—a low rib cage, Joey's mother, Kelley, called the family trait—and here he was, shirt sticking out, and he strutted that sideline football strut that his grandfather made his own. Joey wore the tie Joe Paterno wore when he won his 300th game. It was his proudest possession. Joey was twelve.

"They beat Bowling Green 48 to 3 that day," he said.

"How about his 324th win, the one that passed the Bear?" I asked him.

"That was 29 to 27 over Ohio State. They came back from 27 to 9."

His 400th win?

"Too easy: 35 to 21 over Northwestern."

His 200th win?

"That was over Bowling Green too, right?" He smiled proudly. In another room, people lined up to touch the casket of Joe Paterno. In this room, Joey bent his head down and looked just like the old man.

• • •

EVERY FAMILY HAS A STORY that can be told without being told. An expression will trigger it. A word. In the Paterno family, they called it the Shyster Story. At family gatherings, all anyone ever had to do was get red-faced and shout "Shyster!" Everyone else would break out laughing.

The Shyster Story went like this: Back in the early 1970s, the Paterno family went to a restaurant, and Diana, the oldest child, ordered an all-you-can-eat salad. Late in the meal, Mary Kay, the second-oldest, reached over and took a cucumber from Diana's plate and started to munch on it.

"What are you doing?" Joe asked Mary Kay.

"I, uh—"

"What are you doing?" he asked again, this time a bit louder. He had that serious look on his face, the one they all knew meant trouble. Mary Kay looked at her father with confusion.

"You just stole from them," Joe said even louder.

Mary Kay looked helplessly around at the table. No one met her eyes. She quietly said she only took a single cucumber. But Joe was off again. When he started on something, nobody could outtalk him, nobody could drown him out; he was like that all his life. "These people work hard to run a business. You are not supposed to share food. It says, very clearly, all *you* can eat. Not all *you and your sister* can eat. You stole from them."

Here a couple of family members tried, tentatively, to speak up on Mary Kay's behalf. It was a single slice of cucumber. Diana wasn't going to eat it anyway. It was just going to go to waste. It was nothing. But Joe could not be stopped. He pounded the table. He ranted. And finally he said, "You all are a bunch of shysters. I don't want anything to do with you." And he stormed out of the restaurant. By the time the kids had chased after him, he had taken the car and was gone.

He drove around the block a few times and came back a few minutes later, just long enough to scare them into believing that he had really left them there.

The Shyster Story. Whenever the story was brought up, Joe held his ground. "I was right," he insisted every time.

AT THE DINING-ROOM TABLE, PATERNO finished reading the report. He asked a few uncomfortable questions that nobody particularly wanted to answer. Then he asked, "So what are they saying about me out there?" He pointed outside, past the living room, through the window, toward the mass of reporters and their notepads and cameras. His children told him that they—not just the media, but many people all across America—were saying that Joe Paterno had covered up for a child predator. They were saying that Paterno knew exactly what Jerry Sandusky had done and what he was about, that Paterno had protected Sandusky instead of those children. They were saying that after more than a half-century of coaching football at Penn State University, Joe Paterno was willing to let children be harmed in unimaginable ways to protect his legacy.

"How could they think that?" he asked, and no one had the heart to answer. "They really think that if I knew someone was hurting kids, I wouldn't stop it?"

They looked at him.

"Don't they know me? Don't they know what my life has been about?"

ACT I: BEFORE

Every kid I knew there, the meek and the tough guys, the word to describe them when they came to mind was always the same: Innocent.

—WILLIAM PETER BLATTY

{ *Prelude* }

Bill Blatty, who later in life would achieve worldwide fame by
writing *The Exorcist*, sat in Otto's, a small sandwich and soda
shop in Brooklyn. It was 1944. Blatty was a sophomore at
Brooklyn Prep, a high school famous for its rigorous academic standards. He had just finished competing in a citywide oratorical contest and had come to Otto's to mope. He was sure he had won. The
people in the audience seemed sure he had won. As best Blatty could
tell, even the competitors thought he had won. But the two judges
were not so sure. They picked someone else to be the victor. Blatty
was shattered.

"I tried drowning my sorrows with a lemon coke and a minced
ham sandwich," he remembered more than sixty years later. "It didn't
work." He started to walk out of Otto's to sulk outside, wearing a hang-
dog expression usually reserved for characters in comic books, over
whose heads gray clouds hover.

Joe Paterno walked in. Blatty described him as swooping in. Joe
Paterno, even then, moved in high contrast, a bright-color blur in a
black-and-white movie. He was the quarterback of the football team,
the captain of the basketball team, and the student council president
at Brooklyn Prep. He was a straight-A student, of course. But there was

something else about him, something that Blatty could see but could not yet put into words. For the rest of Paterno's life, people would tell breathless stories about him, and the quality that connected these stories was their plainness. These would not be stories of Paterno pulling someone out of a fire or saving a cat stuck in a tree. No, the stories were about his doing the simplest things: uttering a kind word, telling a small joke, offering his seat to a near-stranger. George H. W. Bush loved to tell about the time Joe Paterno got him a drink. "He served me!" the president said, wonder in his voice. It's hard to define that kind of magnetism, the sort that makes the simplest gestures feel extraordinary, even to U.S. presidents. It is fair to say that it's a mixed gift.

Whatever makes up that sort of charisma, Paterno already had it when he was eighteen years old. Blatty felt awe when Paterno walked over. He recognized Blatty from a school play.

"What's wrong?" Paterno asked.

Blatty told him about the contest and how he was sure he had won. He had been robbed. He had been cheated of his destiny. He went on for a while, and Paterno listened carefully.

"Then," Blatty said years later, "he leaned over close to my face, took hold of my arm with one hand, and said in a tone of care and sincerity that even Doubting Thomas would have believed: 'Bill, you know you won. What else matters?' "

Brooklyn Prep quarterback Joe Paterno tries to outrun defender John Carbone of St. John's Prep *(Courtesy of Tom Carbone)*

Brooklyn

Giuseppe," Joe Paterno said, and he began to cough. He held up his hand in a silent request to let him finish. In his final months, the violent cough would come and go, like Pennsylvania thunderstorms. He seemed angrier at the cough's spontaneity than its strength. He never liked surprises. He demanded order and routine; if you worked for him or played for him or simply wanted to be his friend, you set your watch by what everyone called Paterno Time. That was ten minutes early. Maybe fifteen. Possibly twenty.

His former players and his family often disagreed about how much Paterno Time differed from reality.

Paterno leaned forward and coughed into a closed fist until his eyes watered. The cough was dry, almost a wheeze. It brought him no relief; coughing was just something that had to be done. When the cough had subsided, he looked up again. "Giuseppe," he said, because this is what he called me, "you picked a hell of a time to write about a football coach."

JOE PATERNO CAME OF AGE in Flatbush, in the heart of Brooklyn, during the Great Depression, when boys calculated the heights and depths of their manhood by how far they could hit a ball with a broomstick. The Brooklyn streets of the 1930s and 1940s, before war and television and highways to the suburbs, have been so glamorized and idealized. Woody Allen made them black and white in his movies; Isaac Asimov wrote dreamily about how the streets looked at night. "If there was a national pastime," the playwright Arthur Miller wrote of his childhood in Brooklyn, "I suppose it was hanging out, simply standing there on the street corner or on the beach, waiting for something to appear around the bend."

It's one thing, though, for writers and artists and people led by their heart to attach longing and wistfulness to those Brooklyn streets. It was quite another for Paterno. He prided himself on being clear-eyed, practical, and unromantic. His wife, Sue, was born on Valentine's Day. Every year Joe would miss both celebrations because February 14 was in the middle of recruiting season. One year he called Sue from the road; he not only remembered her birthday but he had gotten her a wonderful gift.

"What is it?" she asked.

"Leo Wisniewski and Dan Rocco." They were two important football recruits.

"I like what my brother got me better," Sue said.

Even Paterno, though, could not help but fall into a sentimental trance when remembering Brooklyn and his childhood. "I wish you had been there," he said as he sat straight up in his hospital bed. In his memory, those streets of Brooklyn lingered untouched by the years. They were rain-swept and bright yellow, soaked in the smell of freshly baked bread and narrated by a New York Metropolitan Opera tenor bursting through static on the radio. Mothers gossiped through open windows; fathers huddled on front stoops; children played stickball. It may have been only vaguely connected to reality, but that was how Paterno remembered Brooklyn.

Oh, he wanted to remember. It was remembering that seemed to offer him small bursts of joy in those last months. Most of the time, he wasn't sad in those final days, and, much to the surprise of people around him, he wasn't angry either. He was tired. His eyelids drooped and his voice dragged. That voice was such a part of his persona. In his early years as a coach, the players not so secretly called him The Rat, at least in part because his high-pitched voice sounded like Mickey Mouse's. That voice would rise higher and shriller the angrier he got. Every player he ever coached did an impression of that voice, squeaking at the highest pitch they could reach.

You all are just a bunch of bums!

If we play like that, we're going to get licked Saturday!

Run to the ball! Geez, fellas, run to the ball!

That was just terrible! Terrible!

After he was fired as coach of Penn State, after he found out that he had lung cancer, after he broke his pelvis, after his hair started falling out and he came to understand that the end was close, his voice lost much of its life and spirit. He would speak in a soft rumble. But when the subject of Brooklyn came up, he was animated again. His hands moved as he talked, and his voice lifted and dropped like the Cyclone roller coaster on Coney Island.

"We never owned a home," he said, as he faded back to Brooklyn. "We moved around from place to place. Oh, I'd say we moved every year or two." This was during the Depression. The Paternos weren't hit as hard as most; Joe's father, Angelo, had steady work as a court clerk. But there were family obligations and friends in need, and there was never quite enough money to go around. The family moved up and down between Eighteenth and Twenty-sixth Street in Florence Paterno's never-ending effort to find someplace just a little bit better and higher up in the world. Sometimes they moved just to stay one step ahead of landlords who raised the rent. Joe did wonder if moving from place to place—so many places he lost count along the way— made him crave stability and shaped the life he would live. But the thought passed quickly. He was happy to remember Brooklyn, but he refused to regret.

As they moved from apartment to apartment, Joe saw the streets of Brooklyn as his real home. On the streets there was no Great Depression; there was no unemployment. There were kids, always, dozens of them, and they argued about the Dodgers and the Yankees, they talked about the movies, they told each other fantastic lies about heroic things they had done. They called each other the worst ethnic slurs they knew—wop, sheeny, mick—and they had fistfights when the name-calling did not feel quite violent enough. They fought their own version of World War II, killing imaginary Nazi and Japanese soldiers who hid behind every fire hydrant. They got in trouble every now and again, but even that sort of trouble was coated with the innocence of the time. Once Joe's younger brother, George, threw a chain at him. Joe was so outraged, he threw it back, missed, and broke a window of the Thom McAn store. Joe, of course, admitted it to his father—like the little George Washington that he was, his brother would say—and Angelo paid for the window. Like Bill Blatty said: they were all so innocent.

More than anything, they played games that fit the streets where they lived: stoopball, punch ball, curb ball, parked-car football, and, of course, stickball. No Brooklyn story is told without mentioning stickball, that city game played with a rubber ball everyone called a Spaldeen. Joe did not have a knack for hitting a Spaldeen with a broomstick. He was fast and had a quick mind, which served him better in football and basketball. (He always thought basketball was his best game.) "Sure, there were kids in the neighborhood that were ten times better at stickball," he said, and again he coughed and again he needed a moment to regain his strength. "But when the wind was blowing right, I could hit two and a half sewers." He meant the ball would sail over two sewer openings and almost to a third. This was a great distance in the mind of a Brooklyn child.

IN THOSE LAST WEEKS OF his life, Paterno found himself thinking often about two men from his childhood. One was his father, Angelo. Joe was one of those lucky people who lived a long life and never met a man he admired more than his father.

Angelo Paterno also grew up in Brooklyn. Angelo's father, Vincent, immigrated to America in 1885 from a small Italian village called Macchia Albanese, between Cosenza and the Ionian Sea. Vincent became a barber. Many people through the years have pointed out the striking connections between Joe Paterno and Vince Lombardi. They were both Italian Americans who grew up Catholic in Brooklyn. They both became football coaches against their parents' will. They had similarly remarkable careers filled with victories and success and a near-cult following. They would even face each other when they were both still young and uncertain of their future. And they were both grandsons of barbers.

But the barber connection was not peculiar. There weren't many jobs an Italian immigrant could hold in America in the latter part of the nineteenth century. Vincent Paterno, like Lombardi's grandfather, Anthony Izzo, cut hair because it was honest work and it was the work he could find. Both wanted much more for their sons.

Angelo had an adventurous spirit. When he thought he was old enough, at seventeen, he dropped out of school, joined the army, and, in his son's words, "went down to Mexico with General Pershing and chased around Pancho Villa." He then went to Europe and fought in some important battles in World War I. When he returned home after the war, he settled down. He married Florence and they started a family. They stayed in Brooklyn. Angelo worked his way through high school, then college, and then law school at St. John's, and throughout, he was never without a job. His oldest son, named Joseph because Angelo was too modest to name his son after himself, would hold close a sharp memory of his father, late at night, his eyelids barely open after a long day working in the courts, sitting at the kitchen table with a thick law book opened in front of him. "As a parent, you can talk about how important education is until you're blue in the face," Joe said. "But seeing my father struggling with those law books at three in the morning—that had a bigger impact on me than a million words."

Angelo got his law degree and, after a couple of stumbles, passed the New York bar exam. He worked his way up to law clerk in the New York State Supreme Court. "Angelo was one of my heroes," said Joe Murphy, one of Joe's childhood friends. "He was just this really solid guy. He had put himself through law school, he was a big guy in the community. And here I was, just this kid, and he was always so nice to me, always asked me how I was doing, always tried to engage me in conversation. He would say, 'What do you think?' Who does that? Who cares what a kid in the neighborhood thinks?"

Murphy's description of Angelo would sound eerily similar to hundreds of stories told when Joe Paterno died, stories about little moments when Joe reached out to a stranger, asked questions, showed he cared, and said just the right thing. Here's just one of those stories: At Paterno's memorial in Harrisburg, a young woman named Kait Sawyer, who had served as a football intern, stood in front of a huge crowd and talked about a cold day in State College when Joe Paterno walked into the football offices. He made sure to catch her eye and say "It's cold out there, heh?" It was nothing profound, but it was a connection, one she would never forget. "He was the legend," she said, sounding so much like Joe Murphy. "And he was talking to me."

Joe Paterno, however, never saw his father's best traits in himself. "No, no, no. My father had an amazing sense of empathy. He always knew just what to say to make people feel better. He'd kid them, he'd listen to them, he'd make them feel better. I'm just the opposite. People give me too much credit because we've had a little success as a football team. No. My father was the genuine article."

Joe looked out the little window in the hospital as he said that. Outside, flakes of snow and ice that looked like falling mosquitoes dropped fast to the ground. He spoke softly. "I remember he used to talk so softly. I never understood that. People all around would be shouting, talking loud, you know, this was an Italian home. There were always people over at the house, always people yelling and arguing and fighting over anything—politics, sports, whatever. And my father would just sit there and listen. And then, when he did say something, he would talk so softly. Years later, I realized why he did that. When you talk softly, people lean in to listen. That's what he wanted. He wanted people to lean in. He knew how to draw people close. I never had that talent. When I talked, I talked loud. I didn't have my father's confidence. I didn't want anyone missing what I was saying."

Florence Paterno had little of her husband's serenity. She, like her oldest son, talked loudly. She would tell anyone who would listen that she was the first Italian ever hired by the New York Telephone Company; whether or not this was true, she did become a telephone operator just after she graduated from high school. Her father ran a successful trucking company built up from a single horse and a buggy. Success, and the pursuit of it, circulated in the Cafieros' blood, and Florence felt a deep pride in her maiden name. Her nephew Eugene went on to run the Chrysler Corporation.

People would often say that Joe Paterno was his mother's son. His brother was more direct: George called Joe a clone of his mother. She hungered for success in every form—fame, fortune, respect—and she expected it of her children. "My mother wanted to win," Joe said. She was the force behind the family's continuous moves from place to place in Flatbush. She overwhelmed Joe with her expectations and demands. He would remember the heat he felt on the back of his neck whenever a teacher asked the class a question. He had to raise his hand first and fastest and always get the answer right; to do anything less was to disgrace his mother. He remembered the intense pressure he felt when there was a spelling bee or a math contest. He had to win. He remembered the arguments in the neighborhood, supposedly fun little arguments meaning nothing at all, but he could not let go, not until everyone admitted that he had won, that his view was right, that he should be the quarterback, he should dribble the basketball up the court, he should lead whatever they happened to be doing.

That was Florence. One of Joe's most famous quotes is this: "The will to win is important. But the will to prepare is vital." People thought he picked up that line from Lombardi or from reading about ancient Rome or from his college coach, Rip Engle. No. He got it from Florence. Her house was immaculate, always. Every morning, long before dawn, Florence would be up washing and ironing clothes so that Joe and George and their sister, also named Florence, would look sharp for school. This was the constant, the image of her that superseded all the others: Florence preparing before sunrise so that everyone would look at the Paterno family as winners. If every family has its own little joke, a punch line that gets to the heart of things, the joke of Joe Paterno's childhood was this: "Our mother would make us put on a tie just to take out the garbage."

Joe spent his life parsing the differences between *excellence* and *success*. It is the theme that emerges and reemerges, in good days and bad, in triumph and in defeat, when his teams never lost and when he was fired. What really matters: excellence or success? Angelo stood for many things, but one of them was quiet excellence: he studied at home, late at night when everyone was asleep; he felt no need to dominate, no need to become rich or famous or blindingly successful in the eyes of the world. And he never did. Some, including Joe himself, wondered if Angelo had enough ambition. He enjoyed a good joke and good company and a sense of family. "Make an impact" was his advice to Joe.

Florence too stood for many things, but perhaps most of all there was her drive for success: she believed great things are accomplished only through the hunger for achievement. She told Joe again and again, in many different ways, that he was as good as anybody—no, he was better than anybody. He could do great things. No. More. He *had* to do great things.

Joe admitted that those two influences often clashed inside him. "I always believed that winning wasn't the most important thing. And yet I always wanted to win more than anybody."

How do you merge those two forces? He wondered about this all the time. Sometimes, when someone had given him a particularly hard time about being an Italian kid, he would go home and tell his mother. Florence would usually respond with her motto: "Every knock is a boost." Self-pity was a crime against your own destiny. Regret was a waste of time and passion. Use their doubts, she counseled, to propel yourself.

Then she would do something else: she would have Joe recite a list of great Italian men. Joe thought she did this for a couple of reasons, one obvious, the other a bit less so. The obvious reason was that she wanted Joe to have pride in his heritage, to understand the greatness in his heritage. But the second reason, one that Joe did not fully understand until much later, was that she was giving him a target. She did not want him just to memorize the name of Leonardo da Vinci, who was always the first person on the list. She wanted him, in his own way, following his own path, to *become* Leonardo da Vinci.

"Leonardo," Joe said as he sat at that kitchen table in his home remembering the list, "Michelangelo, Garibaldi, Galileo, Dante, Columbus, Toscanini, Vivaldi . . ."

JOE PATERNO WAS A NATURAL left-hander. Few people knew this about him because when he played football—on the street, on the playground, later on the fields of Brooklyn Prep and Brown University—he threw right-handed. He taught himself to throw right-handed through endless drills and an obsessive will. He taught himself to throw right-handed because he believed that quarterbacks were supposed to be right-handed. He never did know for sure how that thought got into his head. Maybe it was because in every photograph of every quarterback he admired as a child they were throwing with their right hand. Whatever the reason, he was never able to completely let go of the bias. In his first thirty-five years as a head coach at Penn State, he started only right-handed quarterbacks.

Still, the point was not about quarterbacks being right-handed or left-handed but about Paterno's deep ambition. His ego—or lack thereof—would be the subject of constant speculation through the years. What drove this man? "In all my life," Don Abbey said, "I never met anyone who cared less about money. . . . He didn't care about winning the most games either."

"Many people think he does care about that stuff but he just doesn't let on," I said.

"No, they don't know what the hell they're taking about. Joe had an enormous ego. Enormous. But it's not an ego for money or fame or any of that."

So what hunger drove that ego? Paterno was left-handed. He threw footballs against brick walls again and again with his right hand. When he found that he could throw the ball passably well (though he never could make the ball spiral with regularity), he gathered his friends and had them run pass patterns so he could practice his timing. He threw so many passes with his right hand that some mornings he would wake up and not be able to lift his right arm without pain.

Why? Paterno was better suited for other positions as a football player. He had marvelous instincts that allowed him to predict how a play would develop. That made him a spectacular defensive back. Sixty years after he graduated from Brown he still held the school record for most interceptions by a player. He was also a fast and shifty runner. "I remember many times watching him make a move that made a tackler fall down," said the sportswriter Bill Conlin, who grew up in Brooklyn and watched Paterno play at Brooklyn Prep.

Those moves and that speed could have made him a wonderful running back.

But Joe had to be the quarterback. This wasn't a choice. It was all well and good to run fast and intercept passes and score touchdowns, but he could not imagine being anything but the quarterback. He needed the ball in his hands. He moved to the center of everything, making all the important decisions, sometimes without even realizing it.

"I'll give you an example of what Joe was like in those days," Joe Murphy said. "In our junior year at Brooklyn Prep, we had a bumpy year. We got knocked around a little bit. We had a lot of guys talking all the time; there wasn't a real leader.

"So Zev Graham, who was our coach, decided that in our senior year we wouldn't have a huddle. And we didn't. We didn't have a single huddle all year. He said, 'Joe will call the plays and that will be that.' We'd have a key number which would change every week. Joe could call, 'Twenty-three, seventy-three, sixty-two,' or whatever, and if the key number was three, then that third number was the play we would run. We did that the whole season. Joe called every play. And we lost just one game."

That one loss deserves a few extra words. It was 1944, Paterno's senior year at Brooklyn Prep. His team had dominated opponents all season. Paterno scored four touchdowns in a game against Cardinal Hayes, and his more powerful brother starred as a runner. ("George really was a better athlete than I was," Paterno would say.) The team was undefeated when it faced St. Cecilia High School from Englewood, New Jersey. St. Cecilia was coached by Vince Lombardi and had not lost a game since 1942. More than eight thousand people attended.

The week before, Paterno had badly hurt his arm. He still played against St. Cecilia, of course. Physical pain embarrassed him; it was to be ignored and overcome. For the rest of his life, sometimes to his detriment, he would have difficulty understanding how injuries, mere pain, could stop young football players. But this time willpower was not enough. The injury rendered his right arm almost useless. He couldn't throw the ball. He couldn't run the ball either.

St. Cecilia played inspired football. Paterno remembered that late in the game, a St. Cecilia player ran over him to score the game-winning touchdown. "I don't know that I ever lived it down," he said.

There was another twist to the story. Years later, Paterno was reminiscing with Lombardi, and Lombardi admitted that before the game he had told his players that people in Brooklyn had been sending him taunting and vicious letters. He read a few of those letters to the players, read how people were calling Lombardi a traitor and his players hoodlums. The players, so outraged by these letters, raced onto the field and played with fury.

"And you know what Lombardi told me?" Paterno asked. "He told me that he had made the whole thing up. There were no letters." At this Paterno laughed and laughed. That was one hell of a motivational trick. Yes, one hell of a trick.

THE OTHER MAN PATERNO FOUND himself thinking about at the end was the Trojan hero Aeneas, son of the goddess Aphrodite and the mortal Anchises. Paterno never tired of saying how strongly he connected with the story of Aeneas founding Rome, a story told by Virgil in the *Aeneid* a couple of decades before the birth of Christ. In Paterno's autobiography, *Paterno: By the Book,* he wrote, "I don't think anybody can get a handle on what makes me tick as a person, and certainly can't get at the roots of how I coach football, without understanding what I learned from the deep relationship I formed with Virgil."

"If anything," he said twenty years later, "I feel that connection even more deeply now."

He formed that relationship with Virgil at Brooklyn Prep, his Catholic school in Crown Heights. To get to The Prep, as students called it, he would walk ten blocks and take a fifteen-minute trolley ride. He had to leave before seven every morning to get to school on time. A public high school, James Madison, was only a block away from where the Paternos lived. It was no ordinary public school. Gary Becker and Robert Solow, who would both win the Nobel Prize for Economics, went there. Martin Perl, who would win the Nobel Prize for Physics, went there. Ruth Bader Ginsburg, who would serve on the U.S. Supreme Court, and Martin Landau, who would win an Academy Award, all went to James Madison.

But James Madison did not fit into Angelo and Florence's plan for Joe. Angelo wanted his oldest son to go to a Catholic high school; Florence wanted her oldest son to go to the best school money could buy. It cost the family twenty dollars a month at a time when Angelo was pulling in maybe five or six thousand dollars a year. "We couldn't really afford it," Joe said. "But there was never a question about it. Nothing mattered more than education. You understand? We couldn't afford a washing machine. We couldn't afford any of the luxuries. None of that mattered. I was going to Brooklyn Prep, and that was it. When my brother, George, was ready, he was going to Brooklyn Prep too. My father worked out a package deal, thirty bucks a month for the both of us."

By the time he arrived at The Prep, Joe was already an over-achiever. He worked in the New York Public Library; he worked as an usher for the Brooklyn Dodgers; he was a baggage checker at Penn Station. He took the lead in school—straight A's, always—and he took the lead in the neighborhood. Everyone who grew up with him remarked on his solemn sense of purpose. They called him "the dog-faced boy" because of his seriousness. "He was a fun guy to be around," his friend Joe Murphy said. "But, absolutely, you could tell he had it in his mind that he was going places. We all recognized it."

Thomas Bermingham recognized this call to greatness in Paterno. He would say it was impossible to miss. In time, Bermingham would become a Jesuit priest and would spend more than fifty years teaching the classics at Fordham University. But he spent his regency period, a

Jesuit's first three years teaching and learning to be part of a community, at Brooklyn Prep. Bermingham was still young then, still seeking his way as a teacher. Joe Paterno was the first student he tried to reach.

"This may sound oversimple," Bermingham's longtime friend Father William O'Malley said, "but Tom was incandescently innocent. Life made him overjoyed. It's difficult to describe, but Tom was—accessibly holy. Anybody who had even the slightest sensibility would sense something sacred about him."

Through Paterno, Bermingham found he had an eye for talent and a knack for finding a connection with students. After Paterno graduated, he reached out to Bill Blatty and (as he had with Paterno) told the young man that he had greatness in him. "It was Bermingham who gave me my love of theater," Blatty said. Bermingham did more than that: he gave Blatty a story that would spark his imagination, a marvelous little story he would use when he wrote *The Exorcist*.

"Berms had called home because his mother was dying," Blatty explained. "Arriving at the house, the attending doctor said he was too late, that she had already passed, whereupon Tom told him he'd go up and say some prayers anyway. When he got to his mother's bedroom, he began saying the prayers of Extreme Unction, when suddenly his 'dead' mother opened one eye and with her usual brogue said, 'Tom, that's very nice, but would you mind getting me a drink?'

"He rushed downstairs, poured a scotch, and brought it back to her. She sipped a little, then looked at him and said, 'You know, Tom, I've never told you this, but you're a wonderful man.' The drink slipped from her fingers and she died. Later the doctor asked Bermingham, 'Listen, could you send me a copy of those prayers you said up there?' "

Bermingham reached out to Blatty using their shared love of the theater and the occult. With Paterno, the link was Aeneas. Before Paterno's senior year began, Bermingham suggested they meet before school every morning and, together, translate the *Aeneid* into English. This hardly sounds like the sort of thing a young man would want to do in his spare time, but Paterno was drawn to exactly these sorts of challenges. "It sounded impossible," he said. And so, every morning, the two men would translate the *Aeneid* word by word, beginning at the beginning:

Arma virumque cano.

I sing of arms and a man.

Paterno was instantly hooked. He craved adventure then, as his father had. He wanted a life beyond the ordinary. His favorite movies starred Errol Flynn as a swashbuckler fighting for the honor of some fair maiden. His favorite books took him to worlds filled with danger and triumph, such as *Treasure Island* and *The Leatherstocking Tales*. He spent much of his young life talking about brave knights and damsels in distress. Now he was reading about Aeneas, a reluctant hero who faced raging storms, an unnerving visit to the underworld, jealous gods, and a climactic fight to fulfill his destiny and found Rome. The *Aeneid*'s twists thrilled him.

But it was the question of destiny, the driving theme of the *Aeneid*, that stayed with Paterno for the rest of his life. Bermingham had explained to Paterno that in Latin *fatum*, which led to the word "fate," means "that which has been spoken" or "divine word." Aeneas's *fatum* wasn't something that happened to him or something that was given to him. He was told by the gods—in divine words—that he was destined to found Rome. How would he do this? He did not know. Was he strong enough to achieve his destiny? He did not know. What would be the price? He did not know. Aeneas tried to follow the *fatum*, but he found that sometimes his instincts lied, sometimes they seemed illogical, sometimes they led him into agony. Sometimes he wanted to stop and give up the chase.

But he kept going. To Paterno, that was the lesson. Aeneas knew that you cannot escape your destiny; you are put in this world to fulfill it. "You have to listen for the divine word that tells you your destiny," Paterno said as he sat in his hospital bed near the end of his life. "And then you have to follow it as best you can."

"Did you hear it?" I asked.

"I don't know. I sure heard something."

Photos Joe Paterno sent home while he served in the army just as World War II was ending *(Courtesy of the Paterno family)*

{ *Intermezzo* }

Paterno did not often talk about the war. Sometimes, in those rare peaceful moments when his grandchildren caught him in the right mood—sitting in a lounge chair under the sun, recruiting season over, spring practice yet to begin, the next season still full of possibility—he might talk a bit about what it was like in Seoul during the rainy season or how it felt to discharge a weapon. But even in those moments, he lost interest in the subject quickly. It was not that he carried scars from his time in the army. He had missed all the fighting. He was at Fort Dix in New Jersey being fitted for his uniform when he heard over a nearby radio that President Truman had dropped the bomb on Hiroshima. He never doubted that Truman did the right thing. "Two great things Harry Truman did. He saved Europe with the Marshall Plan, and he ended the war when he dropped the bomb."

Paterno did not talk often about the war: "Who wants to hear my silly little war stories?" He was a Hemingway man at heart—grace under pressure and all that—and those years were his own cross to bear. He was nineteen years old when he was drafted; he had stayed an extra term at Brooklyn Prep so he could play the 1944 football season. He was a good enough football player that he had been offered an all-expenses-paid scholarship to Brown University by a zealous alum, but Brown and football had to wait. First he was sent to New Jersey to train while the war closed. Then he was shipped off to Korea. His letters home to his parents, his brother, and his sister, who was nine years younger, were those of a wide-eyed Brooklyn kid experiencing life outside the borough for the first time.

February 21, 1946

Hi Folks,

Well, I guess this will be the last letter you'll get from me for a long time. Tomorrow we ship out. Where? I don't know or on what ship but we were told the trip would take 17 to 20 days.

This morning I signed up for a couple of those educational courses the Army offers. I'm taking College Physics, American Literature, Medieval History and Physical Science. The way they work it is they give you the textbooks and you study on your own and when you think that you are ready for the test they give it to you. If you pass the test you can apply to a college for credits in that subject. At least I'll have something to keep me busy.

The trip here was really interesting. The Rockies are the most beautiful thing I've ever seen. You remember how pretty Vermont was, well that's nothing compared to the Rockies.

*I never knew or realized how large this country is. Boy, it really
impressed me.*

*There isn't much more to say except don't worry about me.
I'll be alright. The time will go fast and I'll be home before you
realize it. Meanwhile, I'll be having an experience I'll never
have another chance probably to go through. Good bye for
now—you probably won't hear from me for a month and a half
or more.*

All my love,
Joe

His letters home flowed with such sentiments: *Don't worry about
me. I'll be alright. The time will go fast. I'll be home soon.* This hardly
made the young Joe Paterno unique, of course. Every soldier wants to
keep the folks back home from worrying. Still, this melody was particularly striking in Paterno's letters. World War II had been so stark,
so certain. The stakes, the enemies, the dangers, the matter of right
and wrong, all of it was clear. But Paterno had been shipped to Korea
to work as a radio operator at the start of the cold war, when purpose
and future were hazier.

He refused to admit such confusion, though. The defining feature
of his letters was their cheerfulness, their opacity, their striking lack of
fear and loneliness. He would believe for the rest of his life that leaders keep their burdens close.

June 7, 1946

*Today I spent all afternoon on the beach and had a swell time.
There were about five of us who went down together. The water
is much nicer than back home. It is so clear that you can see the
bottom very clearly at depths up to 13 feet. It is a little cold but
refreshing.*

June 9, 1946

The food is still swell. We get plenty to eat, no worry about that. This business about me writing cheerful letters, that's the bunk. It really is nice here. I have nothing to do as far as work is concerned and there's plenty of recreation.

June 16, 1946

I am sincere when I tell you I have the life of a king. We have a house boy to clean our rooms and do our washing. The Gov. pays him. Every once in a while we give him a pack of cigarettes. . . . Sometimes I wonder if it's possible to have such an easy life.

June 19, 1946

Well here I go again, the old personality kid. . . . So you're worried about my hair, Mom. Don't be silly. The climate is no different and as for not getting enough vitamins, that's absurd. I eat plenty and everything. We get all kinds of vegetables. Please don't worry about anything. Everything is as nice as it can possibly be, not being home and all that! I am happy and I get a kick out of all these letters telling me how swell I am.

June 29, 1946

Just a short note before chow from that dashing son of yours. I am still in wonderful health and wonderful spirits. . . . I don't even ask how Sis made out on the exams. After all she takes after me. All the fellows think she looks a lot like me. The lucky kid! They thought George looked like me too but that he was kind of skinny. Not near as husky as I. But who is? As you can see I'm still the modest little fellow that I always was.

At this point in his life, Paterno would remember having no thoughts about becoming a football coach. But there are places in his letters home where the roots of the man he would become seem obvious. His fascination with practice — "The will to win is important, but the will to prepare is vital" — comes across in a letter he wrote about the 31st Infantry Regiment:

July 13, 1946

Eisenhower is in Seoul, and he's staying until Saturday. I haven't seen him yet, but I will tomorrow. The outfit next to us are going to be reviewed by him. This outfit, the 31st Infantry Regiment, is a training outfit and the best marchers in Korea. They are really good and they should be. They practice every day, and every night they have a retreat parade. Whenever anybody comes around, the Division commander calls on the 31st to impress them.

His self-deprecating nature is in every letter, such as this one about playing softball:

June 11, 1946

We played the Hospital in softball again and, hold on to your seats, believe it or not, we won 6–2. And, another believe it or not, yours truly got a couple of hits. Just to show you how indispensable my buddy and I are to a softball team, I will tell you what happened to Hdgs. Co. softball team when we left. When we played on the team, it won a game and lost around 6. The other day one of the fellows from Hdgs. Co. was up here. He told me that since Tony and I left, the team has won 6 straight games. I knew they couldn't do it without us (ha ha).

For the most part, though, the letters home tell the story of a brash young man who wanted to get going but was not entirely sure where to. Like most soldiers, Paterno sought out the familiar. He asked about the Brooklyn Dodgers. He wondered if his brother was still dating a girl named Mal. He worried about his father's health, encouraged his mother to buy some clothes and take some time away from work, asked often about the old neighborhood. This was how he remembered himself in the army: "I was driven to succeed. But succeed in what? I didn't know. I talk to these people who always knew they were going to become a coach or always knew they were going to write or whatever. I didn't know. I assumed I would go into the law, and live in Brooklyn, and be like my father."

"Rip" Engle, center, is surrounded (*from left to right*) by assistant coaches J. T. White, Joe Paterno, and Joe McMullen *(Penn State University Archives, Pennsylvania State University Libraries)*

Engle

They called Everett Arnold "Busy" because he wouldn't shut up. The nickname went back to when he was a boy in Providence, Rhode Island. He talked constantly in class. He would butt into conversations, even teachers' conversations. He interrupted anyone to offer his opinion. The teachers called him "Busybody." The kids in class shortened it to "Busy." He was called Busy Arnold for the rest of his life. And he never did shut up.

Busy Arnold became a comic-book titan. That was a time in

the American story when you could become a titan of more or less anything: Conrad Hilton was a hotel titan, Stanley C. Allyn a cash-register titan, Milton Hershey a chocolate titan, Daniel F. Gerber a baby-food titan. Busy Arnold worked his way from selling color printing presses to printing comic books. He gained a reputation, rare in the comic-book world, of giving artists creative freedom and paying them a fair wage. He hired the artist Rube Goldberg. He hired Will Eisner, who would become famous for creating a hero called The Spirit. Busy Arnold made a fortune.

He spent his money well. He liked being in the middle of the New York scene. He wore the finest suits and was often seen at hot spots like the Stork Club with beautiful women who shared the distinction of not being his wife. He also became known for some of the wild parties he threw.

How does Busy Arnold, comic-book titan, enter our story? As much as he loved money and women and being photographed, Busy Arnold's greatest love may have been his alma mater, Brown University. He wanted the Brown football team to win. He wanted this so badly that he personally looked for talented football players he could send to Brown on an unofficial Busy Arnold scholarship.

This was not against regulations in the mid-1940s; there really weren't any college football regulations in the 1940s. The National Collegiate Athletic Association did not have an executive director until 1951. In the 1940s, many schools, including what was then known as Pennsylvania State College, did not offer football scholarships. So there was an opportunity for industrious alumni to find talented football players and pay for their tuition and books and maybe a little extra. Busy Arnold was just such an alum. Joe Paterno was just such a player.

Arnold became friends with various high school coaches around New York, including Brooklyn Prep's football coach, Zev Graham, whose real name was Earl, but nobody called him that. Graham had gone to Fordham to play baseball in 1923, but he showed such blazing speed as a football player that he became a starter even though he was just five-foot-six. After his first game, a New York sportswriter nick-named him Zev after the Kentucky Derby winner in 1923, and he was Zev for the rest of his life. He became an All-American and one of the biggest college football stars of his era. Years later he would become coach at Brooklyn Prep and the man who turned his team over to a smart quarterback who couldn't throw.

"Busy Arnold really must have trusted Zev," Paterno's old team-mate Joe Murphy said, "because it seems like he sent half our team to Brown."

Arnold paid for Brooklyn Prep's football stars Joe Murphy, Chuck Nelson, Bucky Walters, Frank Mahoney, and George Paterno to play football at Brown. And, of course, he also paid the cost of room and board and books for Joe Paterno. "Those were different times," Paterno recalled. "There was no way for a guy like me to go to an Ivy League school. We couldn't afford it. Nobody in the Ivy League was giving out athletic scholarships. When Zev Graham told me that Mr. Arnold wanted to send me to Brown to play football, it was like a dream."

The irony wasn't lost on Paterno. He would spend his coaching life publicly railing against overbearing alumni eager to pay talented football players under the table and the coaches who looked the other way. He made it clear to Penn State alumni that he would not stand for that. "We want your money," he often told alumni, "but we don't want your two cents."

And yet Paterno's college football career, and the remarkable coaching career that followed, happened in large part because of an overbearing Brown alumnus willing to do anything to help his alma mater win. Busy Arnold paid Paterno's tuition and introduced him to Brown's coach, Rip Engle. And for Paterno, Rip Engle changed everything.

CHARLES A. ENGLE WAS CALLED Rip because of the many times he ripped his jeans as a child. The nickname fit: Rip Engle forever expected bad things to happen to him. It was his nature. He did not drink; he did not swear. He worried. People called him the "King of Gloom." "To Engle," Walter Bingham wrote in *Sports Illustrated*, "no sky is completely blue, no rose without its thorn." One of his rival coaches, Ben Schwartzwalder of Syracuse, uttered this classic: "Rip Engle is not happy unless he's sad."

In Engle's mind and heart, every victory was luck, every loss inevitable, every opponent more frightening than the last. To entertain alumni and friends, he would tell stories not of football glory but of growing up in a town so small that the speed bump was considered a city treasure, and of the two years he spent playing football for a starcrossed team at little Blue Ridge College. Friends would call these "Rip's Humble Talks." Engle would say that the first football game he ever saw was the first football game he played for Blue Ridge; that's how terrible the team was. He would invent wonderful and hilarious stories about the team's incompetence; he said that Blue Ridge lost every game, never scored a point, and eventually closed down to become a bus company. First, though, he said they lost to Temple by more than a hundred points. Of these, only the last was true: Temple did beat Blue Ridge 110–0 in 1927.

Much of this kvetching and brooding cloaked Engle's talents and competitive nature: he was one hell of a football coach. He was an innovator—a training game he invented called Angleball was still being played thirty years after his death—and he had a knack for getting players to work hard and play together. In his years at Penn State, his teams never had a losing record. When he retired, he was inducted into the College Football Hall of Fame.

Joe Paterno sensed these coaching qualities the first time he met Engle, when he was a high school student looking for a place to go to college. Paterno had a piercing intuition about people from a young age. Over time he would sharpen the gift, harness it, and develop what seemed to other coaches an almost magical ability to see through a player in only a few minutes and tell if he had the right stuff. In this way, Paterno and his coaches found overlooked and undervalued football stars probably more often than any coaching staff in college football history. Then, like all gifts, Paterno sometimes took his for granted, especially in his later years. "Joe wasn't always right," one assistant coach said, "but he was always sure."

Paterno knew when he met Engle that he wanted to go to Brown. His father had some doubts about Joe's going to a non-Catholic school, but Joe wanted to play football for Rip Engle. "Rip just had this nice way about him," Paterno said. "On the outside, we were very different. I was this fiery kid from Brooklyn, always sure I was right, always getting into little scraps with people. Rip was different. He was a gentleman. On the inside, we probably weren't too different."

Engle grew up in a small town in southwestern Pennsylvania called Elk Lick. (In later years, perhaps sensibly, the town changed its name to Salisbury.) His father left the family when Engle was a boy. His mother, Cora, was intensely religious; she worshiped in the Church of the Brethren, a religion built largely around the ideal of peace. (Its dictum: "Continuing the work of Jesus. Peacefully. Simply. Together.") Engle worked a mule in the coal mines when he was just fourteen; the legal age for working in the mines was sixteen, but he was big for his age. When he realized that the mines were not for him, he left to play football at Western Maryland College, and that's where the unlikely chain of events began. At Western Maryland, he played for a coach named Dick Harlow, who would become a legendary coach at Harvard. Engle started to think about a life of coaching. So, if you want to summarize the story, it might go like this: Harlow inspired Engle and convinced him (against his better judgment) to become a coach. Engle inspired Paterno and convinced him (against his better judgment) to become a coach. Pennsylvania State College became Penn State. And fifty years later, 107,000 people would regularly gather in State College to watch football games that seemed to matter more than anything.

PATERNO LOVED AND DESPISED BROWN University in somewhat equal parts. He would say that he never felt more alive than he did in college. At first, he majored in engineering on the advice of a practical uncle, but he quickly came to know his own limitations ("Joe couldn't fix a sandwich," his wife would say) and switched to English lit. The humanities suited him better. He was enthralled by gracefully written sentences; some of them stuck with him long after he left Brown. To the end of his life, he could recite from memory Hamlet's soliloquy, large portions of "Ode on a Grecian Urn," and the last paragraph of *The Great Gatsby*.

"I sometimes wonder if I could have been a writer," he said three weeks before he died. "I tried to write some now and again. But I never really put my heart into it. Who had the time? I would scribble a few things down now and again—ideas, lines, you know. I don't know, maybe I had some talent for it. [My son] Jay has a great talent for writing. [My youngest son] Scott does too. He does a different kind of writing, but he's very good. Maybe now, after I get through all this, I will do some writing. . . . I hope so."

Paterno cherished the feeling of being surrounded by knowledge and curiosity and intellectual power at Brown. He remembered with joy the late-night arguments he and his friends had about Hemingway and Socrates, the infallibility of the pope, and the government's responsibility to help the poor. As a coach, this was the intellectual atmosphere he encouraged his players to embrace. "This is supposed to be the best time of your life," he would tell them. "Don't miss out."

There was, however, another side of Brown University that Paterno also never forgot. Brown was founded before the Revolutionary War, and many of the students came from old money and prominent families. This was Paterno's first clash with snobbery and exclusion, and such things tore at him. The name-calling in Brooklyn had been surface stuff—blatant, hot, and unmistakable—and it could be answered with fists and wit. At Brown, though, snobbery, elitism, and prejudice hid behind the eyes and was whispered under the breath. Paterno often told the story of the white sweater. When he was a freshman, he went to an Alpha Delta Phi fraternity party. He wore the nicest sweater he owned, a white sweater his mother had given him, and the moment he walked into what he called "that room filled with blue blazers and martinis" he felt every eye turn to him and his sweater. This was the Brown fraternity of steel titans Arthur B. Homer and John D. Rockefeller. He recalled hearing someone whisper, "Who invited that dago?" The looks of the young men in the room pierced him. "I still see and feel that room, those people, fingering their cocktails, studying me out of the corners of their eyes," he wrote in his autobiography forty years after he left Brown. "No, I never forgot what it felt like to walk into that room," he said in the hospital in his last days.

In some ways, those penetrating stares and hushed snubs molded his outlook on life even more than his success as a Brown football player. He was a marvelous player. The sportswriter and editor Stanley Woodward purportedly wrote, "Paterno, the Brown quarterback, can't run. He can't pass. All he can do is think—and win." Woodward's pithy line, which later seemed exactly the sort of thing someone would write about Paterno, was quoted often after Paterno became head coach at Penn State and ad nauseam after his teams won. It's likely, however, that Woodward never wrote the line. Paterno never knew of anyone who had actually seen the quote, and though his family had clipped many of the stories written about Paterno as a player, no copy of Woodward's quote was found.

Sometimes, though, myth has its place. Stanley Woodward certainly could have written the line. Paterno couldn't pass, but he could run pretty well and his teams did win. Engle's Brown teams had thirteen wins, seventeen losses, and four ties before Paterno's junior season. That year Paterno starred on defense and as a punt returner—he set what was then the school record for most yards returned on punts—and Engle often put him in as quarterback to spark the team. Brown won seven of nine games that year. The next year, with Paterno entrenched as the starting quarterback, Brown went 8-1, its best season in decades.

"There was something particularly close about that coach-quarterback relation," the *Providence Bulletin* columnist Jerry Prior wrote days after Paterno graduated in 1950, "for the latter had come close to the ideal as a coach's player, loyal, quick-witted, inspirational and a hard worker. The last line is especially true, for Brooklyn Joe was always working to make himself deserving of the confidence Engle had in him."

Paterno's football career at Brown ended with perhaps his most illustrious performance, in a game against Colgate. Before that game, Joe's brother, George—a bigger and better athlete than Joe but, by his own admission, not nearly as driven—told a reporter that he thought he still had his best game left in him. Joe overheard. When Colgate, a team that had lost seven games in a row, took a 26–7 lead early in the third quarter, an enraged Joe Paterno turned to his younger brother and said, "We're going to have to do this."

The Paternos led Brown on a remarkable comeback. George broke through for a 37-yard touchdown run. Joe ran for 42 yards and threw a touchdown pass. Joe intercepted a pass and raced 40 yards. George ran hard for a 15-yard touchdown. And so on. George ended up rushing for 162 yards, by far the most productive game of his career. Brown scored 34 points in the last seventeen minutes of the game for a rousing and overwhelming victory that clinched one of the best seasons in the school's history.

And Joe? He didn't score a touchdown. He didn't put up impressive statistics. When the season ended, he did not get picked for the All–Ivy League team. Maybe this troubled him a bit at the time; the young Joe was not averse to seeing his name in the newspaper. But he would not remember feeling troubled. "You know what I liked best about Aeneas? He was a team player. He didn't care for individual glory. He didn't care about getting the credit. He simply wanted to be a part of something larger than himself. That appealed to me."

THE STORY OF HOW JOE Paterno became a football coach was told so many times through the years that in time it lost its power and honesty. The story evolved into something of a folktale that went like this: Joe Paterno had intended to go to law school to fulfill his parents' wishes. But then Rip Engle offered him a job as an assistant coach at a cow college called Penn State. Paterno, the Brooklyn kid through and through, reluctantly took the job to pay off some debts. He saw this as a temporary detour toward the law. At first, he despised this little hamlet in the middle of nowhere called State College (where they put celery in the spaghetti sauce), but gradually he began to appreciate its small-town charms and grew to see that he was destined to be a football coach. He stayed in State College for the rest of his life and coached football there until a terrible series of events sparked a national scandal, and then cancer killed him.

The folktale, like all folktales, oversimplifies. But that's not the real problem. The problem is that it strips the humanity out of what really happened.

It seems likely that Paterno did not want to become a lawyer. He was almost twenty-four when he graduated from Brown. He had served in the army, he had read the classics, he had been a football star. He craved a life of excitement. He knew full well that his parents expected great things from him; this had been a persistent and overpowering theme of his young life. He had applied to law school and was accepted at Boston University. But, though he was careful not to admit it at the time, the signs pointed to a young man who was hoping for something to save him from what seemed his inevitable fate.

"It's particularly pleasant to learn today that a young fellow named Joe Paterno will serve as an assistant backfield coach to Engle in his new post at Penn State," Jerry Prior wrote in the *Providence Bulletin* in May 1950. "Joe, in order to make the move, had to shelve, temporarily, at least, a plan to enter law school. But he had hoped all along to go into coaching if he found the right opening."

There is the key phrase: *He had hoped all along.* When the 1949 season ended, Engle asked Paterno as a favor to work with the quarterbacks who would replace him at Brown. He loved it. Here was a calling that spoke to his highest aspirations: teaching, pushing for perfection, making an impact on people's lives. Here was also a calling that fed some of his more earthbound ambitions: winning, being in charge, having the last word. Paterno said he spent those few weeks of coaching as a diversion to fill the time before law school began. But this might be his memory playing tricks. He had read the *Aeneid*; it seems likely that he hoped for the Fates to step in and change the course of his life.

And the Fates came through. Rip Engle was offered the head coaching job at Penn State University. He had been offered coaching jobs at schools before, and he turned them down, but this one was different. For one, his coach and mentor Dick Harlow had played for Penn State. For another, Engle was from a small Pennsylvania town and knew the territory. But perhaps most significantly, Penn State had determined, after a long hiatus, to give full scholarships to football players. This was a chance for Engle to recruit top athletes and coach big-time football. And Engle, gloomy and modest though he might be, had ambition.

He took the job, but there was a stipulation in the offer: Engle had to keep the entire coaching staff intact. Penn State officials worried about losing the mission of college sports (which is why they had stopped giving out football scholarships in the first place). School administrators liked to think of coaches as professors, so much so that they offered their coaches tenure. They did not want coaches fired for losing games; theirs was to be a higher calling. If Engle wanted the job, and the tenure that came with it, he would have to take on the assistant coaches too.

Engle agreed but pleaded for the chance to bring in one new coach. He wanted to teach the players his own complicated version of the Winged-T offense, and none of the Penn State coaches knew it. The school granted him this request, and Engle tried to hire his first assistant coach, Gus Zitrides, but Zitrides decided to stay on as head coach at Brown. (It was a doomed move for him: Zitrides's team lost eight of nine games, and he was promptly fired and went to work for the government.) Engle then tried to hire his second assistant, Bill Doolittle, but he decided to stay with Zitrides at Brown.

Engle was stuck. He was out of assistant coaches. (Another of his coaches, Weeb Ewbank, had become an assistant coach for Paul Brown and the Cleveland Browns; he would go on to a Hall of Fame coaching career in the National Football League.) In desperation, Engle convinced his graduating quarterback and favorite player, Joe Paterno, to come with him to Penn State and help him get the program off the ground.

Paterno would entertain countless dinner audiences, men's clubs, and alumni gatherings with the story of his drive with Engle through the mountains on the way to State College. "Rip kept talking about how clean the barns were. I remember that's the thing he kept saying. 'Oh, the barns there are so clean, you could eat off the floors.' I was a kid from Brooklyn, what the heck did I know or care about barns? And then we actually got there, and those barns stunk like you wouldn't believe. Eat off the floors? I couldn't eat within two miles."

Paterno would tell interviewer after interviewer that coaching at Penn State was a fluke, a temporary thing, a holding pattern until he had made a few dollars and could go to law school and follow in his father's footsteps. That was certainly the story he told his parents at the time. Angelo was typically kind and understanding when Joe brought up coaching, at least at first. Angelo had hoped his son might achieve great things; he had told Joe that he might be president someday. But here, in the pivotal moment, he told his son to follow his heart. "I never made a lot of money," Joe remembered his father saying, "but I tried to do the thing I loved. If this is what you want to do, try it."

Florence was typically skeptical. "What did we send you to college for?" she asked.

Over the years, Paterno came to believe the folktale version of his own story, came to believe that on the way to law school he lucked into a coaching gig and sort of drifted into his life as a legendary football coach. But he had to know the story did not go quite like that. Paterno was not the sort of man to float aimlessly toward his destiny. He coached his football players to "make something happen." He taught his children to "make an impact." He read books about

Churchill and Patton and Alexander the Great—"you know," he said, "the doers."

If you go deep into the Brown University Archives, you can find a 1949 Football Press Guide. This was written before the 1949 football season began, months before Penn State hired Rip Engle, months before Boston University accepted Paterno to law school. The Joe Paterno blurb did not get everything right—it called him an economics major, for instance—but it had a fascinating conclusion:

> *Big brother Joe Paterno is one half of Brown's first set of co-captains since 1940. This popular leader from Brooklyn, New York is an excellent field general on offense and a tough man to go through or over on defense. Also used to run back punts and kickoffs, Joe rated with the best in the country. A halfback at Brooklyn Prep, he made the All-Metropolitan squad in 1944. He also captained the school basketball team. At Brown, he was switched to the "down-under" position. He is an economics major, a member of Delta Kappa Epsilon fraternity, and hopes to become a football coach after graduation.*

"When they first told me that, I was surprised," Paterno would say at the end. "I guess maybe I did want to be a football coach. I just didn't think it would happen."

Requiem

In October 1945, when Joe was at Fort Dix, and two months after the bomb was dropped on Nagasaki, Angelo Paterno was director of Interfaith Movement Inc., an interracial group formed just before the war with the pledge of "allegiance to the kingdom of truth, the brotherhood of all mankind, and a world indivisible, with liberty and justice for all." He stood in front of a group of about 250 people gathered at the Barbizon Plaza Hotel overlooking Central Park to honor Colonel Clarence Eymer, who had led troops at Omaha Beach. There were other speakers. Rabbi Max Felshin of the Radio City Synagogue spoke; so did Judge Arthur Markewich, who years later would preside on the panel of judges that disbarred Richard Nixon.

This appears to be the only time Angelo ever spoke in front of the Interfaith crowd. "Realizing that the program for the evening is quite lengthy," he began, "I do not propose to take one minute longer than is absolutely necessary for me to convey to you assembled here this evening my thoughts in reference to this worthy interfaith movement."

Joe did not recall his father's being particularly eloquent or forceful. Angelo usually lost the arguments at home to Florence. Joe did not remember many enduring quotes from his father. He remembered that his father said "Make an impact" and that when he came home from playing a sport, Angelo always asked "Did you have fun?" (and never "Did you win?"). Angelo's wisdom breathed in the silences. Joe worried, even at the end of his life, that he had not done his father's memory justice, that he had not lived up to his father's silent hopes, that he had not expressed well enough Angelo Paterno's depth of character.

Maybe this was because Angelo was not one to make grand speeches, not one to preach to his children about the Golden Rule or, as one of Joe's contemporaries and heroes Martin Luther King famously said, that people should be judged not by the color of their skin but by the content of their character. These lessons, Angelo seemed to think, were too big to be taught with words.

Some people look upon the Movement as an outlet for prodigious writings wherein they extol the virtues of our cause; others expound the theories of Interfaith by loquacious and lengthy discourses. . . . To me, Interfaith has only one meaning. To me, it signifies the opportunity to manifest our consideration for our fellow beings by our conduct. All the talking and all of the literature in behalf of tolerance are wasted energies unless accompanied by overt acts.

George Paterno found this speech many years later and put it in the introduction to his book, *Joe Paterno: The Coach from Byzantium.* George too found it difficult to sum up the wonder of his father. There were easy enough descriptions. Angelo was a disciple of FDR, so much so that he named a son Franklin Delano Paterno, who died at eighteen months. Angelo was a devotee of the law, a tough semipro football player, a veteran of war, the uncle and cousin that everyone called when they needed help. He believed that tough people overcome. But, again, these are only words.

Stripped of all descriptive phrases and divested of its many interpretations, Interfaith means just that: Do unto others as you would want them to do unto you. This movement should emanate from our hearts. The propelling force will then be strong enough to enable us to overcome all the obstacles placed in our paths. . . .

We must all act as missionaries, and we must preach to our fellow men, night and day, of the evils of this hydrated monster of bigotry. The forces of intolerance and hate are on the march today. The seed of hate and discord is being sown all around us. It is our task to inculcate our worthy ideals into the warped minds of the weakling before this seed takes root. . . .

As we leave this assembly hall tonight, let us make a solemn pledge to the thousands of American youth, white and black, Protestant, Catholic and Jew, who had made the supreme sacrifice, that we will carry on those ideals for which they paid so dearly. They died that we might live and enjoy the benefits of this great and glorious country.

In conclusion, let me urge you who are assembled here this evening to rededicate your lives to the proposition that all of the forces of intolerance must be expunged from our midst and that you will become a crusader in this most worthy cause.

On September 29, 1955, almost exactly ten years after he spoke to the Interfaith Movement, Angelo Paterno suffered a massive heart attack and died. He was fifty-eight years old and had been talking about retiring. At the time, Joe was an unknown assistant football coach barely making a living wage in State College. He was twenty-eight, unmarried, and he lived in the basement of the home of another assistant coach. His law school invitation had long since expired, and his Brown degree in English literature rusted in the morning dew of football practice. Joe never did conquer the empty feeling that he had not lived up to his father's ideals. He never did conquer the sadness that Angelo did not live to share in his triumphs.

"My father was a great man," Joe said. "I don't think I've ever explained it well enough. He had no hatred inside him. Of all of the things he taught me, I think maybe that was the biggest one. He believed that if you give somebody a fair chance—whatever their color, whatever their religion—that they might be able to do great things."

At Angelo's wake, there were about a hundred white people in the room when a black man walked in. Nobody in the room knew him. He cleared his throat to get everyone's attention and said, "I want everybody to listen." With that he offered a small but breathtakingly beautiful eulogy of Angelo Paterno. Joe recalled his saying, "Every day, Mr. Paterno treated me with respect. Every day."

"I hope, if nothing else," Joe said near the end of his own life, "I gave a few people a chance to do great things."

Joe and Sue Paterno relax on the flight home from the 1967 Gator Bowl *(Penn State University Archives, Pennsylvania State University Libraries)*

Sue

During the last three months of Paterno's life, after the scandal and the firing and the cancer turned them inside out, they were funny and sublime, Sue and Joe, the way they finished each other's sentences, the way they rolled their eyes at stories they had heard too many times, the way they corrected each other. She was outraged; he was pragmatic. She was optimistic; he was stoic. She worried about him; he worried about her even more. It was as if they had lived fifty years together in training for the last act.

Joe was an assistant coach and Sue a freshman at Penn State when they first talked in the football study hall in the library they would rebuild together decades later. Sue was dating one of the players, someone she knew from high school. Study hall was more or less the only time they could see each other. "It was nothing serious," she said, while Joe listened and nodded. "It was just—we were freshmen."

Joe would tell the story of that first meeting a bit differently each time, though the year stayed constant. It was 1959. He had been coaching for Engle and Penn State for nine years. He was thirty-two and making hardly any money. He had lived with Engle at first, then moved into the home of an assistant coach and onetime Penn State football star, Steve Suhey. Then he lived with the family of another assistant coach, Jim O'Hora, for almost a decade. "He lost himself to coaching," O'Hora told a local writer and character named Ridge Riley.

Paterno spent almost no time living; it seemed like all he did was coach. To players of the day, Assistant Coach Paterno seemed to be ever present. He was there when they went to class and there when they walked out. He was there when they ate, when they joked around, when they went on dates. Milt Plum, one of Penn State's star quarterbacks, recalled, "On Friday nights before games you would be walking around and then all of a sudden there would be Joe, out of nowhere, and he would be shouting, 'Get off your feet!' "

Paterno spent his days watching films of opponents, preparing practice schedules, arguing with his fellow coaches (who followed the lead of former coach Joe Bedenk and called Paterno a "whippersnapper"), chasing football players around to make sure they were doing the right things, and constantly trying to strike up football conversations. He was inexhaustible. At night, he wrote countless notes (all his life, he was a compulsive note-taker) about football ideas he wanted to try, plays he wanted to run, techniques he wanted to teach, improvements he wanted to make, thoughts about leadership that crossed his mind. He wrote so many notes to himself that every month or so, Betts O'Hora, Jim's wife, would drop him a note of her own saying, "Clean this up, or move out."

He was such a force of will that people just bent to his way of thinking. Friends remembered him getting into furious shouting matches with Penn State's athletic director, Ernie McCoy, blaming McCoy for holding back the football team. But McCoy seemed to take it all in stride. (He would eventually hire Paterno as head coach.) In newspaper interviews, Paterno played it small, always acquiesced to Engle and the other assistant coaches, but in the closed circle of the program everyone understood that it was Paterno's drive and single-mindedness that powered Penn State football.

His first conversation with Suzanne Pohland had to do with football.

"He's your boyfriend, right?" Joe asked her as she began to leave for the night.

"Yes," Sue said.

"Well, listen, you better get him to study or he isn't going to be here much longer."

Joe was not sure that the conversation happened in the library. Sometimes he remembered asking Sue to meet him somewhere else to discuss her boyfriend. Sometimes his memory supplemented that brief exchange with small talk. "You remember," Sue said, "you told me I wasn't in love with him."

"I didn't say that," Joe said.

"Yes, you did. You said, 'You're not in love with him,' and I said, 'How do you know?'"

Joe shook his head, with the comic timing of a Marx brother. Truth is, that first conversation, whatever it happened to be, didn't have much of an impact on him. She was a freshman from Latrobe, Pennsylvania, hoping to become a teacher. He was a thirty-two-year-old assistant coach perpetually worried about the next game. The one thing he remembered for certain, the one thing that stuck with him through the years, was that the football player Sue dated did fail out of school. "Shame," Joe said. "He was a talented kid."

• • •

RIP ENGLE'S DEFINING QUALITY AS a coach was his gentle nature. It was certainly not his only quality; he could be stern, he often raged at officials and players on the sideline, and the reporters knew him best for his entertaining gloominess and pessimism. But his gentleness stood out to his players and assistant coaches. And it was gentleness that had the largest impact on the young Joe Paterno, perhaps because Paterno himself was so ungentle.

Here's an example: Football coaches often talk about having a player "cheat" to one side, meaning that they want the player to stand a step or two closer to that side in anticipation of a certain play. Engle refused to use the word "cheat," and he would not allow any of his coaches to use it. He believed that the word had no place in fair competition. Instead, at Penn State, they would talk of having players "fudge" to one side.

This may sound ridiculous, but little quirks like this were the bricks of Engle's day-to-day coaching style. There were many other examples. Football has a position called "monster back," usually a player who stands behind the linebackers and is given the freedom to roam all over the field in pursuit of the football. Well, to Engle, "monster" was an even less suitable word than "cheat," and so at Penn State they called the position a "hero back."

Or this: One day they were trying to come up with a name for the linebacker who sets up on what's called the weak side, the side where the offense has fewer blockers. Engle did not want to call the position a "weakside linebacker," as most coaches do, because that had connotations of weakness and frailty. The coaches sat around for far too long trying to come up with a good name for this position, when finally Engle said, "Okay, enough of this. The next idea someone comes up with, we're going with that." To which Paterno said something like "Well, while we are waiting for that brilliant idea, can we go ahead and order some pizza from Fritz?" The man who ran Home Delivery Pizza in town was Fritz DeFluri. And so, from that day forward, the weakside linebacker at Penn State (and numerous other copycat pro-grams) was called the Fritz linebacker.

Engle's compassion and kindness permeated everything he did. He constantly reminded his coaches, "It's the players' team, not ours," a mantra Paterno repeated to himself when he was at his lowest points. Engle almost never swore, almost never tore down a player, almost never fought with one of his coaches. He deflected credit and entertained the media with stories in which he inevitably ended up playing the sucker.

Paterno watched Engle's style closely. He was not like Engle. He was, in his own words, "a loudmouth." When he first came to State College as an Ivy League–educated Brooklyn street fighter, he felt en-tirely out of place. "It was too quiet to sleep," he said, repeating some vaudeville line from his memory. He got into ferocious arguments with fellow coaches, including Engle. Some of those arguments were so vicious and heated that an outsider might wonder how Paterno kept his job. "I was a pain in the neck," he confessed. "I just knew I was right all the time."

Of course, as Paterno readily admitted, he never lost that part of his personality. But over sixteen years as Engle's assistant coach, he did temper it. Some of Engle's nature penetrated him. While he trusted his own strategic football judgment over anyone else's (that too never really changed), he saw how Engle could get his point across without screaming. He noticed the respect Engle quietly built. He learned about the power of consensus, even if he never fully embraced it. Engle had some Angelo in him. And though Paterno coached with more passion and wrath and authority and certainty than Engle, he did soften over the years. He stopped swearing. He learned how to em-power others. He never took the credit. In time, he also began to see some of the beauty of State College. Well, that did take some time.

After the 1956 season, when Penn State won six of nine games, the University of Southern California's legendary Jess Hill called Engle. Hill had played Major League Baseball, had been a star running back on USC's 1928 national championship team, and had won two national championships as coach of USC's track team. He had also been the football coach at USC, but he decided to give it up. He called Engle and asked him to be the new coach. Engle was flattered, but he was not sure the school was a good fit for him. Paterno was absolutely sure. He told Engle that this was their chance to go big time. Engle decided to put it up for a vote. "And then," Paterno said, "I started to talk to the other coaches. You know how people call me a great politician? Well, I used my political skills." He hammered away at Engle, telling him again and again how much easier it would be to recruit great players at USC and how much better their chances would be to play in a great game like the Rose Bowl. He lobbied his fellow coaches. He begged and pleaded, threatened and cajoled, charmed and bullied. He did everything in his power to get Engle to take the whole lot of them west, where they could coach football in the sun.

When the votes were counted, all the coaches except Paterno voted to stay in State College. "It's a good thing I didn't go into politics," Paterno said.

After the USC letdown, Paterno began to look at State College as home. To his surprise, he found that there were many things about the place he liked. He liked the ease of things, the comfort, the way he could focus on football without the inconveniences of daily life to distract him. He liked the routine so much that he did not leave the O'Hora home. The end of that living arrangement came only when Jim O'Hora sat Paterno down and gave him a speech that Paterno remembered for the rest of his life. In Paterno's memory, this is what O'Hora said:

"You know, Joe, when my father came from Ireland, and my cousins would come over, they'd stay with us for three or four months. And my Dad would say, 'You've been with us four months now. It's time to get out, cut yourself from us, go and live your life.' . . . Joe, you've been with us ten years. Get the hell out of here."

To which Paterno remembered asking, "Have I been here that long?"

The continuity and regularity of the seasons comforted him. The students stayed young and eager and were less spoiled than they had been at Brown. He liked the ice cream at the historic Creamery on campus; in time, their most popular flavor would be Peachy Paterno. He found that he loved to walk around the town; the beauty of Mount Nittany and the surrounding forests did not inspire him to write nature poems, but he could think clearly as he walked along the familiar streets, friendly people waving as he walked briskly past. The anger and commotion of the day seeped out of him. Ideas and football plays crystallized in his mind. Those walks around Happy Valley would calm and energize Paterno for the rest of his life.

THE PERSONA THAT WOULD BECOME so familiar to college football fans was coming into focus when Paterno first met Sue Pohland. He was argumentative, certainly, and obsessive and always certain, but he was also charming and funny and smart. He was a popular speaker on campus and around Pennsylvania. Reporters generally loved him. Players, even those he speared with sarcasm in his high-pitched voice, could not help but be drawn in by his energy.

His passion for education was apparent from the start. He hated the idea of players coming to college only to play football. He also hated the idea of teachers treating football players differently from other students. In his mind—and Engle believed this too—coaches were professors and football was a particularly intense class designed to teach discipline, focus, and various life lessons. For the rest of his life, Paterno would publicly uphold this ideal, graduating 80 to 90 percent of his players and influencing young men who would become doctors, lawyers, chemists, and teachers.

His purpose was so public that many people, especially late in his life, would wonder if he exaggerated his commitment to education or, worse, was an out-and-out phony. But it seems no matter how deeply you dig into the life of Joe Paterno, no matter how many players or professors you talk with, you find a man driven by the cause of education and repelled both by schools who took advantage of football players and by football players who did not take advantage of their opportunity to learn. "I don't see why people can't just realize that Joe is who he says he is," Sue said. "He isn't perfect. But he tried to teach young men how to live."

This passion was in place from the start. Here's part of a letter a young Joe Paterno wrote in 1952 to a recruit named Earl Shumaker:

Dear Earl,

As I told you last December we definitely feel that you are the type of boy we want at Penn State—a good student as well as a good football player. All the people I have talk[ed] to about you have told me the same thing—you are interested in going to college to get an education first and to play football second. That's the way it should be and we are only interested in boys who feel this way. Always remember you can only play football a few years, and if all you get out of college is four years of football you are getting cheated. No matter where you decide to go to school make sure that you will get an education that will enable you to have a happy and well-rounded life.

Sincerely
Joe Paterno

As an assistant coach, Paterno developed a reputation as a molder of quarterbacks. Football was a different game in the 1950s and 1960s; quarterbacks did not throw nearly as often as they would forty and fifty years later, and they called their own plays, a responsibility that coaches later took for themselves. It was important, then, to teach quarterbacks how to think, how to feel the game, how to anticipate what the defense might try. Paterno loved coaching like this; he did not want players to be like robots. He wanted them to develop their own rhythms and styles, to learn from their own mistakes.

He also believed in simplicity. If a play worked, he wanted his quarterbacks to try it again. If the play worked again, he wanted his quarterbacks to try it yet again. He was not opposed to an occasional trick play; he developed the belief that a surprising gadget play such as a reverse or a halfback pass could turn the tide of close games. But like his Brooklyn counterpart Lombardi, Paterno believed that you did not win games by tricking teams; you won with precise execution of plays and by making fewer mistakes than your opponent.

His first great quarterback success was Milt Plum, whom he personally recruited. Plum was such a versatile athlete that he played quarterback, running back, defensive back, punter, and kicker. But he was a disappointment during his sophomore and much of his junior seasons. Paterno wrote about Plum in his autobiography, expressing his feelings about the mysteries of football and his own passion for teaching in a single paragraph:

> *In our first six games that season [1955] we broke even, confirming the mediocrity of both our team and our quarterback. If the electricity a quarterback transmits (or doesn't) to a team defies analysis, another imponderable is what happens when that current suddenly transforms. In our seventh game of 1955, all the teaching, drilling, and praying I had pumped into Plum miraculously fused with his natural talent. He took charge. His passes clicked. His confidence lit the field and charged through the team. We surprised the experts in the press box by slipping past Syracuse 21–20, when we were scheduled to be crushed by them. On that day, Milt Plum became a star quarterback—and my first visible success.*

Plum was brilliant in 1956. He threw the ball only seventy-five times the whole season, fewer than nine times a game. Forty years later, there would be quarterbacks who would throw that often in a single game. But Plum ran well, tackled hard on defense, intercepted seven passes, and one of his punts against Ohio State went 73 yards and stopped at the 3-yard line, perhaps the decisive play in Penn State's shocking 7–6 upset victory, one many Penn State historians believe started the modern success of the school's football program. Plum would go on to a long and successful career as a pro quarterback.

Paterno's next quarterback project would prove even more successful. Richie Lucas grew up in Glassport, just outside of Pittsburgh. Paterno believed that he saw Lucas's great talent before anyone else did, before he even became a quarterback. Paterno was watching films of a more highly touted quarterback, Jerry Eisman of nearby Bethel, when he noticed Lucas, a player on the opposing team. Other schools soon noticed him too, and there was a recruiting battle to get him. Paterno won the battle, as he would hundreds of times through the years, by captivating Lucas's parents, in particular his mother.

Riverboat Richie Lucas, as he came to be called, became a Penn State legend. He fit Paterno's ideal of a quarterback perfectly: he was fast and tough, had a good arm, and could make good decisions quickly. But there was something else: as his nickname suggested, he also had a bit of the gambler in him. He liked to take chances, throw the ball downfield, go against conventional thinking. The conservative Paterno was quietly thrilled at this. He did not want quarterbacks who always did the "right" thing; sometimes, as he would tell players, you need to forget what you were taught and just make a play. Lucas instinctively understood that. In 1959 Lucas led Penn State to nine victories in eleven games and finished second in the Heisman Trophy voting behind Louisiana State's Billy Cannon. He would eventually be inducted into College Football's Hall of Fame.

Lucas's senior year was the year Paterno had his first conversation with Sue Pohland. It was also the year other coaches around the country began to notice him. Weeb Ewbank, who coached Paterno at Brown, wanted him to become an assistant coach for the Baltimore Colts. Nick Skorich asked Paterno to be an assistant coach with the Philadelphia Eagles. Boston College invited him to interview for the head coaching job. And there were other offers. The only job that appealed to him was when the Yale head coaching job opened up in 1962. Paterno was thirty-five, about to be married, and he saw the potential to fulfill his destiny there. Yale had a rich football history; it had fielded one of the first college football teams and was the nation's most dominant football program before World War I. The program's success had been sporadic after World War II, but Paterno thought he could rebuild some of the magic. "I wanted that job pretty badly," he remembered. "The idea of being Yale's coach for fifteen or twenty years was very appealing to me. I thought we could win some games, we could do it the right way, we could have an impact on some of the bright young men who would help form the future. If they had offered me that job then, I think I might have taken it."

Yale did not offer the job in 1962. Two years later, however, the job opened up again, and this time they offered it to Paterno first. Many things had changed in two years, though. Joe and Sue were married, they had a baby daughter, and Paterno's axis had shifted. He now saw his future more clearly. He wanted to be head coach at Penn State. Rip Engle told Paterno he was going to retire soon. Engle named him associate head coach, making him the clear succession candidate, and Athletic Director Ernie McCoy told Paterno that he was next in line. They all went to see the school's president, Eric Walker, to get final assurances. "I want to know what my chances are to get the job," Paterno remembered telling Walker.

"If you're good enough, you'll get the job," Walker replied.

And Paterno, certain he was good enough, stayed at Penn State. "I'd just as soon stay here the rest of my life," he told a reporter at the Penn State newspaper, the *Daily Collegian*.

There was one other job offer whose story is worth telling. During this time, a fellow Brooklyn native named Al Davis asked Paterno to be an assistant coach for the Oakland Raiders. Davis, however, never just asked for something he wanted; he went on the attack. But that story needs to wait because it's more about Sue Paterno than about Joe.

• • •

SUE AND JOE SAW EACH other around campus, and they talked every now and again about their mutual love of literature. Neither could remember exactly when their casual friendship became attraction or when attraction became love. They remembered seeing each other at a lecture on campus by the controversial literary critic Leslie Fiedler. They talked for a long time after that.

Joe said he fell first. After Sue's sophomore year, in the summer of 1960, she worked as a waitress at the American Hotel on the Jersey Shore, in a five-block square with the magical name Avon-by-the-Sea. One day, at the house where she was staying with "sixteen girls, five bunk beds, one phone," Joe called to say that he was in the area ("I don't even remember what excuse he used," Sue said) and wanted to meet her for pizza. She already had a date, and she thought so little of Joe's call that she invited her date to come along. "No, I don't think so," he said.

"Oh, it's okay," Sue said. "He's just a friend. You'll see. He's an old man."

Joe was almost thirty-four. Sue was twenty. They saw each other around campus the next year, but it wasn't until the summer of 1961 that their relationship shifted. Sue went back to work on the shore, Paterno rented a house a couple of towns away, and they would spend their free time together on the beach, reading books, discussing them, arguing, laughing. It's easy to see what Joe saw in Sue: she was pretty and smart, energetic and forceful. What Sue saw in Joe is a bit more complicated. She could have seen a middle-aged assistant coach who still lived in the basement of another family's home. (Jim O'Hora had had his "It's time to leave, Joe" chat in June of that year.) Instead she saw a brilliant, kind man with honest intentions and ambitions to do something great. She was pinned to someone else, but that summer she fell in love with Joe Paterno.

"I figured," Sue explained, "you know, 'Dick's really good-looking and really a good dancer but why spend the rest of your life with a petroleum and natural gas engineer?' " In other words, she was not attracted to stability and the expected; she craved an unpredictable life. Joe Paterno offered that. At summer's end, he asked Sue to marry him, and she accepted. They intended to get married three weeks later, before Sue graduated from Penn State.

First, though, they would have to tell Sue's parents, Alma and August Pohland, and that turned out to be an adventure. The Pohlands had gone to New York to see one of Sue's sisters and to catch a show, and so Sue and Joe went there to tell them the good news. They all met at the Hotel Astor in Times Square. Alma Pohland was a sensible woman; she hardly ever drank, and she was a devout Catholic. They had dinner and planned to see the show *Irma La Douce* at the Plymouth Theater. The conversation they had in the restaurant of the Hotel Astor wouldn't have sounded out of place on Broadway.

> *Joe:* Would you like to have a drink?
> *Alma:* No thank you.
> *Joe:* We would like to get married in three weeks.
> *Alma:* I'll have a whiskey sour.
> *Sue:* Well, we . . .
> *Alma (grabbing Sue):* We're going to the ladies' room.

Sue's parents convinced her to graduate before she and Joe got married. Then, because Penn State qualified for a bowl game, the wedding was pushed back to May 1962. One of Paterno's favorite and most polished bits when speaking to alumni groups and after-dinner functions was about their honeymoon. "We planned to go to Europe for two months. But we couldn't afford it. So we decided on a few weeks in Bermuda. But there were a couple of things that came up with the football team, so that shrunk to two weeks in Bermuda, which became ten days in Florida, and then we settled on a week in Sea Isle, Georgia. The bottom line was that we spent five wonderful days in Virginia Beach—well, four days, because we had to detour to Somerset to see a recruit. Sue waited in the car. We lost him to Miami."

"That's true," Sue said in her own retelling. "I think his name was Jack White or something. I don't remember. I read a book in the car. Whatever."

That was the word Sue would use many times through the years: *whatever.* She was not a particularly devoted football fan before meeting Joe, and she had no idea what life as a coach's wife would be. But that was part of the attraction. "After about two years of marriage, I thought, I wasn't *courted,* I was *recruited.* In those days, you used to be able to take out the recruits' families for dinner, get the mother flowers, whatever. So that's what Joe did for me, and I thought, I wasn't courted, I was recruited. Only it wasn't for four years."

PENN STATE NAMED JOE PATERNO head coach in 1966, a few months before his fortieth birthday. But before then, Al Davis made his push to hire Paterno and make him a coaching star. There were, as mentioned, many offers in the early 1960s, but this one was different because of Al Davis. Even in 1963—long before Davis had become the owner of the Oakland Raiders, the purveyor of a philosophy he called "Commitment to Excellence," a pro football legend and villain in equal parts—he was a whirlwind.

Like Paterno, he had grown up on the streets of Flatbush, playing stickball and dreaming big dreams. He became an assistant football coach at a small military college in South Carolina called The Citadel, and there he reinvented the way colleges recruit high school players. He was, as best anyone can tell, the first college coach to send cards to high school coaches asking for information not only about the coach's own players but about the players his teams had faced. He knew more about players than anyone else. And he recruited ferociously; Paterno first became aware of Davis the year they competed for an Italian American tight end from New Jersey. Davis won the recruiting battle. That's the kind of salesman he was even then: he coaxed an Italian American football player from New Jersey to come south to play at a military school rather than play for Joe Paterno.

Paterno had dreamed of going west to coach at Southern California in 1957, but it was actually Davis who got the job. By 1963, Davis had become head coach of the Oakland Raiders, and he decided that Paterno had to be his offensive coordinator. He offered to triple Paterno's salary, from roughly six thousand to eighteen thousand dollars, to get him a new car, and to put him on track to be the next Vince Lombardi in professional football.

Paterno said no. He remembered telling Davis, " 'Al, you know what? You and I would have a tough time getting along.' He said, 'Why?' I said, 'Because I'm smarter than you, and you would never admit it.' " But this was more of Paterno's vaudeville patter; the real reason was Sue. And Al Davis knew it. Sue had a vision about their life together, a blurry vision to be sure, but one that involved family and college and being at the heart of a community. She had fallen in love with State College the first day she arrived on campus as a student, and though Joe did not know it yet, the rest of his life would be guided by her vision. Joe was cocky, ambitious, principled, smart, consumed by football, and determined to win; those qualities and others would make him a great football coach. But he would become a legend by seeing the world through Sue's eyes.

"Sue," Davis said, because of course he called her after Joe turned him down, "I have to tell you this, and I want you to think about it. You are holding your husband back."

He could not have been more wrong.

ACT II: EXCELLENCE

I don't belong anywhere where celebrity equals merit or money means talent or wealth proves achievement.

—IRISH ACTOR DONAL McCANN

Paterno addresses Penn State's graduating seniors at the 1973 commencement ceremonies *(Penn State University Archives, Pennsylvania State University Libraries)*

{ *Aria* }

Joe Paterno
commencement address to Penn State's graduating seniors
June 16, 1973

I chuckle at people who blame the "system" for our problems, just as I laugh at those who claim that we should have blind faith in our government and institutions. What is this notorious "system"?

In my game, people talk about offensive formations as the cure-all. After we lost to Oklahoma in the Sugar Bowl, many people asked: "Are you going to switch to the wishbone formation?" Believe me: It isn't the plays of the offensive system which get the job done. It is the quality of the players which makes the formation effective.

And it is you who will make the organization work for you and you who will become victims of this system, if you fail to execute your responsibility to yourself and your fellow human beings. You have a part to play and if you loaf or quit, don't sit back and complain that our method is no good.

The system, the organization, the method, the government IS you.

If each of us is easily seduced by expediency, by selfishness, by ambition regardless of cost to our principles, then the spectacle of Watergate will surely mark the end of this grand experiment in Democracy. One of the tragedies of Watergate is to see so many bright young men, barely over thirty, who have so quickly prostituted their honor and decency in order to get ahead. To be admired. To stay on the "team." These same young men, within the short period of the last ten years, sat in on convocations such as this. They were ready to change the world. They didn't trust the over-thirty generation.

I warn you: Don't underestimate the world. It can corrupt quickly and completely.

And heed Walter Lippmann, who wrote several years ago: "It is a mistake to suppose that there is satisfaction and the joy of life in a self-indulgent generation, in one interested primarily in the pursuit of private wealth and private pleasure and private success. We are very rich but we are not having a good time—for our life, though it is full of things, is empty of the kind of purpose and effort that gives to life its flavor and meaning."

What Lippmann wants us to realize is that money alone will not make you happy. Success without honor is an unseasoned dish. It will satisfy your hunger. But it won't taste good.

Paterno screamed "Go to the ball!" Here, eight Penn State defenders, including Dennis Onkotz (35), George Landis (31), Jack Ham (33), Gary Hull (80), and John Ebersole (89), swarm a Colorado player during the 1969 season (*Penn State University Archives, Pennsylvania State University Libraries*)

The Other Thing

Paterno sat in the upstairs office of his small house in State College and felt something like desperation. Scraps of graph paper blanketed the thirteen-dollar desk Sue had found at an auction, and on each scrap were pencil scribblings in feverish cursive. Paterno had been head football coach of Penn State University for one year. One disappointing year. He picked up one scrap of paper, read it, then another, a third, pulled out a notepad, scrawled something, threw it down, picked up another piece of paper, read it, crumpled it. He stared out the window for long stretches of time.

Sue had never seen him like this. She had known him to be driven, of course, but this was something different, and a bit frightening. He woke up at 5:30 every morning, went into the room he used as an office, closed the door, and stayed in there all day. This was the spring and summer of 1967. The Paternos had three small children: Diana, the oldest, was four; Mary Kay was two; David was not even a year old. Joe did not seem to know them. He stayed in that makeshift office, often through lunch, often all afternoon, and when he emerged for dinner he had a dazed look, like a child coming out of a dark movie theater. He would look at Sue and the kids with an expression that seemed to say "Hey, what are you all doing here?" More often than not, he would take his dinner back to the office.

He called the project The Other Thing. Well, he did not actually have a name for it, but he would often tell Sue, "I gotta go work on the other thing" or "I have a meeting, and then I need to get on the other thing." Sue worried about The Other Thing. She worried about him. She worried about herself. It was a summer of worrying. She took the children to Welch Pool for four and five hours at a time, just to get them out of the house, just to get them away from the tension and strain that seemed to rise off their father like steam. Joe did not seem aware of when they were home or when they were gone. He lost weight. He walked around oblivious. He was unresponsive, even to his young children.

"We could have moved out," Sue said, "and he wouldn't have noticed. He might have noticed when he came out and there was no dinner there for him. But he might not even have noticed that. He was in his own world."

"I always tell our players that you can't be scared to lose," Joe said. "That summer, if I'm being honest with myself, I was scared to death."

• • •

HIS FIRST GAME AS HEAD coach ended without a handshake. Nobody had been surprised when Penn State hired Paterno in February 1966; that had been an inevitability ever since he turned down the Yale job. But it's also true that nobody knew him as anything other than the quirky assistant coach who yelled a lot and told funny stories and obsessed over the game.

"He wanted to be like Lombardi," said Don Abbey, one of Paterno's first recruits. "At that time he was all scream-y, swear-y. Later I would hear players say that Joe Paterno never swore. Well, I can tell you he grew into that. At first, he was vicious on the field. Vicious. He would get in players' faces and yell, 'You're a fucking coward' and that sort of thing. Nothing like the 'real Joe.' Nothing like Joe became."

Ambition consumed him. At the end of his life, he would appreciate that there were complicated and conflicting things clashing around inside him when he was named Penn State's head coach. He was thirty-nine; many of his friends had long before achieved their professional success. He had never come to grips with the wishes, or the death, of his father. And he was not even sure that he could be successful. He was a head football coach at a school in a remote Pennsylvania town with a football team that, though a consistent winner, had made little impact on the national college football scene. Even the hiring process felt small and insignificant. "We would like you to be Penn State's football coach," Athletic Director Ernie McCoy had said.

"I'd like that," Paterno said. "I think it's the best job in the country."

"Good," McCoy said. "We'll pay you twenty thousand a year."

They shook hands and that was it. No contract. No haggling. No promises. Four or five years later, Alabama's legendary coach Bear Bryant, peerless among football coaches in his ability to consolidate power, was mortified to learn that Paterno still did not have a contract. "You get yourself a contract," he ordered. "And you be sure that you get them to include two hundred tickets in there."

"Two hundred tickets?" Paterno asked. "Why?"

Bryant smiled. Paterno would remember that smile the rest of his life. His fascination and curiosity about the great coach never faded. Bryant, the old southern politician, said plainly, "Two hundred tickets will get you a lot of favors."

That was all much later. In that first year Paterno felt inadequate. He did not trust his future to any other coach, so he called all the plays, offensive and defensive. He did not trust his players to play their best, so he worked them harder than he ever would again. When I asked him at the end if he felt such a desperate need to achieve because his father had died young, or because of the driving personality of his mother, or because achievement had been the overpowering theme of his life, Paterno shrugged. He did not like to be analyzed. He simply said, "Yeah, sure, all of that."

All of that. The players in that first year had conflicting memories of Paterno. The consensus sided with Abbey: that Paterno mimicked Lombardi, played the role of a tyrant who worked them beyond the point of exhaustion and demanded of them something just beyond perfection. Dave Rowe, a marvelous defensive guard who played with such joy that his teammates called him "Hap," was thrown off the team briefly for breaking curfew. This might not be worth noting—football players get thrown off teams all the time for breaking curfew—but in Rowe's case he was out late on the night after a game. Coaches rarely even have curfews the night after a game. And Rowe was spending that time with his new wife.

"Interestingly, I carried being thrown off the team through my thirteen years in the NFL," Rowe said. "In the pros, I *never* broke a rule. I know that sounds unbelievable, but I remember how devastated I was when I was thrown off and realized how much football meant to me."

Then again, not everyone remembered Paterno as a tyrant in that first year. Mike Irwin, who was co-captain of that team and later coached under Paterno, remembered that Paterno had actually gotten too loose and mellow and had lost the fire that made him such a force as an assistant coach.

Either way, the larger point remains: Paterno was not himself that first year. His style was unformed. The assistant coach who always believed he was right turned spectacularly indecisive as a head coach. He changed the offense from Rip Engle's Wing-T—the offense Paterno had led at Brown, the offense that had brought him to State College in the first place—to the more modern I formation, where two running backs line up behind the quarterback as if waiting in a line for coffee. He then changed back. He switched quarterbacks. One minute he seemed eager to prove that he was not at all like Engle, and when that felt wrong he tried to be more understanding and calm, and when that felt wrong he switched again.

Penn State did win Paterno's first game against Maryland, but it was such a miserable performance by both teams that the Maryland coach, a character named Lou Saban, did not even show up for the traditional postgame handshake. Saban called two days later to semi-apologize. "Ah, I shoulda shook your hand," Paterno would remember him saying, "but you guys stunk so bad, we stunk worse, it just didn't seem right to shake hands about it."

Paterno didn't disagree. The next week, his team was destroyed 42–8 by the top-ranked team in the country, Michigan State. That told Paterno how far away his team was from greatness. The week after that, Penn State lost to Army 11–0. That told Penn State fans how far his team was from even being good.

"After that Army game, you wouldn't believe some of the letters I got," Paterno said. "In all the years I was at Penn State, I would say some of the most vicious letters I got were in that first year after we got shut out against Army." His first thought was that he could somehow joke people out of their rage—that was how arguments were handled on the streets of Brooklyn. But this was a different level of anger than he had ever endured. People called Paterno's home (his number was listed, and would remain listed throughout his life) and screamed at Sue. A doctor in East Stroudsburg sent letters filled with such contempt that Paterno would remember them for the rest of his life. "Oh, I knew enough even then not to worry about what people said. But I wouldn't be entirely truthful if I didn't add that it was a bit eye-opening. Here it was, I had only coached three games, and people had decided I had no idea what I was doing. Maybe they were right, but it wasn't like we had been a great team the year or two before."

Two weeks after the Army debacle, Paterno decided to entirely change his team's defense in an effort to stop a talented UCLA offense featuring a future Heisman Trophy winner, quarterback Gary Beban. This move foreshadowed what would be a Paterno trademark: his willingness to start over and do whatever was necessary strategically to win. But it would also demonstrate just how raw he was as a coach, that he didn't yet understand his own limitations. The staff was still trying to teach the players the new defense on Friday, the day before the game, which, as Paterno would say, "is way too late. If you're still teaching on Friday, you're dead before you get started." He learned that lesson. In later years, he would be at his most relaxed on Fridays, because by then, in one of his favorite Latin phrases, *Alea iacta est*. The die is cast.

But he did not know that yet, and his defensive players were utterly confused. The Bruins destroyed Penn State 49–11, and to make things more agonizing, UCLA's coach, Tommy Prothro, ordered a late onside kick, a play that is used almost exclusively when a team is trailing and in a desperate situation. Paterno believed Prothro was trying to embarrass him and his team, and it made him seethe.

Little went right. The week of the Syracuse game, Sue Paterno came up with a plan to liven things up. On Thursday night, she, Sandra Welsh (wife of assistant coach George Welsh), and Nancy Radakovich (wife of assistant coach Dan Radakovich) sneaked over to the Nittany Lion statue at the heart of campus and splattered a little washable orange paint on it, Syracuse's color, and strung up a few orange streamers. Their idea was to get the Penn State students riled up and ready for Syracuse. "It was way too quiet," Sue explained. "Nobody was showing any spirit at all." The wives were so nervous they didn't realize that most of the paint had ended up on their own coats.

The next morning, the radio news announced that the Nittany

Lion statue had been painted orange and the police knew the identity of the criminals; jail time was being considered. Joe flipped. He had so many other problems, and now his wife might go to jail for painting the most beloved statue on campus orange. It was more than he could handle. He called home to tell Sue that she was going to be arrested.

"Joe was mad," Sue recalled. "I mean he was really mad. I had thought it was just some good clean fun, but Joe was never like that. He has always had the strongest sense of right and wrong—the strongest sense of anyone I have ever known. He was outraged. If they had sent me to jail, I don't even think Joe would have fought it. He even told me, 'If you go to jail, I'll have to find someone to take care of the kids.' "

As it turned out, the wives had splashed only a little bit of paint on the statue, probably even less than they remembered, considering how nervous they were. But then, perhaps inspired by the idea, some Syracuse students had come along and painted the Nittany Lion orange from mane to tail, and they had done the job in oil paint. In the end, three Syracuse fans did a little jail time, Sue's prank would be retold every year, gaining new and more exciting details all the time, and every homecoming week Penn State students would make a show of protecting the Nittany Lion from fans of the opposing team.

Even with all of that, Syracuse beat Penn State 12–10.

Penn State came together well enough to beat the University of Pittsburgh in the last game of the season to salvage a 5-5 record; this mattered because the school had not had a losing season since 1938. But Paterno took no comfort from this. Years before, he had followed his *fatum*, his inner voice, and it had taken him away from law school, away from New York, away from the life of accomplishment his parents had planned for him. The voice had taken him to State College to be an assistant coach for sixteen years. Why? He had to believe it was for something great. Then, in his first year as head coach, the team had lost as many games as it won, and many people thought he was overmatched as a head coach. He had to admit to himself that he was not even a good football coach, much less a great one.

"I'll tell you what I think happened that first year," Paterno would say in a rousing soliloquy. "I was pointed in the wrong direction. I wanted to be successful. That was my mistake. I wanted to be one of the great ones. I wanted to be as big as Lombardi, as big as Bear, as big as Woody Hayes or Bobby Dodd. I had forgotten Rip's lesson: 'It's not our team. It's their team.'

"And so, that first year I was acting like a coach. I had watched the great coaches closely, and I was doing things the way I thought they did them. I wasn't a dumb kid, you know? I was almost forty years old, and I knew a lot about football. I knew how to win. But I didn't know how to infuse that into the players. I had a lot of doubt, my coaches had a lot of doubt, it all trickled down.

"A good coach, a good manager, a good leader of any kind shows no doubt. And they can make players understand that the greatest thing in the world is to lose yourself to something bigger. How could I ask my players to do that when I wasn't willing to do it? I kept thinking of it as *my* team. But it wasn't *my* team. That's not a bad title for your book: 'It Was Never My Team.' "

THE OTHER THING WAS PATERNO'S strategic plan to prove that he was a great coach. To everyone. To himself. It was nothing less than his attempt to reinvent the game of football.

Though Paterno had achieved much of his playing success as a quarterback and his greatest coaching success as a molder of quarterbacks, he had come to believe that the best way to win football games was with a great defense. This was something many football coaches believed, but for Paterno it would become a guiding philosophy. Years later, he would scribble a fascinating little note to himself, sort of a miniature Socratic discussion about how to win:

There are two ways to build a football team.
1. Solid kicking.
   Dominant defense.

Limited offense that doesn't take chances because it doesn't have to.

OR

2. Solid kicking.

An offense that is all over the place—big plays—deep passes—take chances because they can, but have to take chances because the defense is going to give up points.

You won't win all of your games playing that second way. You have a bad game throwing it. You fall behind and never catch up. You have to go the length of the field.

It is rare to go to a Rose Bowl and win a national championship without a great defense. The only way to control a game is with a great defense.

After the 1966 season, Paterno felt certain the way to make Penn State a great football program was to build that great defense. He shut himself into that upstairs office, shut the door, sat at that thirteen-dollar desk, and worked on designing a defense that had never been seen before. That was The Other Thing, a new kind of defense, and to build it Paterno would have to go deeper inside himself than he ever had in his life.

THE FUNDAMENTAL DIFFICULTY WITH COACHING defense is this: You don't know what the offense will try to do. That may sound obvious and simple, but this is the challenge that has baffled and inspired defensive football coaches since the game was invented.

The offensive team calls a play, and all eleven players know the play. They know what they want to do. They know where they are supposed to go. They act.

Defensive players must react. "On offense, you only think about one play, the play you're running," Paterno explained. "On defense, you have to think about a lot of plays. You have to be ready for anything."

The struggles of the 1966 season convinced Paterno of two things. First, he wanted his best athletes playing defense. This would become a Paterno staple; for the rest of his career he would take great offensive players from high school and put them on defense. There is example after example; he even put one of his greatest offensive players, Heisman Trophy winner John Cappelletti, on defense for a while. Perhaps the most extreme example happened when Paterno tried to recruit a brilliant high school quarterback named Jim Kelly. Paterno wanted him to play linebacker. Kelly wanted to stay at quarterback. He became a star at the University of Miami, led the Buffalo Bills to four Super Bowls, and was inducted into the Pro Football Hall of Fame. As a quarterback.

When a friend kidded Paterno about being the coach who wanted to shift Kelly to linebacker, he remained defiant: "You don't know. He might have been an even better linebacker."

But improving the defensive talent was only the first step. The second: Paterno wanted to conjure up a defense that would baffle and frustrate coaches for years. People will argue whether he invented something new at that desk in his home over that Summer of Love, or if he simply cobbled together some of the better ideas already in circulation. Either way, he called his new defense the 4-4-3. And for the next few years, the Penn State defense would terminate every offensive plan thrown its way.

Here was Paterno's thinking: For many years, teams lined up seven defensive players close to the line of scrimmage. The combination of players changed—it might be three defensive linemen and four linebackers, or four defensive linemen and three linebackers, or some other blend—but the core number stayed the same: seven. This was important because it left four players downfield to protect against deeper passes and to act as a last line of defense should an offensive player break through the front lines. Defensive coaches tinkered with the alignment, but in general this was the accepted philosophy: seven in front, four in what was called the secondary.

Paterno wanted eight players in front. He figured that with eight close to the line of scrimmage, his team could attack the offense in a whole new way. The most devastating offensive play of the late 1960s was the option, where the quarterback runs parallel with the line and then either turns upfield himself or (as an option) pitches the ball to a trailing running back. A good offensive football coach, like a good general, figures out ways to outflank the defense, to get outside of them (to "break contain," in the language of football), and this is how so many of the biggest offensive plays happen. Paterno believed if he had that eighth man up front, his defense would not be outflanked, and teams would be unable to run around them.

Of course, he was not the first coach to think of putting an extra man up front; coaches had long done that when it was clear the opponent wanted to run the ball. But as far as Paterno knew, nobody had kept eight up front for entire games, and the reason was obvious: doing so would leave only three in the back. How could a team defend against the big play with only three in the secondary? Wouldn't quarterbacks complete deep pass after deep pass? Wouldn't teams break long runs against a secondary spread too thin?

This, then, was Paterno's challenge: to turn three players into four. He was designing a magic trick. This was what kept him in a spare bedroom fifteen hours a day, what prompted him to ignore his family for weeks at a time, what sent him into such a deep level of obsession that friends worried about him.

"This was how Joe's mind worked," Sue said. "It was always like that. He would have something in there, and he just had to work it out. It was like a train coming through.

"I remember that some days that summer he would work something out in his mind, and he would come out and be like a human being again. He'd be joking and fun again. He would ask us to name some of the new plays, and that was fun. Then, another train would come through, and he wouldn't say another word to us for two weeks. There were times after that when we saw that side of him, but I don't think he was ever quite like that again."

What Paterno worked out came from different places in his life, but his most important breakthrough came from baseball. He had grown up watching the Brooklyn Dodgers—he had even been an usher at Ebbets Field one summer—and he was fascinated by the way outfielders worked in tandem. When a ball was hit to left-center field, for instance, the left fielder and center fielder would go after it. But the right fielder would also run in that direction to back up the play. This, of course, left no one in right field. But the team obviously did not need anyone in right field: the ball wasn't there.

But was this concept true only for baseball? Paterno did not think so; he believed that it was true in all sports. The defense followed the ball. All that mattered was the ball. And this inspired in Paterno a four-word phrase that he would scream at his players so many times through the years that they would swear to hearing it in their sleep.

"Go to the ball," Hall of Fame linebacker Jack Ham said.

"Go to the ball," All-Pro linebacker Shane Conlan said.

"I heard him say it a thousand times at least: 'Go to the ball,' " All-Pro linebacker Matt Millen said.

"Go to the ball," Penn State star and Hall of Fame running back Franco Harris said. Those words had a particular effect on his life. As a running back for the Pittsburgh Steelers, Harris was the key player in what came to be called the "Immaculate Reception." In the final seconds of a playoff game, the ball deflected into the air and Harris ran to it ("Go to the ball!"), caught it, and scored perhaps the most famous touchdown in pro football history.

Go to the ball. Paterno devised an ever-shifting rotation of his defensive backs based on where the ball was most likely to go. He had his players attack the middle of the field in waves so that runners could not break through. He changed the way his defense looked to the quarterback before the ball was snapped, which confused matters even more.

"Confusion," Paterno would say, "plays defense."

• • •

WAS IT REVOLUTIONARY? WHEN IT comes to sports—and life too, probably—there is always somebody who claims to have done something first. In baseball, there are at least a half dozen people who could claim, with some credibility, that they invented the curveball. In football, there are several who may have invented the option play. Paterno's defensive innovations would in time become widely copied; his design would be at the heart of the two-deep zone defense that many consider the soundest ever developed. But Paterno would not claim that he invented any of it. "You know what they say: There's nothing new under the sun."

What is undeniable is that his new defense worked wonders for Penn State. There were some doubters at first, even among his own coaches and players. The assistant coaches challenged Paterno, threw countless imaginary scenarios at him, and some were dubious about his answers. The players, especially the older ones, wondered if such desperation was a sign that their coach was cracking. Penn State played tentatively and without confidence and lost the first game of the 1967 season to Navy. Paterno lost all patience. "I've got to get rid of those older guys," Sue remembered him saying. "We can't win with them."

The next game, at Miami, Paterno gradually removed many of his senior players and replaced them with talented younger men. But it wasn't their talent he was thinking about. He sent in the younger players because they believed in what he was teaching. Penn State beat Miami 17–8 in a spectacular defensive show. That surprising and dominant performance won over some fans and reporters. What Paterno did after the game won over the team.

At the airport after the game, Paterno saw two of his seniors having a beer in a bar. This was against a Paterno rule; football players were never to be seen in a bar during the season because it reflected poorly on them and the team. The players—not unreasonably, perhaps— pointed out that they were of drinking age and they did not think the no-drinking rule carried over to a Miami airport. Nobody knew them in Miami. It was just one beer. Paterno was unmoved. One of the players had been in minor trouble before, and now Paterno threw him off the team; he suspended the other for two games.

Back on campus, the Penn State captains, Tom Sherman and Bill Lenkaitis, went to Paterno to protest. They told him the team had discussed it, and they believed his ruling was unfair. Paterno addressed the team. "I told the team that all their life they would have to live by rules, whether they agreed with them or not. They might not see the wisdom in a speed limit or in getting taxes in by midnight on tax day. I told them that the rule was there to protect them, but it didn't matter if they agreed with me. There are consequences for breaking rules. And by breaking those rules you are accepting those consequences."

He then challenged the team: "If you can't live with it, go." Paterno walked out to give the players a chance to leave. He returned a couple of minutes later. Every player stayed.

Penn State lost the next week to a UCLA team ranked No. 3 in America, but this time they scared the heck out of Tommy Prothro. UCLA needed a blocked punt to squeak out a 17–15 victory. The Other Thing defense had again proven commanding.

Penn State did not lose again for almost three years.

{ *Intermezzo* }

Here is how a Joe Paterno after-dinner story came about: Penn State won eight of ten games in 1967 and so was offered a chance to play in a bowl game. This was not an insubstantial thing in 1967; there were only nine bowl games. Years later there would be so many bowl games that almost every Division I football team in the country with a winning record received an invitation. But in the late 1960s bowl invitations meant something.

Penn State played Florida State in Jacksonville and dominated the game for the first half, leading 17–0. The defense had overwhelmed Florida State's players. Then, with less than a yard to go from their own 15-yard line, Penn State faced a fourth down. The obvious decision was to punt the ball; in fact to call it an "obvious decision" is to undervalue the word "obvious." A punt was more or less the only call, so much so that Paterno's friend Jim Tarman would always remember the reaction in the press box of Penn State's athletic director Ernie McCoy and President Eric Walker (as recalled in Ridge Riley's book *Road to Number One*).

"Joe's going for it," Tarman said.

"He'd never," McCoy said.

"He'd better not," Walker said.

He did. Near the end of his life, Paterno would talk nostalgically about his decision to go for a first down, as if remembering the choice of an old friend. "I'll tell you what I was thinking. I was still a young coach, understand. And I had convinced myself that the only way to win was to be unafraid of losing. That's what I used to tell the guys."

With this Paterno stood up. We were in his kitchen, and he had just been released from the hospital after breaking his pelvis. He was going through chemotherapy and radiation treatments. He had lost weight, and his face sagged a bit, and that beautiful voice of his had grown faint. But now he stood up.

"You can't be afraid to lose!" he shouted with a jolt of force, and he pointed at me. "You will not win all the time in life. Sometimes the other team's gonna lick ya. But you have to believe you will win. You know who wins in this world? I don't care if it's football or politics or business. The bold people win. The audacious people. People who are afraid to lose, they beat themselves. They lose before they ever get started. They have their excuses before the game is even played."

Then he sat down. The fury had subsided. "I went for it on fourth down because I refused to be afraid to lose," he said softly. "But what I didn't understand then is that while you don't want to be afraid of losing, you want to have a healthy respect for it."

Paterno's gamble failed. Penn State was stopped on fourth down—or anyway, that's how the officials saw it. Penn State's quarterback Tom Sherman would always believe he had gained the first down. He dived forward and felt sure he had pushed the ball well past the first-down line. But the officials gave the ball to Florida State, which put together a rather remarkable comeback. At the end of the game, Florida State was in position to gamble, to go for victory on fourth down, but Seminoles coach Bill Peterson decided that his team had played too well to lose, and so they kicked a field goal and the game ended tied 17–17.

Media people sided with the conservative Peterson and attacked Paterno. *Sports Illustrated* called his decision to go for it on fourth down the bonehead play of the year. Columnist after columnist confirmed the brainlessness of the decision. Sue Paterno found herself on an elevator with a man who was muttering to himself, "Stupid. Stupid." Even Paterno himself said after the game, "It was my call. I blew it."

On the plane ride home, he was despondent. Though he would forever after talk about how that bold and fateful decision served a larger purpose by convincing his team that they should always play to win, he felt humbled by the moment. He had allowed his bravado to cost his team a game. He blamed himself for allowing Florida State to tie the game.

Paterno would recall two versions of what happened next. In the first version, Jack Curry, an excellent Penn State receiver, walked to the back of the plane, where Paterno was sitting, and said, "Joe, the guys wanted me to tell you something."

Paterno looked up. He waited for the consoling words.

"You blew it," Curry said. "Everybody on the team thinks so." And he turned and walked off.

Over time, Paterno would add details, build up the drama, and punch up the punch line until the second version became one of his after-dinner staples:

> *Most of you are too young to remember this, but I was once the dumbest coach in America. Some people would say I'm still the dumbest, but believe me, I'm smarter than I used to be.*
>
> *My second year as coach, we went to the Gator Bowl. That was my first bowl game as a head coach, and I really wanted to win it. We went up 17–0, and I was feeling pretty good about myself. I was thinking, "Hey, we must be pretty good." Then we had fourth down and one from our own 15-yard line. And the players were saying, "Go for it!" Well, players always want to go for it. Every time they come off the field, we could be fourth and 100, the quarterback will tell me, "Coach, we can get it."*

But this time, I was feeling pretty good. And I thought, "Yeah, we can make that. It's less than a yard." So I say, "What the heck! Go for it!" I wanted to be unconventional.

Of course, we don't make it. I'll never forget that. We don't make it, and Florida State comes all the way back and ties us 17–17. Now I feel terrible. I cost my team the game. Most of the guys said, "That's okay." But they're really thinking, "Paterno, you blew it."

I'm sitting in the back of the plane, feeling sorry for myself. I'm sitting there with Sue, and then Jack Curry comes back. Jack was the team clown. He was a great guy and a great receiver. So he comes back, and he said, "Don't feel bad about it. There's good in everything."

I look up at him. And he says: "Before the game started, nobody knew who coached Penn State. But after you went for it, everybody in the country shouted: 'Who in the hell coaches Penn State?'"

So what's the real punch line? Jack Curry said neither version is accurate. In fact, he says, it wasn't even Paterno's idea to go for it on fourth down. He said that Paterno sent the punter onto the field, but the players themselves sent the punter back to the sideline and went for it. "Joe took the blame," Curry said. "But there was nothing he could do about it." So there was no reason to say anything at all to Joe on the plane.

But Curry didn't mind the stories Paterno told. He especially liked the "Who the hell coaches Penn State?" version. It made a lot of people laugh.

Paterno at Beaver Stadium in the late 1960s *(Penn State University Archives, Pennsylvania State University Libraries)*

The Grand Experiment

When the 1968 college football season began, Joe Paterno was virtually unknown outside of Penn State. Within five years, he would be the most famous and admired coach in America. He would become more than that, really. Rich men would throw absurd sums of money at him. Editorial pages across the country glorified him. Many students looked to him as an example of sanity. So did their parents; thousands wrote letters to Paterno asking for guidance and perspective and even salvation for their sons. Paterno, with his thick glasses, wisecracking Brooklyn accent, and seemingly unshakable ethics, stood for something people feared had been lost.

It is hard for any man, even a plainspoken Brooklyn kid determined never to lose his bearings, to hold on to what matters when people start to see him as a saint.

THE WINNING CAME FIRST. PATERNO had miraculous teams in 1968 and 1969. The Nittany Lions did not lose a game either year. Their 31-game unbeaten streak eventually would capture the attention of President Nixon (though not exactly in the way Paterno wanted). Their deceptively simple and conservative offense—run the ball, run the ball, run the ball—overpowered opponents. Their ever-shifting defenses folded and unfolded and left quarterbacks and coaches bewildered. This was how Paterno had imagined football in the many hours he spent scribbling plays and thoughts on graph paper, devising The Other Thing; his teams in 1968 and 1969 seemed to spring directly from his imagination. The Nittany Lions outplayed team after team, and if they could not outplay a team on a certain day, well, they helped those teams beat themselves.

It was this—making teams beat themselves—that marked Paterno's career, not only in the late 1960s but throughout his coaching life. Time after time teams would lose to Penn State and leave the field believing that they should have won. "We had a chance to beat Penn," Miami coach Charlie Tate said after a 22–7 loss in 1968. (Notice how he called Penn State "Penn." It would be a few years before Penn State became a brand name.) "But the injury to [our quarterback] and the blocked punt hurt."

"The big thing is they didn't make mistakes," Kansas State coach Vince Gibson said after his team lost 17–14.

"The fumbles killed us," Syracuse coach Ben Schwartzwalder griped after his team's 15–14 loss.

Two words, *if only*, haunted Penn State opponents for more than forty years. If only we hadn't fumbled. If only we hadn't committed that penalty. If only we had made that field goal. This was no accident, and because it happened time after time, it was not luck either.

Paterno's overriding philosophy was simple and boring, and through the years fans often complained about it: Your best chance at winning is not losing. You prevail in football and in life by making fewer mistakes than your opponent. You triumph not with grand heroics and individual brilliance and the sorcery of strategy. No, football teams win, he told his players again and again, because of the small details you get right and the other guys get wrong. You trust your teammate a little bit more than the other guy trusts his. You sacrifice a little bit more for the good of the team. You hold on to the football, and you don't take unnecessary chances, and you don't jump offside in the big moment.

Again and again, over and over, Paterno told them: Take care of the little things, and the big things will take care of themselves.

"I know it's boring," Paterno would say. "I know fans don't want to hear it. They want to win every game 55–0. They want to throw the ball all over the field. They want gimmick plays. Sometimes that stuff will work. But that's not how you win championships. That's not how you get to the top. If there's one thing I learned it's that teams lose games far more often than they win. A good punt will win you more games than a great catch. I know people will say, 'Ah, Paterno, you're full of it.' But I'll take my chances with my way."

His way guided Penn State through the 1968 season undefeated. The final victory, a dramatic 15–14 triumph over Kansas in the Orange Bowl on New Year's Day, was typical. Penn State did not play well; the Nittany Lions committed four turnovers, a stunning breakdown for a Paterno team. Because of these mistakes Kansas led 14–7 with one minute, thirty seconds left in the game.

Then the Penn State players put together a series of winning plays. Neal Smith blocked a punt. Quarterback Chuck Burkhart, who was not flashy and would take much abuse throughout his college career because of it, threw a long pass to Bob Campbell to move the ball to the Kansas 3-yard line. After a couple of failed attempts to get the ball into the end zone—and with less than twenty seconds left—Burkhart changed the play just before the snap, kept the ball, and powered into the end zone. Burkhart was supposed to hand the ball off to Penn State's star running back, Charlie Pittman, but he was sure he saw a small opening, and he ran through it. It was risky; Burkhart was such a limited runner that he had not scored a single touchdown all season. But Paterno said that what Burkhart lacked in pure talent he more than made up for with his nearly flawless instincts. He scored the first touchdown of his career.

"This will sound like a contradiction because I believe you win with teamwork," Paterno said. "But football is a contradiction. Life is a contradiction. Sometimes you have to ignore what the coaches tell you, what the players tell you, what anybody tells you, and you have to go out and make the winning play. People thought Chuck wasn't much of a quarterback because he didn't throw the ball that well and he didn't run it that well either. But Chuck understood what it took to win games as well as anybody I ever coached."

Paterno had his team go for the 2-point play and the victory. He never considered settling for a tie; that would have gone against everything he believed about being unafraid to lose. The 2-point attempt failed; Burkhart's pass fell incomplete. The game was lost. And then it wasn't. Kansas had twelve men on the field. A review of film would show that Kansas actually had twelve men on the field for the two previous plays as well, but the referees had not realized it. This time they noticed. The penalty gave Penn State another chance. This time, running back Bob Campbell took a handoff and scored the 2 points that won the game.

"The penalty was the big play," Kansas coach Pepper Rodgers grumbled about his own team's blunder. He would not be the last coach to mutter those words after facing Joe Paterno.

HERE IS A STORY ABOUT luck. In the spring of 1967, Joe Paterno called a sophomore football player named Steve Smear to his office. Smear had played offense in high school, but Paterno switched him to the defensive line, one of the many times he shifted a talented player to defense and made him into a star. Smear would become captain of the undefeated 1968 and 1969 teams, a second-team All-American, and one of the legends of Penn State football.

"I remember that first he told me not to get discouraged by my new position," Smear said. But this was not the point of the conversation. Paterno told Smear that a Penn State recruit had decided at the last minute to go to another school, and this had opened up a football scholarship. Paterno wanted to know a little bit more about a high school teammate of Smear's. He asked Smear two questions.

"Is he a hard worker?"

"Yes, coach, absolutely," Smear said.

"Is he a good guy?"

"Yes."

"Okay," Paterno said. "Thanks, Steve. See you at practice."

That was it. End of discussion. Paterno did not ask any questions about the young man's talent as a football player. After the conversation, he made Smear's old friend a last-minute scholarship offer. One of Paterno's great strengths—and perhaps one of his great flaws—was his fierce loyalty and absolute trust in the people closest to him. Though he had coached Smear for only a year, he had unqualified faith in his judgment. "I knew Steve was a good guy. I knew he would tell me the truth."

"It's not always easy to get his trust," said Tom Bradley, who played and coached for Paterno for thirty-five years. "But once you have it, you have it all."

Smear's former teammate and friend happily accepted the scholarship—he did not have many other offers—and when he got to campus Paterno moved him from the offensive line to linebacker. (Yes, another player shifted to defense; the story repeats again and again for the next forty years.) Paterno watched the player in spring practice for only a few minutes and then called in his graduate assistant coach, a young man named Jerry Sandusky, and said, "Here's how I want you to coach him. Don't coach him! Leave him alone! Don't change a single thing!"

The new kid was Jack Ham, who would play with wild abandon for Penn State and the Pittsburgh Steelers and, in time, be inducted into both the College Football of Hall of Fame and the Pro Football Hall of Fame. Some football experts still call him the best linebacker in the history of football.

Jack Ham might be the best player Paterno ever found, but he did not spend any time recruiting Ham—he ended up with Ham after the recruiting period ended. It seems impossible to call this anything other than luck, but if something happens again and again, can you still call it luck? Paterno had a startling series of recruiting success stories in the mid- to late 1960s. Other schools certainly offered money under the table, freedom from academic pressures, and guarantees of future stardom, while Paterno offered only a scholarship and the promise of a good education. Is it luck? How often must good fortune happen before it becomes something larger than luck?

The college football recruiting scene was raw in the late 1960s. There were far fewer regulations and penalties than there are now. "It was the Wild Wild West" is how Paterno put it. Cheating was rampant and only cosmetically camouflaged. Top football recruits drove expensive new cars around campuses across the country and worked at well-paying and largely fictitious jobs such as making sure the sprinklers worked. A representative case might be Joe Namath, a western Pennsylvania high school legend whom Paterno ignored because "he wasn't much of a student." Other coaches were not so picky. "It was strange," Namath famously told *Playboy* magazine, "coming out of high school and having colleges offer me as much as my father made in a year."

Academic standards were preposterously low when it came to football stars. The National Collegiate Athletic Association had set the grade standard for scholarship athletes at 1.6 out of a possible 4.0—barely passing. Even with a bar that low, schools were famous for putting their football players in trumped-up classes that newspaper columnists invariably called "Basket Weaving 101" and "Elements of Bottle Washing." All of these forms of cheating and others would remain a part of college football throughout Paterno's life, but the cheating was never quite so brazen and unabashed as in the late 1960s.

Paterno hated the cheating. The most conspicuous reason for this was his undisguised impulse to value right over wrong. There's a story Paterno would tell sometimes: When he was in the Delta Kappa Epsilon fraternity at Brown, there was a secret and contentious vote over a pledge named Steve Fenn, who was Jewish. There had never been a Jewish member of a Brown fraternity. The way Paterno remembered it, two frat brothers secretly blackballed Fenn. Paterno and his friends learned who one of the blackballers was and convinced him to rescind his objection, but they could not discover the identity of the other. This told Paterno that the man was both a bigot and a coward, two qualities he abhorred. When the secret voting started again, Paterno stepped forward and announced, "I'm embarrassed to say this, but I voted the blackball. I would like to withdraw it now."

In many ways, that story describes not only Paterno's sense of fairness but also his strategic sensibilities. He liked to challenge people. Everyone in the fraternity had to know Paterno did not vote the blackball. The ruse was transparent; Paterno had been one of Fenn's most vocal supporters. But this did not reduce the power of the strategy; the only way the blackballer could call out Paterno as a liar was to reveal himself as a bigot. As Paterno told his quarterbacks through the years, "It doesn't matter if they know a play is coming if they can't stop it." He expected that the anti-Semitic frat brother would stay shamefully silent, and he did. Fenn was admitted into the fraternity.

From more or less his first day as a head coach, Paterno called out those coaches at other schools who cheated and committed academic fraud. He railed against paying players large sums of money, not only because it was against the rules but because he thought it was no way to teach young men about the realities of life. Every one of his five children got jobs in college, even long after he had made his first million. He believed giving too much to an eighteen- or nineteen-year-old—whether in the form of fame, expectations, or riches—could leave permanent scars.

For Paterno, college football was supposed to be about teaching young men how to live. He would say all the time, "I know this sounds corny" or "People may not believe me," but this idea was his North Star. Teaching young men how to live. He insisted that schools should—*must*—challenge football players academically. He believed deeply in education. He may have carried some grudges from his years at Brown, but he also saw his time there as the most intellectually stimulating of his life. "When else in your life do you wake up every morning and the main goal is to learn?" He believed college football players should be challenged and taxed and inspired. He wanted them to be bone-tired at the end of practice. He also wanted them stretching their mental limits trying to decipher Virgil or to consider Napoleon's motivations or to wrestle with physics formulas long after dark.

College football worked, he believed, only if the trade was even. At Penn State, a player would give his heart and body to the team, and along the way help make millions of dollars for the school and spark joy and passion in hundreds of thousands of Penn State fans. Paterno understood that was a large sacrifice for a player. In return, the player deserved a matching reward, the biggest any school could offer: his players would leave Penn State prepared to live a full life. What could mean more? That was the only way the trade was fair. Yes, he expected players to get their degrees—between 80 and 90 percent of Penn State football players graduated over the years—but that was only part of the deal. More, much more, he wanted players to be prepared for all that followed, to learn how to be successful, to be good husbands, good fathers, to know how to fight through the hard times and overcome mistakes and achieve more than they thought possible. This was Paterno's deal, and if colleges failed those students, the deal was broken. Paterno looked at those schools who gave players money and grades and easy ways out, and it disgusted him.

"You will hear people talk about paying the players," he explained. "And I think football players should get a little stipend, some spending money so they can go to the movies and go out with their friends without feeling embarrassed. But you can't turn college football into professional football. The formula doesn't work. If you pay a big star $100,000 to play college football, and you don't discipline him and make him a better person, you are getting him on the cheap. You are using him. You are failing him."

Paterno's sense of fair play would strike people differently through the years. Some thought him holier-than-thou. His own brother, George, complained about what he considered Joe's sanctimony. Others thought he was simply lying about his commitment to education or Penn State's vigilance about not paying college players or his utopian dreams for college football. Every misstep he made, especially those at the end of his life, would confirm the hypocrisy charges to the critics and the cynics and the people who found themselves unmoved and unconvinced by his stand on ethics and academics.

But there are more than forty years of stories and testimonials that show Paterno lived what he believed. The interview files for this book are bursting with player quotes like this, from the 1986 team captain Bob White: "You understood that if you didn't go to class, you didn't play. That wasn't a punishment. In Joe's mind, it was all the same thing." Or this from tight end Mickey Shuler, who told Paterno he was hoping to play in the NFL: "He looked at me kind of surprised . . . then he shocked me by saying he didn't know I wanted to play professional football. He thought I wanted to be a teacher and coach like my dad. . . . It wasn't until later in life that I realized Joe didn't just see me as a football player, but as someone with potential to be whatever I wanted to be."

And so on. There are so many quotes like these from former players that after a while they lose their power; they sound alike and induce involuntary eye rolls. Paterno impressed upon so many of his players, through so many years, exactly the same thing: *Go to class. Be on time. Don't make excuses. Get up after you fall. Play to win. A* sportswriter named Charles Culpepper hit on something when challenged about Paterno's friend and rival Bobby Bowden, Florida State's football coach. Bowden coached college football for fifty years, and he was an impossibly charming and jovial man with a wonderful sense of humor, both about himself and the world. "The guy's a phony," a Florida State hater said to Culpepper.

"Yeah?" Culpepper replied. "Well, to do it that long, it's one hell of an act."

PATERNO CALLED HIS ATTEMPT TO marry football, academics, and life lessons "a grand experiment." In short order, those three words would become capitalized, and "a" would be replaced by "The." These simple changes reshape the meaning, no? "The Grand Experiment" sounds so much more certain and cocksure and presumptuous. There's a reason for this. Paterno first talked about his bold ideas with a Philadelphia sportswriter named Bill Conlin, who was, well, certain and cocksure and presumptuous. Paterno may have referred to it as "a grand experiment," but Conlin pierced through the timidity and called it "The Grand Experiment." Conlin had grown up in Brooklyn, had seen Paterno play football in high school, had gone to Brooklyn Prep, and so even though the men were very different, they understood each other. Conlin's life as a sportswriter was big and bold, full of arrogance and brilliance. His career would end right around the time Paterno's coaching career ended, with a long story in a Philadelphia newspaper reporting accusations that he had molested children many years earlier. Conlin denied the charges and, shortly afterward, suffered a nervous breakdown. Even after that, though, in an email exchange with me, he wanted it remembered that he had coined "The Grand Experiment."

The Grand Experiment was built on Paterno's beliefs about education and fair play, of course, but there was also a powerful third reason, perhaps the most powerful one of all: The Grand Experiment worked. Paterno understood that he did not have the charisma of Bear

Bryant or the molten fury of Ohio State's Woody Hayes or the studious calm of UCLA's basketball coach John Wooden. What Paterno had was confidence and a clear vision. He was honest. He used that honesty, cultivated it. Other coaches recruited the players; Paterno recruited the parents. Other coaches made promises; Paterno made demands. Other coaches made their recruiting trips fun and exhilarating; player after player after player said that their Penn State recruiting visits were boring beyond exaggeration.

Paterno's honesty came from a real place, of course: from the Brooklyn streets, from his insistent mother, from what his brother called his "pathological need to do the right thing." But he was shrewd enough to see how well it worked for him. The players who were drawn to his frank observations were exactly the sort of players he wanted in the first place. For instance, Lydell Mitchell was a star high school running back from New Jersey. Paterno happened to have a surplus of star running backs already. The great running back Charlie Pittman was already on his team; another gifted high school star from New Jersey, Franco Harris, seemed intent on committing to Penn State. But Paterno still wanted Mitchell, not only because of his speed and talent but also because "he was such a great person."

Mitchell, though, had decided to go to Ohio State. Or, anyway, that's what he thought he had decided. One day after he had made his decision, Mitchell heard his name over the high school intercom and was told to report to the office. When he got there, he saw Joe Paterno waiting. He braced himself for an uncomfortable conversation.

"Um, Coach, thanks for coming," Mitchell said. "But I'm not interested in going to Penn State. I'm going to Ohio State."

"I know," Paterno said. "You're afraid to come to Penn State because Charlie Pittman is there and you can't compete with him."

Whatever Mitchell might have been expecting Paterno to say, that wasn't it. He was furious. "Yeah?" he said. "I'll come up there and break every Penn State record there is."

That's just what Lydell Mitchell did.

Honesty worked with the kind of players Paterno wanted to coach.

He did not promise players they would start. He told them plainly that they had to go to class or they wouldn't play. He would often say, "We would like to have you come to Penn State. But we don't *need* you." He challenged them to reach for something bigger within themselves. Every time he gathered together a bunch of recruits, he would give the same speech: "Not all of you are cut out for Penn State. Here, we go to class. Here we wear ties when we travel. Here we wear plain uniforms, and we don't showboat, and we follow rules. If that doesn't appeal to you, I understand, and I suggest you go somewhere else." That kind of recruiting pitch may not sound all that appealing, but it had three powerful pulls.

One: It appealed to parents.

Two: It appealed to the kind of players Paterno wanted at Penn State and eliminated many he did not. Any player who recoiled from his challenges was a player Paterno did not want anyway.

Three: Perhaps most significantly, Paterno's directness had a muscular salesmanship of its own. "Young men crave discipline," he said many, many times.

"Joe Paterno didn't lie to me," Steve Smear said, and dozens of others said the same thing. It turned out that many players did not want to be told how great they were. It turned out many wanted to go to college and be challenged mentally as well as physically. Many found themselves drawn to Paterno's ideal of "being part of something bigger than yourself." When Joe Paterno recruited you, player after player said, it felt like Penn State was offering something just a little bit more honorable than what the other schools were selling.

PATERNO PROSELYTIZED PENN STATE FOOTBALL. In those days, the power of college football was concentrated in the South, the Midwest, a bit out West, more or less everywhere but in the Northeast. The stars of coaching were Bear Bryant at Alabama, Woody Hayes at Ohio State, Darrell Royal at Texas, John McKay at Southern California, and Ara Parseghian at Notre Dame in Indiana. To people around

America, eastern football sparked images of undersized Ivy League kids bashing into each other between classes on Chaucer. When Paterno became head coach at Penn State, there were 46,000 seats at Beaver Stadium, and many of those were empty on game day.

So Paterno preached. He and Penn State's sports information director, Jim Tarman, traveled to Philadelphia, Harrisburg, Cleveland, and New York—and also to smaller places like Altoona and Scranton and Hazleton—and they gave speeches, told jokes, shook hands, and, most of all, wooed reporters. They carried heavy suitcases filled with bottles of whiskey, just enough to loosen the conversation, and they traveled to every Optimists Club and Rotary Club and Alumni Club they could find. The reporters inevitably showed up at the hotel, where Paterno turned on his Brooklyn charm. The reporters enjoyed the liquor but also found a football coach unlike any they had ever encountered. He talked with them about Greek mythology and the writing style of Fitzgerald and the politics of Nixon. He did not hide his disdain for corruption in college sports (a favorite topic for newspaper reporters), and he refused to speak in clichés (a favorite trait of newspaper reporters). Paterno loved to argue, and he found that newspaper reporters and columnists generally enjoyed doing so as well. "Joe turns it on," the longtime Philadelphia sports columnist Bill Lyon warned, "and you're dead."

Later, especially in the last fifteen years of his life, Paterno would wage a cold war with the media. He would become secretive, dismissive, and cranky. In response, many of the reporters became distrusting and snarky. It's hard to tell who turned first or hardest, and in the end it did not matter. College football had changed. The media had changed. The world had changed. And, though it sounds simplistic, perhaps Paterno did not want to change. "We used to be a lot closer," he would say, not without regret in his voice.

It's true: in those early years, reporters loved Joe Paterno, and he loved them, and together they built up the aura and importance and wonder of Penn State football. "You do a little research," the longtime Wisconsin football coach Barry Alvarez said, "and you see what Knute Rockne did for Notre Dame. He took that little school and he crisscrossed the country on a train before we had media like we have today. So the big newspapers are writing about this midwest Catholic school Notre Dame like it was some bastion of learning and a huge university. . . . Joe did the same thing at Penn State. To put it on the map, to get people around the country to know who Penn State is, and to have him stamp that school as one of the best football schools—I think he did the same thing Rockne did."

In November 1968, toward the end of Paterno's first undefeated season, Dan Jenkins wrote a story for *Sports Illustrated* whose soaring opening paragraph created the template for the Joe Paterno stories that would follow for three decades:

> A Beethoven symphony swirls through the mind of a defensive tackle. A linebacker earnestly dashes to physics class on the morning of a game. Test tubes intrigue a cornerback; math fascinates a center; engineering problems make a safety swoon. And while the youthful keeper of these characters, 41-year-old Penn State coach Joe Paterno, should be fretting about his team's possible climb toward No. 1 or an Orange Bowl bid, he stares at the boutique-colored leaves of the pastoral Alleghenies, thinks about Romantic poets and longs to drive his kids over to Waddle or Martha Furnace or Tusseyville so they can sit down and talk to a cow.

Jenkins was a famously sardonic writer—he was the author of the raunchy and hilarious football novels *Semi-Tough* and *Life Its Ownself*—and yet even he could not help but fall for what seemed sweet and old-fashioned and enlightened about Joe Paterno and the program he was building. Paterno never did drive his kids to Waddle to talk to cows, nor did he spend much time staring at leaves, but after Jenkins, writer after writer celebrated his ambitions.

Mike Reid was that defensive tackle who heard Beethoven playing in his mind. Reid had grown up in Altoona, about forty miles from

State College, and he was a terrifying and marvelous football player. "Mike Reid was the only guy I really—I don't say I feared him, but I stayed away," his teammate Don Abbey said. But Reid was not typical. He never wanted football to take up too much of his life. He never believed the coach's stuff about football defining character.

Reid loved music. He would often joke that for him football was the sissy game, and music was the manly endeavor. When he was twelve, he bought an organ for $1,500, saving pennies from his paper route for two years to pay for it, and he spent every free minute playing, tinkering, listening to the sounds. He was a star football player and an eastern collegiate heavyweight wrestling champion, so people found it hard to understand how much music moved him.

But it did. Abbey remembered the time he and Reid went to see *2001: A Space Odyssey*. When the music began for the famous space ballet involving docking stations, Reid said admiringly, "Johann Strauss's 'The Blue Danube.' " In front of them a couple of kids snickered loudly. When the movie ended and the two kids started to leave, Reid stood up, pushed them back in their seats, and made them understand that they had just been listening to beautiful music.

Paterno was the ideal coach for Reid. He encouraged Reid to follow his musical dreams even if it meant missing practice, as it often did. Paterno made it clear that he expected Reid to think beyond football, to chase hard after his muse and what mattered to him most. After graduation, Reid became a pro football star in Cincinnati, but at twenty-seven, he quit football to concentrate on his music. In time he became a renowned songwriter and an admired composer. Though he would lose touch with Paterno and Penn State football as both of them became more celebrated, he always believed that Paterno had helped him become a man. "I had a fear of Joe," Reid told reporter Bob Hertzel of the *Times West Virginian*. "And it certainly wasn't physical because any one of us could have grabbed his scrawny little neck and wrung it. . . . I lived in fear of disappointing him, the same way I did with my Mom and Dad."

Dennis Onkotz was the linebacker who insisted on taking a physics exam on the day of a game. "I won't sleep anyway," he had told Paterno. In many ways he and Reid defined The Grand Experiment as much as Paterno did. Onkotz was both an All-American and an Academic All-American. He led the team in tackles and posted a 3.5 grade point average. Paterno had this utopian ideal of what college football could be, but Reid and Onkotz and others were living it. They were showing him possibilities beyond his own aspirations.

"Everything is changing," he told Dan Jenkins. "And the kids want to change the world."

Nixon

When the 1968 football season ended, Paterno was offered what he called a staggering amount of money to become the coach of the Pittsburgh Steelers. It was a tempting offer for many reasons, money being only one of them. Sue had grown up in Latrobe, about forty miles from Pittsburgh. Art Rooney, who owned the Steelers, was a tough former boxer whom Paterno admired deeply. The chance to coach the greatest players tempted the strategic side of him. But he turned it down. "I think coaching should be fun, and I'm not sure I could get that out of pro football," he told reporters. It wasn't a particularly big story in 1968. The Steelers hired a relatively obscure Baltimore Colts assistant named Chuck Noll, who would lead them to four Super Bowl victories. The next big offer for Paterno would stun America.

Paterno had relatively little trouble turning down the Steelers because he knew that "unless we become fatheads" his 1969 team would be one of the best in the country. Deep down he believed it would be *the* best team in the country. Penn State's defense—featuring Jack Ham, Mike Reid, Dennis Onkotz, and Steve Smear, among other stars—would prove almost impossible to score against. The offense was built around three great running backs—Charlie Pittman, Franco

Harris, and the motivated Lydell Mitchell—and a quarterback who had never lost a college game, Chuck Burkhart. It was a dream team, and Paterno thought he might never get to coach one quite as gifted. He believed that Penn State could again win every game. And he believed that this time, unlike in 1968, when his undefeated team finished second in the national rankings, they could finish as the No. 1 team in America.

On the field, things went more or less the way Paterno had envisioned. Penn State outscored opponents 312 to 87 over the season. They shut out West Virginia and Maryland. Only two games all year were close, and one of those was only cosmetically close; the Nittany Lions led Kansas State 17–0 before resting their starters and settling for a closer-than-it-was 17–14 score. The other game was legitimately close, a comeback 15–14 victory over Syracuse that left Coach Ben Schwartzwalder seething about the officiating. "If there were three or five bad calls, there would be no reason to complain," he said after the game. "This isn't five or six or even seven calls. This is a case of twenty-five or more bad calls. And it was seemingly unending."

Schwartzwalder charged Paterno with cursing and intimidating the officials. That set off Paterno's fierce temper. Through the years, he would sometimes act rashly when he believed his honor or authority were being questioned. "It is one part of my personality I've never been able to conquer," he said with regret in his voice.

As for Schwartzwalder's sour grapes, Paterno told the *New York Times*, "It's disappointing that a leading member of our coaching profession would resort to this type of attack after such a great game by two outstanding teams." As for the complaints about his cursing and intimidating, he said, "I'm not going to even waste time to dignify such an accusation."

That bit of ugliness aside, Penn State breezed through a marvelous season. After Syracuse, no team came within 20 points of the Nittany Lions. But the larger story, at least at the time, was how little respect the so-called experts had for eastern football. Penn State had started the season No. 3 in the polls and had moved up to No. 2 before the close victories against Kansas State and Syracuse. After those, the Nittany Lions dropped all the way to eighth in the Associated Press poll (voted by sportswriters), and they were not in the top five in the United Press International poll (voted by football coaches). Even when they moved up to No. 4 in late November, Paterno griped, "This has got to be the first time in history a team wins every game for two straight seasons and doesn't get a No. 1 ranking a single week."

In those days, bowl games recruited teams the way teams recruited players. There were four major bowl games—Rose, Orange, Sugar, and Cotton—and a handful of minor bowls, such as the Tangerine Bowl in Orlando and the Astro-Bluebonnet Bowl in Houston. There were complicating factors involved in the invitations; for instance, a convoluted agreement with the Big Ten Conference stipulated that a team could not go to the Rose Bowl in back-to-back years. But for the most part, bowl scouts in labeled jackets crisscrossed the country in an effort to identify and then woo the right team to come play in their game.

Both the Cotton Bowl and the Orange Bowl wanted Penn State. So, in the third week of November, Paterno and his players had a decision to make. If they went to the Cotton Bowl in Dallas, they would play the winner of the Texas–Arkansas game. Both of those teams were undefeated, so that would make for a fascinating matchup, but it would also mean Penn State would play Texas or Arkansas in the Southwest in front of a mostly hostile crowd. The other option was to go back to the Orange Bowl in Miami, an experience the players had enjoyed the season before.

When it came to the national rankings, it did not seem to matter which game they chose. Ohio State was undefeated and all but locked in as No. 1. Many people were calling that Ohio State team the best ever, but because of the strange agreement the Big Ten had with the Rose Bowl, the Buckeyes were not going to *any* bowl game. They would surely end the season undefeated and would undoubtedly win their second straight consensus national championship. Everyone else was playing for No. 2.

This made Penn State's decision superfluous—or so it seemed. The players wanted to go to Miami again for various reasons. Some of the black players, such as Pittman, Mitchell, and Harris, were reluctant to go to the Cotton Bowl in Dallas, which they had heard to be a racist city, and which they still associated with the assassination of President Kennedy a little more than five years earlier. Other players simply thought Miami was a more exciting destination. Paterno probably did not feel especially moved to play Texas or Arkansas in their home territory when the national championship was already decided. In the end, Penn State announced that it would play Missouri, considered by many to be the best offensive team in the country, in the Orange Bowl.

Then, five days after the announcement, Ohio State was stunned by Michigan and its new coach Bo Schembechler, once Woody Hayes's key assistant. That changed everything. The Associated Press poll suddenly looked like this:

1. Texas
2. Arkansas
3. Penn State
4. Ohio State
5. Southern California

Suddenly, Penn State's decision to play in the Orange Bowl looked disastrous. Texas and Arkansas would play each other the next week, and the winner of that game would unquestionably be ranked No. 1, with Penn State ranked No. 2. If Penn State had chosen to play in the Cotton Bowl, they would have had a chance to play for the national championship. "We can't worry about it now," Steve Smear told a UPI reporter. "But I sure wish we could change our mind."

They could not change their minds; they had committed to the Orange Bowl. Instead Paterno thought it best that Penn State go on a public relations attack. He gave interview after interview about how good his team was, how amazing its winning streak was, how Penn State had as good a case as Texas or Arkansas or anybody else to be voted No. 1.

And then the president of the United States stepped in.

PATERNO REMEMBERED THAT YEAR, 1969, as a time when everything felt heightened, when young people and old shouted and it seemed no one was listening: "Everybody was protesting everything."

The Texas–Arkansas game received a lot of hype. It pitted the No. 1 team against the No. 2 team in what was being celebrated as the hundredth year of college football. So, yes, it was inevitable that the game would be on the radar of President Richard Nixon. For one thing, Nixon was a huge football fan. He had played football at Whittier College (more to the point, he was on the team). He idolized players and coaches. As David Maraniss writes in his biography of Vince Lombardi, *When Pride Still Mattered*, Nixon had his counselor John Mitchell do a background check on Lombardi as a possible running mate in the 1968 presidential election. (That idea went nowhere; Mitchell found out that Lombardi was a Kennedy Democrat.)

It may have been Nixon's great love of football that inspired him to get in the middle of the Texas–Arkansas extravaganza, but perhaps even more significant was his love of votes. Nixon had lost Texas by a slim margin in the 1968 election, and he had been crushed by third-party candidate George Wallace in Arkansas. He had no real footing in the South. What better way to gain ground in Texas and Arkansas than through college football?

On the Saturday morning of the game, Nixon flew into Fort Smith, Arkansas, where a sizable crowd welcomed him. "To get this kind of welcome, in the heart of the country, right here in Arkansas, means a great deal to me," he proclaimed. "All that I know is that we are going to see today, in this one-hundredth anniversary of football, one of the great football games of all time, and both of them I wish could be number one. But at the end, whichever is number one will deserve it, and the number two team will still go to a bowl and be a great team."

Paterno was unaware of this speech, which not only gave the official White House No. 1 spot to the Texas–Arkansas game winner but suggested strongly that the loser was the No. 2 team. Apparently Penn State did not even merit mention. The worst indignity for Paterno and Penn State, however, was yet to come.

The Texas–Arkansas game was a classic—at least, that's how it was portrayed. Texas turned the ball over six times and fell behind 14–0. Then the Longhorns scored a touchdown and added a 2-point conversion. Arkansas quarterback Bill Montgomery, with his team deep in Texas territory, tried an ill-advised pass that was intercepted. This gave Texas the ball and the chance to drive for a touchdown that gave them a 15–14 lead. Montgomery threw another interception in the last minute, and Texas won by the same score with which Penn State had beaten Kansas in the Orange Bowl. People almost immediately began calling it "The Game of the Century."

Nixon was omnipresent. During halftime he chatted happily with ABC announcer Chris Schenkel and Bud Wilkinson, the legendary former coach at Oklahoma whom Nixon had hired as a special consultant. "Great stuff," White House Chief of Staff H. R. Haldeman would write in his diary. "Especially at half-time, when P gave thorough analysis of the game so far, and outlook for second half, which proved 100% accurate. And some really good stuff in the locker rooms, talking to the players. A real coup with the sports fans."

After the game, Nixon visited the victorious locker room and—to the horror of Joe Paterno, his team, and the state of Pennsylvania— presented Texas coach Darrell Royal with a presidential plaque. "For a team to be behind 14 to 0 and then not lose its cool and to go on to win, that proves that you deserve to be number one, and that is what you are."

This wasn't even the worst of it. Between the time Nixon landed in Fort Smith and the time he spoke with Royal, it had been suggested to him that Pennsylvania (another state he lost in 1968) might not take too kindly to being snubbed. A solution was slapped together, one that would become college football legend.

"If I could add one thing while we're talking here," Nixon said to Royal. "I do want to say that Penn State, of course, felt that I was a little premature in suggesting this. So we are going to present a plaque to Penn State in the one hundredth year with the longest undefeated, untied record. Is that fair enough?"

"That is fair enough," Royal answered.

Paterno, unsurprisingly, did not find this fair enough. Or anything close to fair. It was bad enough that Nixon had taken it upon himself to put the power of the presidency behind Texas as the No. 1 football team in the country. But for him to offer Penn State a ludicrous consolation prize for having the nation's longest unbeaten streak was more than he could handle. Paterno immediately called Penn State's PR man Jim Tarman and said he wanted to release a statement. Tarman tried to calm him down, but Paterno's temper was in full bloom. He was not going to take this, not from anybody, not even from the president of the United States.

The statement Paterno released was cushioned by Tarman, but his biting rage still managed to come through:

> *First, I wish to congratulate Coach Royal, not only on a great victory, but for having the courage to go for two points. This will stand him in good stead in the Cotton Bowl. It appears that Texas and Arkansas read the script from our Orange Bowl game last year and from our win over Syracuse.*
>
> *In response to numerous telephone calls I received today regarding President Nixon's television remarks concerning a plaque to Penn State for having the nation's longest unbeaten streak, I have heard nothing official about any such plaque.*
>
> *Before accepting such a plaque, I would have to confer with my squad. I'm sure they would be disappointed at this time, as would the Missouri squad, to receive anything other than a*

*plaque for the No. 1 team. And the No. 1 team following the
bowl games could be Penn State or Missouri.*

*To accept any other plaque prior to the bowl games, which
are supposedly to determine the final No. 1 team, would be a dis-
service to our squad, to Pennsylvania and to the East, which we
represent, and perhaps most important to Missouri, which might
just be the best team in the country.*

*Due to the fact that I had to babysit with our four children
while trying to watch today's game I did not get to hear all of
President Nixon's remarks. But it would seem a waste of his very
valuable time to present Penn State with a plaque for something
we already have undisputed possession of—the nation's longest
winning and unbeaten streaks.*

It was this last sentence that Tarman worried about most, but
Paterno would not leave it out. He found it insulting to be given a
plaque for something that "any idiot consulting a record book could
see." He found it incredible that the president of the United States
would butt in to the already preposterous college football system,
where champions were picked by ballot and undefeated teams like
his were told that they were second best because they didn't look good
enough. For the rest of his life, Paterno fought for a college football
playoff, so that, in his words, "the champion could be decided on the
field." Yet even though people would assign great, even unlimited
power to Joe Paterno, this was one of many battles he did not win.

Penn State beat Missouri in the Orange Bowl 10–3 in a defensive display so dazzling and overwhelming that Tigers coach Dan
Devine called Penn State the best defense he'd seen in twenty years
of coaching. Paterno then made his final pleas to the media. None of
it mattered when the votes were tallied. Texas came from behind in
the last minute and beat a not overly impressive Notre Dame in the
Cotton Bowl and was named the national champion by the sportswriters. The coaches had already named Texas No. 1 in the UPI poll; in
those days they chose their national champion before the bowls even

began. Penn State was undefeated, untied, and No. 2 again. For his part, Nixon was a bit sheepish about the whole thing; at the National Football Foundation's Gold Medal Dinner just a few days after the Texas–Arkansas game, he admitted that maybe naming a team No. 1 wasn't the smartest thing for a president to do.

In his early years as an assistant coach at Penn State, his mother and father would sometimes say to Joe, with disappointment in their voices, "I thought you were going to be president." In 1970, Paterno had become known across the country as the football coach with the gall and guts to take on the president.

PATERNO NEVER FORGAVE THE SLIGHT. In 1973, the year he achieved secular sainthood, he said this about Richard Nixon: "I'd like to know how the president could know so much about college football and so little about Watergate."

In 2012, two weeks before he died, Paterno said, "With all due respect to the office of the president, which I respect very much, President Nixon should have kept his big mouth shut."

Race

Mike Cooper was a talented young quarterback from Harrisburg. For his first two years playing at Penn State, he was a backup to Chuck Burkhart, the quarterback who threw wobbly passes but never lost. This troubled Cooper; he felt sure he threw better than Burkhart, ran faster than Burkhart, and could move the team better than Burkhart. But he understood that, with Burkhart winning every game, it was difficult to argue that he could do better. "I thought I was better than Burkhart," he told the Penn State student newspaper just before he graduated. "But we were winning with him." When Cooper was a senior in 1970, after Burkhart had graduated, Paterno named him starter.

That made Mike Cooper the first black starting quarterback in Penn State history.

PATERNO SPENT HIS COACHING LIFE at a school where only a tiny percentage of the students—fewer than 2 percent in his early years, still fewer than 5 percent at the end—were African American. This created tensions. There were years when the Penn State football team did not have many black players, and there were black players

Paterno tried to recruit who said they did not feel comfortable on the State College campus. After the 1979 Sugar Bowl, where Penn State played Alabama, Charlie Pittman complained to his former coach that Alabama—*Alabama, which did not have its first black player until 1971*—had more African Americans than Penn State. "I know," Paterno said. "We have to do better."

Through the years people would express many different opinions about Paterno's views on race. Some thought him a bleeding heart; others called him a racist. The criticisms weighed on him as few criticisms did.

He came to Penn State as an assistant coach before *Brown v. Board of Education,* before Emmett Till was murdered, before Rosa Parks refused to go to the back of the bus. The civil rights movement inspired him. His father, president of the Interfaith Movement, inspired him. He expressed his strong feelings about racial equality in conversations with friends, to the point where sometimes he sounded naïve and even patronizing. "I wish I was black," he often told Jim O'Hora and other coaches and friends. But he tried to be part of the fight. In 1962, when Penn State played in the Gator Bowl in still-segregated Florida, an airport restaurant in Orlando refused to allow his star Dave Robinson to sit with the white players. The entire team left the restaurant in protest, but Robinson still had nowhere to go.

"Come with me," Paterno told him, and together they walked to a coffee shop. Robinson, who would become one of pro football's most respected players with the Green Bay Packers, remembered the determination on his coach's face. Here was someone who would not allow him to be treated as anything less than a human being. "Joe Paterno cared," he said. But perhaps what he said in private means even more. "A football coach can have such a powerful influence," Robinson's friend Bill Curry said. "Dave Robinson told me that Joe Paterno helped make him into a man."

From his early years as head coach, Paterno saw his effort to bring more African Americans to State College, to be involved in their lives, as a cause. He was always at his best when he had a cause. He raged against schools he felt were using black players without taking their education seriously. He fought to raise academic standards, believing that to expect less from young men, white or black, was to bury them with second-rate expectations. Penn State football's graduation rate for black athletes was always among the highest, and sometimes was the highest, among big-time college football programs. Just one example: In Paterno's last year, according to the New America Foundation, Penn State showed no achievement gap between white and black football players, and called that "very rare for Division I football." It was a hallmark of Joe Paterno's Penn State teams.

But some pointed to the low number of black players on Paterno's teams, especially at key positions such as inside linebacker, and said that Paterno's words did not equate to action. "It's like everything else," Paterno said. "All you can do is try your best. For a long time, we would lose many of the black players we recruited to Ivy League schools. In later years, we did better. But we never did well enough. I would never say we did well enough. I hope that the players we did get, we had a positive impact on their lives."

PATERNO RECRUITED MIKE COOPER WITH the intention of making him the first black quarterback in the school's history. He wanted very much to shatter that barrier. "Mike Cooper was a wonderful and talented young man," he said. "And what happened to him still makes me sad."

Cooper started the first game of 1970 and played well; the 55–7 victory over Navy was Penn State's twenty-third victory in a row. But then things went bad. Penn State went to Colorado and were pounded 41–13. Though it was the Nittany Lions' first loss in almost three years—"Let them have their glory; we've had our share," Paterno said in the locker room—Paterno remembered that the atmosphere in State College immediately turned sour. A week later, the team was thumped again, this time by Wisconsin. Two weeks after that, on homecoming, they were beaten soundly by Syracuse. Letters poured into Penn State. The phone rang constantly in the Paterno home. Fans booed their own team during the Syracuse game. The message was clear: people wanted the black quarterback benched.

Paterno struggled with what to do. He did not want to cave in to the pressure, especially pressure so racially charged. ("Some of the letters I got have haunted me for forty years," he would say.) On the other hand, Cooper was not playing well. Paterno had hoped that Cooper's confidence would kick in, but after the Syracuse loss he had to concede that it might not happen.

After that season, Cooper said of the racism, "I didn't consciously think about it. But subconsciously, I guess it did affect me. I didn't play up to what I thought my potential was."

Penn State had a promising sophomore quarterback named John Hufnagel. Paterno was so certain that Cooper would succeed that he had moved Hufnagel to defense. Now, though, he decided to bring Hufnagel back over to offense. It was a winning football move. With Hufnagel leading, and Cooper and Bob Parsons playing backup, Penn State won its last five games, scoring at least 30 points in each. In time, Hufnagel became an All-American.

Now letters poured in calling Paterno a racist. He thought that Cooper never really understood or forgave him for not staying with him. Cooper graduated from Penn State and moved back to Harrisburg, where he worked for the Pennsylvania Housing Finance Agency. Teammates rarely heard from him. Penn State would not have a black starting quarterback again until the 1990s.

Kenny Jackson, who played wide receiver for Paterno, coached with him, and became a close family friend, watched the way people projected society's shortcomings on Paterno. "I loved Joe Paterno. He did not see color. He saw a young man he could help and mold. That's it. He would not treat you different for being black, but he would not treat you special either. It was honest. Joe was honest. Think how much better the world would be if everybody was like that."

Joe and Sue Paterno with their daughters, Diana and Mary Kay (in Sue's lap)
(*Penn State University Archives, Pennsylvania State University Libraries*)

{ *Intermezzo* }

George Scott Paterno was the miracle child. Well, the first miracle child; another would come later. The Paternos had four children in five years—Diana, Mary Kay, David, and Joseph Jr., called Jay—and Sue then suffered three miscarriages. It was while she was in the hospital after the third miscarriage that doctors told her she would never have another child. "You can't keep doing this to yourself."

"I want more children," she said.

"Well, we don't think you'll be able to carry a child."

"I know you're doctors," Sue told them, "but you're not God."

By the time Scott was born in 1972, family life had been more or less resolved. Sue was in charge of everything at home. There were things Joe could do, such as read to the children at bedtime, and there were things Joe couldn't do, such as everything else. His one attempt to give the diaper-wearing toddlers baths—complete with crying and confusion and Joe griping, "They don't get undressed! I told them to get undressed and get in the tub!"—became family legend. His ineptitude around the home was the seed of countless family stories. Once, he decided to help Sue break down the dining-room table after guests had left. In one deft motion, he pulled out the middle leaf of the table, smashed it against the chandelier, broke three globes, and watched helplessly as glass rained down all around him. He then stood against the wall, watching Sue sweep up the glass and then vacuum any remaining tiny shards. When she was finished, he asked simply, "Is there anything else I can do?"

Still, Joe was an overwhelming presence in his family. The kitchen table was their center. Every evening—at different times, depending on the day's practice schedule, but still every evening—the entire family sat around the kitchen table, ate dinner, and talked until bedtime. No Paterno child ever ate dinner at someone else's house. "That table was my childhood," said Scott. There Joe would allow conversations on any topic—school, friends, politics, history, literature, religion—except football.

"Dad would always take the opposite view of whatever opinion a kid would express," David remembered. "And by doing so, he taught us to defend, explain, and convince not just ourselves but everyone at the table why we thought our idea was the right one. It taught us to think deeper about what we believed, and it taught us to challenge him too—because you can be sure we quickly learned to pull the same skepticism on his ideas."

Lessons were dished out like pasta. Arguments filled the evenings.

The complete set of the *World Book Encyclopedia* that Sue placed on a shelf next to the kitchen table was the referee for all arguments.

Joe Paterno the father, like Joe Paterno the coach, had tenets that he would repeat again and again. He hated foul language, for instance. "It's a sign of poor intelligence." He was, his daughter Mary Kay remembered, particularly put off by the word "fart." He often threatened to wash out the kids' mouths with soap, and once actually followed through, though he proved to be a somewhat less than effective schoolmarm. "He barely touched the soap to our tongues—you didn't even feel it," Mary Kay said.

Yet many of the players of the late 1960s recalled Paterno swearing often, a jolting change from Rip Engle, who never said anything south of "gosh." Like most things in Paterno's life, his decision to stop swearing grew out of a story. In the late 1960s, Paterno did a lot of recruiting on a school-purchased telephone in his home office. As he talked with recruits on the phone, his toddler son Jay, the son most drawn to football, would often sit on the floor, playing with little football figures and designing plays for them to run. Because recruiting is a tough game, many players would tell Joe they had decided to go to another school. He was always gracious when they gave him the bad news; he told them he was disappointed, but the school they had chosen was a good one, and they would have a great career there—and hey, don't forget to hit the books. He meant all that, but Joe was a competitor, and losing made him crazy. As soon as he hung up the phone, he would grumble to himself, "Son of a bitch! I hope you hate it there."

One time, Joe hung up the phone, and before he could say a word, Jay piped up in his squeaky voice, "Son of a bitch! I hope you hate it there!" Everyone in the family says that's when Joe, on the whole, stopped swearing. (In 1995, when a Rutgers coach charged Paterno with running up the score, Paterno lost his head and shouted on camera, "That's bullshit!" This created a brief scandal in Pennsylvania, and family members and players, many who said they had never heard him use an off-color word, would not let him live it down.)

Joe was devoted to rules and regulations. The same man who

walked out of the restaurant when his daughters shared a cucumber from an all-you-can-eat salad bar would not allow his children to use the pencils he brought home from work because, he said, "that's university property." He hammered his children with the same phrase he used on his players and everyone who ever saw him at a coaching clinic: "It's not enough to be fair. You must *appear* to be fair." This was a constant force in his fatherhood. Doing the right thing was not enough, he told his children. They had to go one step higher than the right thing. This, as much as anything, is what his children thought about at the end.

When everyone in the family looked back, they agreed that Joe wasn't around all that much. Sue was the everyday presence in their lives. She cooked, cleaned, helped with homework, and dealt with every school issue, friend issue, and life issue. Joe would show up for dinner. In many ways, they understood that their role was to not bother him, to not weigh him down, to free him up to do his work. When his fame grew, he could not watch Diana's cheerleading or Mary Kay's gymnastics without being bombarded by autograph requests and photo hounds. Once, when he tried to take the family to the amusement park in nearby Hershey, he was so overrun with well-wishers and fans that at some point he went back to the car and designed plays while the family rode the rides. "It's not fair," more than one of the kids said. "He's *our* father."

But they learned to accept it, the way children of famous people do. They prayed for the team to win. They stayed out of their father's way, especially when his mind started whirring. They lived by his schedule. And as their father became more famous and more beloved, they found their own ways to live with the most famous last name in college football. Diana, for instance, would interrupt teachers taking attendance before they called out her last name. "I'm here!" she would shout before the last syllable in *Diana* was voiced. On their first date, Mary Kay's future husband, Chris, was unaware of her last name.

As for Joe, he felt bad about the time not spent, the way fathers often do at the end of their lives. "I should have been there more," he admitted, but he knew that he could not have been there more and still be Joe Paterno. He loved them and taught them in his own way. And they knew: he had to coach football. It had not begun as an obsession, but it became one over the years. Coaching young men into great football teams was at the very heart of his existence.

Joe Paterno and Joey Cappelletti *(Penn State University Archives, Pennsylvania State University Libraries)*

Sainthood

Joe Paterno became a public saint in 1973, with all the praise and aspersions that go with such a title, but his path to sainthood probably began four years earlier, when he sat in the living room of John and Anne Cappelletti of Upper Darby, Pennsylvania. Their son, John Jr., was one of the best high school football players in the state, and Paterno wanted him to play for Penn State. Paterno spoke a little Italian to Anne, impressing her. He and assistant coach George Welsh explained their approach to football and academics, impressing the father. Paterno had done this so many times, as an assistant coach for Rip Engle, as a head coach and closer, that he was like a veteran stage actor on his hundredth performance. He did not just know the words, he knew the rhythms. He expected that John Cappelletti would come to Penn State.

Then he noticed that John's seven-year-old brother, Joey, was slouched on the couch. "What's wrong?" he whispered to Anne. She told him that Joey had leukemia, and that this was one of his down days.

With that, Paterno walked over to the couch and sat down next to Joey, and they spent the rest of the evening talking. Welsh was left to sell the rest of the family on Penn State and great football and the importance of college. Joe talked to Joey.

In this story, as with so many of Paterno's actions, you can see the beauty or you can see the self-interest. Do you see a man who came across a child in pain and decided that the most important thing he could do that evening was try to bring a little joy into his life? Or do you see a man who determined that the best way he could recruit John Cappelletti to play at Penn State was to spend the evening talking to his sick younger brother? In many ways, this would be the riddle that would follow Paterno throughout his life. Was it real or was it a show?

"Why," Sue would ask, "is it so hard for people to understand that we are who we are and Joe is who he is?"

THE SAINTHOOD YEAR OF 1973 began with an offer. Billy Sullivan owned the New England Patriots, an NFL team that played its games in Foxborough, Massachusetts, between Boston and Providence. Football owners, especially in the years to follow, were billionaires looking for a profitable little diversion. But Sullivan was different; he was not a rich man. When the owners of the old American Football League met for the first time, he told the writer Mickey Herskowitz, "I was the only man in the room who could not be described as independently wealthy. Or for that matter, even dependently wealthy. At the time, I had $8,000 to my name, not all of it in cash."

Sullivan had been a sportswriter in Boston and later, befitting his manic personality, a publicity man for the Boston Braves baseball team and Notre Dame football. He was so relentless in flooding sportswriters with press releases that America's most famous sportswriter, Red Smith, called him the Maître De Mimeograph. Later Sullivan tried to get into the oil business, with less than limited success. He never did make enough money in his life to stay ahead. Over the years, he would lose control of the Patriots, win it back, go into bankruptcy, fight his way out, and more.

But money did not drive Billy Sullivan. Buzz motivated him. Fame moved him. Heck, that's why he had called them the Patriots in the first place: he wanted them to be America's team. In the early years he tried to hire some big-name college coaches like President Nixon's friend Bud Wilkinson and Notre Dame's former coach Frank Leahy, but he got nowhere with them. He tried many different promotions, but no matter what he did he just could not grab people's attention.

In late 1972, Sullivan had his most inspired idea, the one that would finally make his team the talk of the country. He decided to hire Penn State's football coach, Joe Paterno.

Of course, Paterno had been pitched before, most memorably by the Pittsburgh Steelers' owner, Art Rooney, after the 1968 season and then by the Green Bay Packers in 1970, a couple of years after Lombardi stepped down. But even counting Al Davis's attempt back in the 1960s, Paterno had never run into a whirlwind quite like Billy Sullivan. When Sullivan's call came, Paterno tried to shrug him off. He said he didn't really want to coach in the NFL. He was happy at Penn State. Sullivan did not seem to be listening. He told Paterno that he was going to make him an offer he simply could not refuse. Enough money to set up his family for life, and to top it off, something that, as far as he knew, had never before been offered a coach: "I'm offering the chance to be part owner of the Patriots."

Paterno stopped cold. At Penn State, he was making about thirty-five thousand a year, maybe a little less, a comfortable enough living for a father of five whose wife darned socks and disliked shopping. Paterno recalled Sullivan offering him a four-year deal worth a total of one million dollars plus a home with two cars in the garage. The newspapers reported the deal to be worth as much as $1.4 million. Plus as much as 5 percent ownership of the Patriots. It was the richest offer ever made to a coach. Paterno searched desperately for a reason to say no. "I'd need to know how much control I'd have, because it . . ."

"You'd have complete control of the whole thing," Sullivan said.

"Complete control?"

"Over the whole thing. You'd be coach and general manager. It would be your show."

Paterno was entirely shaken. Things like this didn't happen. He had been a successful college coach, no question about it. After the unbeaten streak ended in 1970, Penn State had won eleven games in 1971, ten more games in 1972, excellent records. He had built his reputation by taking on Nixon and by speaking out against corruption in college sports. "Too good to be true," the New York Times called him. Even so, this offer seemed out of touch with Paterno's life. He was not sure he wanted to take the job, but he did not see any way he could turn it down.

To complicate matters, the offer came just as Penn State was to play Oklahoma in the Sugar Bowl. Throughout his life, Paterno hated distractions. In his mind, his job was to coach football, and that was all he ever really wanted to do. He did the other stuff—the interviews, the speeches, the recruiting, the schmoozing—because he knew that it was part of building a great football program. But he resented much of it. In the last fifteen or so years of his life, after he had built Penn State into one of the nation's most respected football programs and there was nothing left to prove, he gradually stopped doing all the other stuff. He delegated everything except the actual coaching. "He would scream at us all the time, 'Would you just let me coach my football team?' " his friend Guido D'Elia would say. "That's all he wanted to do. Every other thing made him crazy."

Now he was trying to get his team ready for the Sugar Bowl, but all people wanted to talk about was the Patriots offer. Billy Sullivan showed up in New Orleans, which amplified the rumors. Back in State College, people were sick with worry that Paterno would leave. A campaign was launched to keep him at Penn State, complete with "Don't Go, Joe" bumper stickers, signs, and buttons. Diana and Mary said this was the first time that everyone at school singled them out as Paternos. They were showered with affection and requests: "Tell your Dad, we love him!" Penn State lost to Oklahoma 14–0, and Paterno was miserable. He felt he had allowed the Patriots talk to distract him and he had let the team down.

But the decision still loomed. Paterno agonized. He had become a decisive coach, but now he found himself wavering like a rookie. Deep down, maybe, he did not want the job. He liked coaching college football. He liked it that Sue felt comfortable in State College; her comfort made him comfortable. He liked the idea that he was a teacher as much as a coach. He liked the players he had recruited; he knew that his team was going to be terrific in 1973, featuring senior John Cappelletti.

Perhaps most of all, he liked the feeling that, in his own way, he was living up to his father's charge to make an impact: he believed he was improving the lives of young men. Could he really make an impact in pro football? His friend Tom Osborne, who had just become coach at Nebraska, would always remember a conversation he'd had with Dallas Cowboys coach Tom Landry: "He told me one time that even after all the wins and all the accomplishments, he really didn't think he made any difference at all in his players' character. He thought by the time he got them in pro football, it was too late."

Paterno, deep down, believed the same thing. What could he teach pro football players about life? How could he honestly call himself anything more than a football coach if he was making a million dollars to coach professionals? He also knew, even if he did not want to admit it, that Sue did not want to move the family from State College. The family acted happy enough. At one point Mary Kay, who was seven, rushed into the house and asked, "Is it true that if Daddy signs a piece of paper, he will get a thousand dollars and coach the Miami Dolphins?"

"No, Mary," Diana said. She was ten. "It's a million dollars and it's the New England Patriots."

"Same thing," Mary said.

Sue told Joe that they could be happy anywhere, they would adjust, and that it was his decision. But Joe knew how she really felt.

"I really didn't want to go, but I felt he's in charge of his career," Sue said. "I just thought where we lived was so comfortable. . . . We met with the Sullivans at the bowl game, and I asked one of the dumbest questions. Scotty was just two months old, and our doctor was just five minutes away. I had very accident-prone children. I looked at Mrs. Sullivan and I said, 'Foxborough? Is that like our town or is that all big roads?' She looked at me like, 'What do you mean, big roads?' So I said, 'Super highways.' She said, 'Oh yeah, you can get anywhere.' I let it go. But I thought that wasn't a very smart question."

Even with these things pulling at him, Paterno knew something else: he couldn't turn this down. It was too much money, too much control, too much glory to pass up. He could coach for a few years, be set for life, and then do whatever he wanted. He could get the house on Cape Cod that all those kids at Brown treated as their birthright. He could set up his family so that they would never have to worry about anything. He could—he had to admit it—he could be a famous coaching hero. Like Lombardi. Paterno had no doubt about what would happen if he took the Patriots job: he would lead the Patriots to the Super Bowl, win the Super Bowl, win more than one Super Bowl. "I had a big ego," he confessed. "I tried to cover that up a little bit, but I thought I was as good a coach as anybody. The Patriots had some good young players—they had just drafted Jim Plunkett with the first pick—and I knew I could go there and win."

Paterno took the job. Sure he did. On Thursday night, he called Sullivan and said he would be proud to be the next coach of the New England Patriots. Penn State sports information director Jim Tarman and his wife, Louise, came over to the house, and the first thing they saw was four-year-old Jay carrying around a Patriots pennant. "I guess he's going," Jim said. Paterno welcomed them with bourbon and Pepsi and asked Tarman to come along to work with the Patriots. Joe had already asked his brother, George, then coaching football at the Merchant Marine Academy, to be an assistant coach. Everything was in place. The Paternos and Tarmans toasted the future and told stories until midnight. At one point, six-year-old David stumbled downstairs. The conversation that followed was recounted for the *Philadelphia Inquirer*:

"You won't go, will you, Daddy?" he asked.

"I'll do whatever you want, Dave," Joe said. "What do you think?"

"Don't go," Dave said.

The night grew a bit somber after that. Voices began to choke a little bit. The humor of the situation began to hit a little too close. "Who wants to coach professionals anyway?" Sue asked, and it sounded a bit too true to be a punch line. But the decision had been made, and though there was some sadness, Paterno insisted on feeling good about it. "How does it feel to be going to bed with a millionaire?" he asked Sue that night, and she smiled without saying a word. Neither of them could sleep. Joe never slept soundly anyway; all his life he woke up several times each night to scribble something down on paper or to let a thought play out in his mind. "Joe needs to work things out," Sue explained. "That's just how he is." This one was hard to work out. He tossed in bed.

Meanwhile Sue woke up and went to another room to feed Scotty. Down the hall, Joe could hear her crying.

That was the moment when Joe Paterno decided who he wanted to be. Years later, as he lay in a hospital bed knowing the end was near, he marveled at the choice that faced him. "I look back on it and think that choice seems obvious. But it didn't feel that way then. You know, I'm not opposed to making money. I didn't take an oath of poverty when I became a football coach. And it was so much money."

At 5 A.M., he called Jim Tarman, who was sleeping. "How can you sleep when I can't?" Joe demanded. Tarman groggily asked what was going on. Paterno told him, "I'm not taking the job."

Shortly after that, when Sue woke up, he told her, "I hope you enjoyed your night sleeping with a millionaire, because it's the last time you will do it."

THE REACTION TO PATERNO'S TURNING down a million dollars to remain a college football coach animated the country. There seemed so little good news in the papers. The war in Vietnam was lost. The Watergate burglary story was beginning its slow but steady march toward the resignation of a president. Eleven Israeli athletes had been murdered in September at the Munich Olympics. The nation was about to be plunged into a recession.

And here was Joe Paterno, the coach who looked like a professor, saying no to money and glory so he could coach young men in college. And why? His quote was reprinted in newspapers across the country: "How much money does one man need?"

"Standards have changed, religion has changed, even baseball has changed," the United Press International reporter began his story. "Joe Paterno has not changed."

"In the long run, it came down to lots of money vs. lots of idealism, and for a change idealism won," the Associated Press wrote.

"Good for Paterno!" was the headline in the *Christian Science Monitor*, complete with the exclamation point.

"In these days of multimillion dollar TV deals with pro clubs, six-figure salaries for athletes and $15 tickets for Super Bowls, money seems the dominant influence in sports," began an editorial in the *Los Angeles Times*. "Thus it's refreshing, as well as almost unprecedented, to see a man like Joe Paterno say no to the big dough."

Though he had not intended it this way, Paterno's decision had given moral authority to The Grand Experiment. His story seemed impervious to cynicism. A couple of sports columnists suggested that he might have been holding out for a job in his beloved New York, but when his former Brown University coach Weeb Ewbank called to see if Paterno had any interest in replacing him as head coach of the Jets, Paterno cut him off. "I'm staying here, Weeb. It's where I'm supposed to be." Governor Milton Shapp of Pennsylvania declared a "Joe Paterno Day." Penn State insisted on giving Paterno a contract—his first with the school—and a big raise, though he had not asked for either. A testimonial dinner was held for him, and alumni gave him a new car and a vacation to anywhere in the world. (He and Sue chose Italy.) Speaking requests poured in, including the biggest of all: he was invited to give Penn State's commencement address.

He was both embarrassed and delighted by the attention. The embarrassment was more public. Again and again, he reminded people that he was just a football coach who liked to design game plans and make sure that his players went to class. "I don't think I'm a better person than anyone else," he told the *Philadelphia Inquirer*. "I just may be smart enough to know when I'm well off." He would always remember, with discomfort, going to a basketball game that winter, and when he stood up the entire arena stood with him and cheered so wildly they had to stop the game for a moment. Paterno was going to the bathroom.

Privately, though, he understood exactly what he had done and how it would be viewed. And he liked being viewed that way. Overnight he had become as famous as any college coach in America, as famous as Alabama's Bear Bryant or Ohio State's Woody Hayes. The recruiting pitch he had repeated in living rooms across America— *Play for the team, not yourself. Be unselfish. There are more important things than individual glory*—was now bolstered by his own life and had a new kind of power. He was being celebrated not for winning games or devising brilliant strategy, but for having his values in order. He thought this, finally, was a tribute to his father. His mother, who lived to be ninety-two and would build much of her life around Joe's career, beamed.

Perhaps most meaningful of all, Paterno felt he had lived up to his ideals. He often worried about that. When reliving the Patriots story almost forty years later, he said, "When I took the job, I found out something about myself. I found that I could be bought. I found out that I had a price." I pointed out to him that, in fact, just the opposite was true: he turned down the Patriots job. He could not be bought. Paterno shook his head and said something curious: "No. They bought me. I took the job. Afterward, because of Sue and the players, I went back and turned it down. Billy Sullivan would have had every right to be angry with me. I broke my word with him. He was a gentleman about it, but I broke my word."

He paused for a long time. When interviewing Paterno, I found, the silences were to be honored because they often led to his saying the thing closest to his heart. Finally, he spoke again. "That was the greatest temptation of my life. When I turned down that job, there was no turning back. I knew exactly what I was supposed to do for the rest of my life."

PATERNO WORKED FOR WEEKS ON his Penn State commencement address. He clipped out articles, scribbled down thoughts, asked the people closest to him for help. For a long time, he had been self-conscious about speaking. He had practiced talking into a tape recorder over and over to rid himself of the Brooklyn whine, until one of the speech professors told him that the accent was part of his charm. He had the ability to entertain crowds with his speeches, in large part because of the piercing one-liners he invented for the occasions.

From a talk at Gettysburg College: "I understand that they are bringing Lincoln's Gettysburg Address back here. I guess a lot of people felt you were going to need it after Paterno gives his Gettysburg Address. Some of our alumni wish I could get four scores in sixty minutes, much less in a twenty-minute speech."

From a talk to a group of orthopedic surgeons: "I've been really nervous about this speech because I figured I'd be talking to some witty, talented, clever guys. But after being with you guys for two days, I feel better."

From a speech to the Quarterback Club in 1979, after his team lost to Alabama in a game for the No. 1 spot: "Everyone wants to hold up that one finger to say 'We're number one!' I still see one finger in my travels today. It's a different finger, and the hand is turned the other way."

From a talk at a political rally in 1974, just after Watergate: "What am I doing here? I'm not a politician. Come to think of it, maybe that's why I'm a Republican."

Yes, Paterno had his way of connecting to audiences quickly. That was an extension of his coaching. But he thought of the 1973 commencement address differently. This was his chance to explain who he was and what he was about, not only to the Penn State students but also to himself. In many ways, the previous twenty-five years had been a blur to him. He had been a quarterback and student at Brown University with the expectation of becoming a lawyer. And then, in a dizzying sequence, he had become a football coach; his father died; he lived in a friend's basement; he did not date much; he met Sue, and they were married, and he was named head coach at Penn State, and the team did not lose for the better part of three years, and people began calling him a genius. He was offered a million dollars. When he turned it down, people started to see him as something larger than life.

For what? What did all this mean? For all his ambition, and for all the effort he spent considering the questions of fate and destiny, Paterno had not spent much time thinking about his own fate and destiny. The New England offer had presented him with perhaps the first difficult choice of his life. Until then, he had allowed himself to float wherever the tide carried him. But now, well, he was not exactly playing it humble when he began his speech by saying, "Some of you have every right to feel let down that after four years of hard work you have to listen to a coach at your graduation." He'd had serious doubts about giving the speech. "But in spite of these and other misgivings, I accepted because I realize that in a day when materialism is rampant, many of you felt that my interest in doing other things besides making money has in some way helped you to reaffirm your ideal of a life of service, of dignity, and a life of meaning."

He made the speech while the Watergate investigation was heating up, and he could not resist what would become his famous jab at Nixon knowing so much about college football and so little about Watergate. But that was mostly where the joking stopped. Joe Paterno had something to say.

I'm sure that it is obvious to all of you that you are going out into a fragmented, disillusioned and oftentimes confused society—a society which has promised more than it is now willing or perhaps able to deliver to our minority groups and, among others, to our poverty victims. There is corruption, fear, mistrust, lack of leadership, unequal justice, privileged economic groups and all the abuses you would expect in a nation without consistent direction—in a country without a common purpose and a people unsure of moral commitments. We are experiencing the frustration of a society, which is desperately struggling with itself, afraid that at any moment it will be ripped apart by deep-rooted racism, which regardless of all our enlightened medication persists as a cancer which defies cure. We cannot get rid of a war we do not want to fight. We cannot wash our hands of the blood that has been shed when we only wish peace and freedom for everybody. We are a decent people struggling with ourselves.

This was Paterno in full bloom: opinionated, thoughtful, forceful, controversial, the man Angelo and Florence Paterno had hoped might someday be president. As the years went on, he showed this side of himself less and less to the outside world. Maybe, Paterno wondered, he became a bit less idealistic, a bit less trusting of the world, a bit less certain of his ability to do much more than affect the lives of his family and football players. More likely, he had been beaten up by the expectations. He grew tired of being called a hypocrite and a moralist, of having critics turn every one of his mistakes and soft spots into a referendum on his character. He retreated inward and built walls around himself and his program. But in 1973, Paterno was open and vulnerable and willing to speak from the heart.

Our forefathers, who carved out this country, had blind faith in America. They had no responsibility to the rest of the world, and they had only to be concerned with what was best for their nation. They had never been beaten and they had supreme confidence. Our state of mind is different. We cannot morally escape our responsibility to the rest of the world, and we can never again do what is right just for America. We will never again have supreme confidence that everything we do is right. Not after Vietnam and Kent State, not after the assassination of Martin Luther King and John Kennedy, not after the death of Bobby Kennedy, and not after Watergate. But this doesn't mean we can be less decisive than our forefathers. We must always act, but when we are wrong, we must be mature enough to realize it and act accordingly. This is where greatness lies.

There is another thing I tell my team. I tell them to keep hustling. Go all out on every play no matter how bad things look—because, if you keep hustling, something good will happen. . . . So keep hustling. You'll do all right. Enjoy yourselves. Enjoy life. Have some fun. Our squad enjoys kidding me because on a nice day before a game I like to walk into the locker room and say, "Boy what a day—oh to be young again."

I cannot adequately describe to you the love that permeates a good football team—a love of one another. Perhaps as one of my players said: "We grow together in love—hating the coach." But to be in a locker room before a big game and to gather a team around and to look at grown men with tears in their eyes . . . huddling close to each [other] . . . reaching out to be a part of each other . . . to look into strong faces which say, "If only we can do it today," . . . *to be with aggressive, ambitious people who have lost themselves in something bigger than they are — this is what living is all about.*

Paterno's speech made news all over America. " 'The System Is You,' Paterno Tells Graduates" was the headline in Charleston, West Virginia. In Centralia, Washington, the headline was "Paterno Speaks Out." *Sports Illustrated* reprinted large chunks of the speech in its "Scorecard" section. "Paterno urged graduates to admit when they are wrong," reported a paper in San Antonio, Texas. The *New York Times* and *Washington Post* each wrote about Paterno's speech in relation to Watergate. "Joe's Penn Statement: Compete!" is how the story was headlined in the *Chicago Tribune*.

Paterno had reached new heights as an icon. Now all that was left was to lead one of the most remarkable and emotional seasons a college football team ever had. And, this being Joe Paterno's sainthood year, that's exactly what happened.

PATERNO KNEW THAT HIS 1973 team would be good. They had won ten of twelve games in 1972 and returned many of their best players, the biggest star being their running back, John Cappelletti. In the first two years of Cappelletti's career at Penn State, he had played defense. The team already had great running backs in Lydell Mitchell and Franco Harris, and Paterno always wanted his best athletes on defense, always preferred winning low-scoring games in which his defense imposed its will. He would have loved for Cappy to become a great defensive player, but he struggled as a defensive back, and when he was a junior in 1972 Paterno relented and put him back on offense.

Few thought that would work. Cappelletti struggled holding on to the football, and for a time people called him "John Fumbletti." But he found his rhythm as the 1972 season went along. He ran for 162 yards against Syracuse, inspiring the Syracuse coach and longtime Penn State doubter Ben Schwartzwalder to whine to *Sports Illustrated*, "Cappelletti sure played better than he did in the movies we looked at." The next week, Cappy carried the ball a school record thirty-four times against West Virginia. His football personality was coming into focus. He was big, strong, and virtually indestructible. He was relentless, always pushing forward for an extra yard, never worrying about himself or his statistics or even his physical well-being. Paterno loved the guy. He would never admit to loving any one player more than the rest, but it's fair to say, based on the way he talked over the years, that he never loved any player more than he loved John Cappelletti.

In truth, he had a special affinity and love for the entire 1973 team. Through the years, whenever people asked Paterno how good his team was, he would borrow the line of legendary coach Bobby Dodd and say, "Ask me in twenty years." He meant that he wanted to see what became of those players, how they lived their lives. It's easy enough to go back and see what happened to those players from 1973.

Quarterback Tom Shuman, who readily admitted that his main job in 1973 was handing the ball to Cappy, remembered getting called into Paterno's office so the coach could tear him apart over grades. Shuman offered a little insight into how Paterno did such things: "[He] very clearly let me know that I had a good bit of talent on the football field, but that I was going to be a huge disappointment to my parents, myself, and the university if I didn't immediately get my nose into my books." This was classic Paterno, using every angle to get inside players' heads. His favorite trick was to use a player's mother as motivation, saying, "I promised your mother that I would make sure that you got an education, and you're making a liar of me." Shuman, like hundreds of others, took the hint, hit the books, made the Dean's List, played pro football for a while, and became a national sales manager.

Fullback Bob Nagle became a systems engineer. Flanker Chuck Herd became a conference planner at Penn State and worked as a personal ministry Bible school teacher. Split end Gary Hayman became an attorney. Tight end Dan Natale owned a sporting goods store. Left tackle Phil LaPorta went into construction.

Left guard Mark Markovich had come to Penn State for the same reason so many did: because he felt Paterno was the first honest coach he had come across. Other coaches had told him he would be a star tight end for their program. Paterno said bluntly, "You're too slow and don't have good enough hands to play tight end. You'll be an offensive lineman." Markovich was taken aback but realized that Paterno was right. He became a second-team All-American offensive lineman and a first-team Academic All-American. He later became president of the Illinois Machine & Tool Works.

Center Jack Baiorunos became a dentist. Right end Buddy Tesner became an orthopedic surgeon, as did cornerback Jim Bradley. In fact Bradley was the longtime team surgeon for the Pittsburgh Steelers. The other cornerback, Buddy Ellis, became a certified public accountant. Linebacker Mike Orsini became an otolaryngologist, or, as Paterno called him, "an ear, nose and throat doctor, what does he need the fancy title?" Kicker Chris Bahr, whose brother Matt also kicked at Penn State and whose father coached soccer at the school, worked as a financial planner. Others were teachers, executives, coaches, and brokers. John Quinn became a high school principal. Woody Petchel became a company president.

Paterno would readily admit he couldn't see the big picture back then. He had this unformed idea in his mind, this idea about the difference between excellence and success. Later his teams would have great success. They would win national championships. They would become so popular that Penn State expanded Beaver Stadium to seat 107,000 people. Paterno himself would be named *Sports Illustrated*'s Sportsman of the Year, and he would make a lot of money. He and Sue would use much of that money to build a library and a student faith center, and they would endow scholarships and fellowships. But Paterno was always careful to say that success and excellence are two different things and not always intertwined. Success is nice, he would say. Excellence, though, is life-affirming.

In 1973 Penn State won every game on its schedule, almost all of them convincingly, and the nation yawned. Perhaps this was because Penn State did not face a single ranked team until it beat Pitt in the final game of the regular season and Louisiana State in the Orange Bowl. But 1973 was an odd season in the annals of college football. Six of America's most beloved teams—Penn State, of course, but also Alabama, Notre Dame, Ohio State, Oklahoma, and Michigan—finished the season undefeated (though Ohio State, Michigan, and Oklahoma had a tie on their records). This left Penn State ranked sixth in the nation.

Paterno insisted, perhaps a bit too intently to be believable, that he didn't care. "I'm not worried about the polls," he said again and again. Penn State outscored opponents 447 to 129, and only two teams all year stayed within a touchdown. Cappelletti was a revelation. He carried the ball thirty-three times in a grueling victory over Air Force ("That was a great feeling, when I looked up and saw there were only seven seconds to go," he recalled.) Two weeks later, before the West Virginia game, Cappy was visited by his younger brother, Joey, who had just turned eleven and whose leukemia was growing more and more aggressive. "What do you want for a birthday present?" John asked.

"Four touchdowns," Joey said promptly.

"I think we'll score four touchdowns."

"No," Joey said. "I want *you* to score four touchdowns."

Cappelletti was not healthy; he had sprained his shoulder. But he was not the complaining kind. In the third quarter, Penn State led 35–14, and Paterno pulled his starters, including Cappy. "You've had a good workout," Cappelletti would remember Joe telling him. At that point, Cappy had scored three touchdowns. He was going to say something to Paterno about wanting to score one more touchdown for Joey, but he did not. He was not the complaining kind. Instead he wandered off to the bench. It was Markovich, his best friend, who explained to Paterno about Joey. Paterno was adamant about keeping his players humble, about preventing his team from becoming fragmented by stars or individual glory. He would say again and again, often with a bite in his voice, that he did not care about personal statistics or achievements. But he loved Joey Cappelletti.

"Cappelletti!" Paterno shouted. "Get back in there." It was like a made-for-TV movie. In fact it would become a hugely popular made-for-TV movie called *Something for Joey*. Cappelletti plunged in from two yards out, his fourth touchdown of the day, the moment that soon would induce tears in living rooms across America. But nobody told that story after the game. Instead Paterno just said, "I don't know if I've been around a greater football player than Cappy."

Against Maryland the next week, Cappy carried the ball thirty-seven times, breaking his own school record. A week after that, he broke the record again, this time carrying the ball forty-one times against North Carolina State. He ran for 220 yards and scored three touchdowns. He seemed to be superhuman. "Cappy just literally took the game over. He just literally carried people," Paterno said. The English lit major was so overwhelmed he used "literally" twice—incorrectly. After that game, Cappelletti was the favorite to win the Heisman Trophy.

The next week, against Ohio University, Cappy ran for 204 yards and again scored four touchdowns. Paterno was now getting into the spirit; he had pulled Cappelletti from the blowout when he had 198 yards and put him back in so he could break the 200-yard mark again. In the last game of the year, Cappelletti carried the ball thirty-seven times in an overpowering victory over rival Pitt. He won the Heisman Trophy in a runaway.

When Penn State beat Louisiana State in a boring 16–9 Orange Bowl, in which Cappelletti played hurt and gained only 50 yards, the national media was unimpressed. "The match was so lackluster," wrote John Crittenden of the *Miami News*, "that I hoped some of the Penn Staters would be honest enough to say, 'We don't deserve to be No. 1.' That didn't happen, though." Not only did that not happen, but Paterno went the other way. "I just held the Paterno Poll," he told reporters after that game. "I did it in our locker room. Our players voted Penn State No. 1. It was unanimous." He then bought championship rings for every player.

Paterno might have been happier coaching the 1973 team than he ever felt again. He would love coaching for the rest of his life, of course, but there was an innocence about 1973 that could not be repeated. *Sports Illustrated*'s William Johnson wrote a long feature on Paterno in November of that year, with the telling lead sentence, "It is arguable whether Joe Paterno, at 46, is an authentic folk hero." That article followed a story line that would be repeated in countless Paterno stories yet to be written: the scholarly coach who lives modestly, babysits his kids, listens to opera as he draws up game plans, rails against cheating, and is most proud of his team's high graduation rate. Yes, it was all true. But over time, it descended into cliché. Nobody's that good. The cynics would pick at his record and his motivations. Some players got in trouble, some failed to graduate, and Paterno was called a hypocrite. The expectations changed. The Paterno children grew up, and their father was too busy to babysit his grandchildren. It would never feel easier or freer than it did in 1973, when everyone was young, when Paterno could speak his heart, and when the game plan was simply to give the ball to John Cappelletti while his younger brother, Joey, watched happily.

THE HEISMAN TROPHY DINNER WAS the crescendo in a year filled with highs. Cappelletti had scribbled part of his speech on the back of an envelope. There was a certain part he wanted to get exactly right; after he thanked his parents, Paterno, his teammates, and others, he reached that part. Paterno knew it was coming. He had told Sue, who was sitting near the back, not to cry.

"The next part," Cappy said, "I'm very happy to do something like this. I thought about it since the Heisman was announced ten days ago. And this is to dedicate a trophy that a lot of people earned, I've earned, my parents and the people I've mentioned and numerous other people that are here tonight and have been with me for a long time. The youngest member of my family, Joseph, is very ill. He has leukemia. If I can dedicate this trophy to him tonight and give him a couple of days of happiness, this is worth everything.

"I think a lot of people think I go through a lot on Saturdays and during the week, as most athletes do, and you get bumps and bruises, and it is a terrific battle out there on the field. Only for me it is only on Saturdays and it's only in the fall. For Joseph, it is all year round, and it is a battle that is unending with him, and he puts up with much more than I'll ever put up with. And I think this trophy is more his than mine because he has been a great inspiration to me."

Sue Paterno did cry. So did everyone else in the New York Hilton ballroom. Vice President Gerald Ford, who everyone suspected would soon be president, teared up. Archbishop Fulton Sheen, who on his death would be considered for sainthood, was there to give the blessing and simply said, "You don't need a blessing. God has already blessed you in John Cappelletti."

Paterno saw Billy Sullivan after the ceremony, after the most re-markable year a college football coach ever had. "Do you see now why I couldn't leave Penn State?" Paterno asked him.

"Yes," Sullivan said. "Yes, I think I do."

"I don't know if he really understood," Paterno would say. "But I did. There was no amount of money that could have made me as proud as seeing John Cappelletti that night."

ACT III: SUCCESS

I would much rather have men ask why I have no statue, than why I have one.

— CATO THE ELDER

{ *Aria* }

Joe Paterno
speech to Penn State Quarterback Club
winter 1979

Let's talk about being number one. The big question is: "Is it worth it?" Personally, I never really felt it was important to be number one. I had always believed deeply in the statement that to travel with hope is something better than to arrive. It might end up being true.

But it wasn't! To get to number one was generally fun. It was great excitement. The game we played against Alabama, though we lost, was a thrilling game to be a part of for everybody involved.

But you never get anything for nothing. And the price of number one can be too high unless we are careful.

You can't turn back the clock. People ... alumni ... subway alumni [alumni that live in big cities like New York and Philadelphia and come in only for games] ... they have had a taste of it and most of them will probably not be happy with less. A two-game losing season might be an unhappy one. These are the new expectations. And in order to stay up with such high expectations, we have to do many things.

We have to have more off-season training by the players. That makes it harder for them to excel in their classes. This is one of the costs.

We must set a tougher schedule so we can be number one. That sounds good, but it means we're never going to win twenty in a row again. The better the competition, the harder it will be to win every week.

This means we need better recruiting in a wider area. If we are going to play a tougher schedule, we must recruit the best.

In order to recruit the best, we have to get better facilities to keep up with the Joneses. We need a bigger weight room, an indoor practice facility, a bigger stadium, a better press box so more of those sportswriters will come and write better stories about us.

We need bigger and better fund raising to protect the integrity of the football program. There are costs here too. This creates ticket problems. Old friends are cast aside for "fat cats." Alumni make way for subway alumni. College football is getting so big. We have a ten million dollar budget. It's almost impossible to run college football the way we used to.

On a personal level, the cost is high. I can't go anywhere now without having to pose for pictures or sign autographs. I'm a private person, and now my family must go out without me because of the attention. I can't protect my family. The game now requires year-round recruiting, seven-days-a-week coaching, there are summer camps and speeches off campus. With success comes interest, visitors, staff. This week alone we've had Virginia, Indiana, New Hampshire, Connecticut and Minnesota high school coaches come to see how we do things.

Is it worth it? Yes. It's worth it because I believe we can

get over our growing pains and build a better organization. I believe we can be number one. And we can do it properly, with academic integrity. We are unique. By being number one, people will know where we are, who we are, what we believe in—and all this on a national scale.

In the end the cheer "We Are Penn State" says it all. We are proud. We are loyal. We are honest. And we are number one in everything, win or lose.

So number one? Is it worth it? I hope so. But if not, it's a helluva lot of fun.

Paterno with his friend and rival, Alabama coach Bear Bryant *(Penn State University Archives, Pennsylvania State University Libraries)*

Bear

Joe Paterno's feelings about Bear Bryant were never simple. He loved the Bear and wanted more than anything to beat him. He admired the Bear and was also repelled by him. He tried to emulate Bear and, at the same time, strove to be his opposite. It was complicated. The only uncomplicated part is that Paterno never beat the Bear.

Paul Bryant, the eighth of nine children, grew up on a farm in Dallas County, Arkansas. His father, Monroe, fell gravely ill when Paul was a boy, and his mother, Ida, generally took care of the farm. ("Miss Ida was always a lady, but she was tough as a sack of nails," her nephew Dean Kilgore was quoted saying in Keith Dunnavant's fine book *Coach*.) Everything about Bryant's life seemed legendary. When he was thirteen, he wrestled a bear at a local carnival for one dollar in prize money. He was never paid the dollar, but he did secure one of the most apt nicknames in American sports history. When he was in the navy during World War II, he disobeyed an order to abandon ship after the S.S. *Uruguay* was struck and sinking, and in disobeying he saved his own life and the lives of his men.

He truly was a bear of a man, six-foot-three, a handshake that buckled men's knees, and a fierce voice that cut through the southern wind. In thirty-eight years, his teams had only one losing season; that was his first year as coach at Texas A&M. Before that season began, he took his team down to a scorching Texas town called Junction and put them through a ten-day summer camp so savage that two-thirds of the players quit. The survivors won only one of ten games. Two years later, though, Texas A&M went undefeated. Two years after that, Bear left to coach at Alabama, where he won six national championships and became the state's living hero. It was said that the most famous thing in the whole state of Alabama was Bear Bryant, and the second most famous was his houndstooth hat.

"He had this—I don't know what you call it, but I guess it was charisma," Paterno said. "It was really bigger than charisma. It's the thing that great generals have. Patton had it. MacArthur had it. He would say, 'Do something,' and people would do it. Why? They were afraid of him. They loved him. They wanted to please him. He just had that thing leaders have."

"Do you have that thing?" I asked Paterno.

"Me? No, no, not like Bear Bryant." And then he told a story he had told many times before. In 1981 Bear Bryant and Alabama came to play in State College. Before the game, Bryant called Paterno. In Paterno's memory the phone call went like this:

Bryant: Joe, you know the governor of Pennsylvania, don't you?
Paterno: Yeah, I know him a little, Bear.

Bryant: Good. We gotta land our plane up in Harrisburg. If you could call up the governor and get him to close off the roads and get us a police escort up there after the game, I'd be appreciative.

"What did you do?" I asked, at which Paterno smiled and replied, "What do you think I did? I called up the governor and told him that Bear Bryant wanted a police escort after the game up to Harrisburg. And he told me, 'It will be a cold day in you-know-where before I'll give those guys from Alabama a police escort.' "

While I laughed Paterno said, "But you know what? You better believe Bear Bryant would have gotten *us* a police escort in Alabama. That's the difference. The only people who listen to me are the ones who have to listen or else I'll bench them. *Everybody* listened to Bear Bryant."

Paterno knew that Bryant was no angel. That's how he would say it: "Hey, the guy was no angel." Bryant drank heavily, and he worked the angles like the most powerful southern politicians. He and Paterno were on opposite sides of college football's purpose. "I used to go along with the idea that football players on scholarship were 'student-athletes,' " Bryant said. "Which is what the NCAA calls them. Meaning a student first, an athlete second. We were kidding ourselves, trying to make it more palatable to the academicians. We don't have to say that and we shouldn't. At the level we play, the boy is really an athlete first and a student second."

"Maybe Bear was more realistic than I was, I don't know," Paterno said. "But I really believed—still believe—that they are students first. I know we tried to make it that way at Penn State. Bear cared about school too. He would suspend players who skipped class, you know. But we probably did see it a little bit differently."

Paterno and Bryant faced each other on New Year's Day 1979 with the national championship on the line, and Paterno wanted to win that game more than any of his life. His teams had continued to win with regularity after the perfect 1973 season. They finished in the top

ten three of the four subsequent years, and there were countless stories written about the football heaven Paterno had built in the place
people called, without irony, "Happy Valley."

But Paterno never enjoyed calm or comfort; he distrusted both.
Whenever the coaches' meetings seemed too agreeable, he would
throw an argument grenade into the room to get people yelling again.
Nothing irritated him more than satisfaction. Guido D'Elia, who
worked with him for more than thirty years, said Paterno never once
thanked him or praised him, not directly. Once, D'Elia's video work
helped Penn State land a big recruit, and as he was walking toward
the football offices Paterno yelled from across the parking lot, "Hey,
I heard you did something not too bad."

D'Elia smiled; from Paterno, this was practically a song of praise.
When Paterno saw that smile he shouted, "Don't let it go to your
head!"

Paterno was compelled by the next challenge, the next task, the
next problem. He liked to think about Hercules' twelve labors, perhaps because they reminded him of a twelve-game football season.
Any one of Hercules' labors was a terrific challenge. But completing
one or two or three wasn't enough. He could not celebrate. "There's
something about me, it's not something I'm proud of: I can't enjoy
success. I just think you should always try for something more. It's like
I tell my kids all the time, I quote Browning that a 'man's reach should
exceed his grasp or what's a heaven for?' "

In 1978, Paterno wanted a special team that would finally be
recognized by everyone in the nation as No. 1. The 1978 team had
rolled through the season. The offense averaged about 30 points a
game, led by quarterback Chuck Fusina, who finished second in the
Heisman Trophy balloting. (He got more first-place votes than the
winner, Oklahoma's Billy Sims.) But as usual for Paterno's Penn State,
it was the defense, featuring future NFL stars Bruce Clark, Matt Millen, and Lance Mehl, that defined the team. Penn State went into
Columbus and shut out Ohio State in its season opener, something

no team had done since 1901. "There wasn't any time in the game we thought Ohio State could hurt us," Paterno chirped happily afterward. The Nittany Lions had back-to-back shutouts against Texas Christian and Kentucky. Late in the year, they played a Maryland team ranked No. 5 in the country and won 27–3.

They finished the season 11–0, undefeated, and, for the first time in Paterno's career, ranked No. 1 in America. They would play Bear Bryant and Alabama in the Sugar Bowl. This was their moment, the chance for Penn State to finally win the national championship that Nixon and voters and eastern football bias had denied them. This was also Paterno's chance to beat the icon, to stake his claim. It mattered to him more than he wanted to admit. "It was clear to all of us how much Joe wanted to win that game," Matt Millen recalled.

"Bear Bryant was the best coach," Paterno said. "John McKay used to say, 'Bear's not *a* coach, he's *the* coach.' I wanted to beat *the* coach. Maybe it was ego. But I wanted to win, and I thought we would win. I thought we had the better team."

Their confidence was surprisingly apparent for a Penn State team. "There isn't anybody on the team that doesn't think we're going to win it," Penn State linebacker Rich Milot told the *Daily Collegian* in a somewhat mangled but unmistakable boast. And then to be clear, he added, "And win it big."

The days leading up to the game were wonderful for Paterno. He spent a lot of time with Bryant, watching the way the great man walked, the way he talked to people, the way he responded to questions, the way he did not even flinch when introduced at the press conference as "the legend in his own time." When David Israel of the *Chicago Tribune* asked if it was hard being a legend, Bryant said, "Son, I don't know. I ain't tried it yet." For Paterno, it was like coaching against a hero out of the movies, like coaching against John Wayne.

At one point, Bryant said, "I'm delighted to be playing Penn State, a great educational institution with a great, deep-rooted football tradition and the leading coach in America." When Paterno was asked what he thought about being called the leading coach in America by the Bear, he smiled and said, "I don't want to argue with him." Yes, it was all great fun. And Paterno thought Penn State would win. "We had such a good team. We didn't underestimate Alabama, we definitely didn't, but I really thought that team could beat anybody in the country."

PENN STATE PLAYED SLOPPILY. CHUCK Fusina threw four interceptions. The offensive line could not do anything against Alabama's great front line; Penn State ran for just 19 yards the whole game. Several penalties hurt the Nittany Lions, especially in the second half. But the stunner was that Paterno himself seemed to wilt in the big moment. With the game still scoreless late in the first half, he uncharacteristically got greedy and called a couple of timeouts in an effort to get the football back for a last-second score. Instead Alabama used the extra time to drive 80 yards for a touchdown and take the lead.

Alabama led 14–7 in the fourth quarter, and with about seven minutes left Penn State drove down to the Alabama 1-yard line. A touchdown and 2-point conversion—and there was never a doubt Paterno would go for 2—would give Penn State the lead. It was fourth down, and then something happened that Paterno would never forget. The coaches were deciding which play to run. Paterno said that in his heart, he wanted to have Fusina, his star quarterback, throw a pass. It made perfect sense to him. Fusina was his best offensive player, his leader, the man he called the greatest winner he had ever coached. And Alabama would not be expecting a pass. This was his chance to win the game, to beat the Bear. "I knew it in my gut," he said.

A couple of coaches disagreed. A pass went against Penn State's enduring philosophy, Paterno's own philosophy, of overpowering teams. They thought Penn State should run the ball, bash it over the line. One even shouted the coaching cliché, "If we can't pick up ten inches when we need it, we don't deserve to be national champion." Paterno rarely let an assistant coach overrule him. He would listen to opinions and consider them, but if he had a strong feeling, as one longtime coach said, "You might as well save your breath."

This time Paterno listened. Why? He explained it in his autobiography this way: "I backed off from a strong instinct and let myself worry about what people might say if a decision was wrong." He explained it to me this way: "I could see the headlines in the next day's paper. It was the only time in my life, the only time, I thought this way. I could see headlines that said, 'Bear Teaches Paterno a Lesson.' When it came down to it, I was afraid to take the chance."

The play called for a handoff to Mike Guman, a fine running back who had picked up a similar short-yardage play in a crucial moment against Pittsburgh that year. Alabama's defense swarmed him and stuffed him. No touchdown. "Alabama just guessed right," Penn State center Chuck Correal lamented. Yes, Bear guessed right again. The photograph of Alabama's powerful defense stopping Mike Guman would hang in sports bars all across Alabama a quarter century later.

Penn State had one more chance, but once again Paterno played a role in the failure. The Penn State defense forced a punt, and just as Alabama's Woody Umphrey set up to kick, Paterno had a moment of panic. He sensed that Penn State had twelve men on the field. He began to count the players with his hands and—this is where Paterno's memory haunts him—he noticed one of the officials watching him. That's when the official decided maybe he ought to count players too. "If I hadn't started counting players," Paterno said, "he would never have even seen it."

Penn State did have twelve men on the field. Umphrey's shanked punt went out of bounds around the Alabama 20-yard line. Had Penn State not committed the penalty they would have had a very real chance to win. Instead the penalty gave the ball back to Alabama, and Bear's team ran out the clock. Alabama won the Associated Press national championship, Bear Bryant's fifth. (Southern California won the national title in the UPI coaches' poll.)

"I don't know a lot about football," Bryant told reporters in that hoarse southern voice of his, "but I know a lot about winning."

Paterno, meanwhile, was left telling after-dinner jokes in which he was the punch line. "My daughter had this riddle for me: What's blue and white and has twenty-four legs? The Penn State punt team."

Though he joked in public, in private he wondered, in a way he never had before, if he was supposed to be coaching college football.

Memento Mori

One of Joe Paterno's favorite movies was the Academy Award–winning *Patton*, starring George C. Scott. Paterno loved that movie because it burst with lines of dialogue that might as well have been written inside his chest. He loved it when Patton said, "Now, an army is a team—it lives, eats, sleeps, fights as a team. This individuality stuff is a bunch of crap." That spoke to Paterno's deepest beliefs about football and about what it takes to win: togetherness, a higher calling, something larger than any one person.

His favorite scene in *Patton*, however, had nothing to do with teamwork or war or togetherness. It was something personal to him. These were the last lines of the movie, narrated by George C. Scott while the camera followed an aging Patton as he walked with his dog along the countryside:

For over a thousand years, Roman conquerors returning from the wars enjoyed the honor of a triumph, a tumultuous parade. In the procession came trumpeters and musicians and strange animals from the conquered territories, together with carts laden with treasure and captured armaments. The conqueror rode in a triumphal chariot, the dazed prisoners walking in chains before him. Sometimes his children, robed in white, stood with him in the chariot or rode the trace horses. A slave stood behind the conqueror, holding a golden crown, and whispering in his ear a warning: That all glory is fleeting.

Paterno felt those words deeply. He would think about that scene more and more as the years went on. He read about those parades and thought that it was probably true that during Roman triumphs slaves would follow conquering heroes and whisper a Latin phrase. The phrase? Nobody knows for sure, but it might have been *Memento mori.* Remember, you are mortal.

Paterno would repeat this story to his son Jay all the time, in an effort to impress upon him how important it was for a person never to get arrogant, never to believe that he is invulnerable or more important than anyone else. *Memento mori.* Remember, you are mortal.

"I think in many ways that was the theme of my childhood," said Jay. "You work hard. And you stay humble. I think Dad really believed if you ever started thinking you were too smart, that was when it would come up and bite you."

By the late 1970s, so many glorious things had been written and said about Joe Paterno that he felt ill at ease about it. The normally hard-hitting news show *60 Minutes* came to State College in 1978 and ended up doing a segment on him so glowing that even Paterno would say, "Geez, my own mother wouldn't say so many nice things about me." Toward the end of the 1978 season, the New York Giants tried to hire Paterno as their coach, and when he again turned down the pros—this time with much less angst, even though the Giants were his hometown team—he received another wave of plaudits and applause across the nation. A book called *Joe Paterno: Football My Way* was written (with Paterno's help) by Mervin Hyman of *Sports Illustrated* and Gordon White of the *New York Times*, and though it was filled with many fascinating insights into Paterno, it also had over-enthusiastic sentences like these:

Bright, intelligent and perceptive to the point of being almost clairvoyant, Paterno has a quick analytical mind that is constantly working.

This is Paterno—a maverick in every sense of the word—and this is what makes him as refreshing as a summer breeze in a profession that is satiated with conformity and dullness.

This, then, is Joe Paterno. Football coach, intellectual, maverick, philosopher, social worker, leader, gambler, idealist, romanticist, humanist, activist.

Hyman and White were hardly alone in doing what sports editor Stanley Woodward had called "godding up the subject." Paterno's combination of football success along with his spoken ideals and his refusal to sell out for the big salary in the NFL inspired overwhelming praise that he found difficult to fend off. "I'm not nearly as good as the media would portray me," he told student reporters after the Alabama loss. "I wish I was as good as that *60 Minutes* show."

When I asked Paterno if there was a story written about him that he always remembered, he at first refused to name one, saying, "I don't read that stuff." But then he picked a surprise: the story Douglas Looney wrote in *Sports Illustrated* in 1980. Why was this a surprise? Because the story was fairly critical and about one of the worst years in Paterno's coaching life. The long headline was a Paterno quote: "There Are a Lot of People Who Think I'm a Phony and Now They Think They Have the Proof."

"I haven't read that story in years," Paterno said. "But I remember when it came out, I thought, 'There. That's an honest story.' "

The story was about how bad things had gone for Paterno and Penn State in 1979. And they did go bad. The trouble began right away, before practice even began, when a player was arrested and charged with committing multiple rapes. Paterno threw him off the team. Just as fall practice began Paterno announced that he was throwing three more players off the team for academic failures, and one of them was Franco Harris's brother Pete, a preseason All-American safety. It had been twelve years since Paterno had to cut a player for bad grades; now he had to cut three. "I'm obviously upset about our situation," he told reporters. "But we've made a commitment to play with student-athletes."

A few days after that, Paterno had perhaps his most famous run-in with a player. Matt Millen was a spirited defensive lineman from just outside Allentown, Pennsylvania. He had grown up with ten brothers and sisters and a father, Harry, who would have them put on boxing gloves to settle their arguments. Matt was the rowdiest of the clan. When Dallas Cowboys star Randy White came to recruit Matt to play for Maryland, they got into a fight. ("I guess you're not going to Maryland now," White told Millen afterward.) When Colorado recruited Millen, he found that there were some perks—he told *Sports Illustrated* about coming back home with a couple hundred more bucks than he left with—and he decided that was the place for him. His sister was all for it; she was in love with Colorado's favorite son, John Denver. Millen signed the Colorado letter of intent with his own blood because he thought it was a cool thing to do. He was that kind of guy.

But Harry Millen was not. And Harry decided that what his son really needed to do was play for Paterno at Penn State, where he might learn a little something about life. So Matt, like so many hardscrabble Pennsylvania kids, played for Paterno because his father told him to.

Millen was a terrific player and a pain in the neck in somewhat equal parts. In one of his first practices, he lined up in a drill against Brad Benson, a starting offensive lineman who would go on to have a distinguished ten-year NFL career. Millen overpowered him. A teammate rushed over and whispered, "Do you know who that is? That's our starting tackle." To which Millen replied, "Uh, we're not going to be very good this year."

Millen clashed with Paterno constantly. He was almost thrown off the team too many times to count. Once, after getting in a fight, he simply left the stadium in full uniform. Many times, after Millen made a good play, he would celebrate, which drove Paterno crazy. "Matt wouldn't believe this, but I got a huge kick out of him. He's extremely intelligent, you know. And he played football with so much energy and enthusiasm. I know people think I want choirboys who do everything right, but that's not how I look at it. I like to spar. I like to help people grow. And Matt had a lot of growing up to do."

Millen was named captain of the team in 1979, but then, on one of the early days of practice, he did not finish the two half-mile runs in the necessary time, mainly because he thought it was a stupid exercise. "When am I going to chase a guy for a half mile?" he would ask more than thirty years later. Paterno responded with force, removing Millen as team captain. Millen completed the runs a couple of days later, but he was not reinstated as captain. The team's leadership never came together. And things fell apart.

"The Great Experiment is kind of in disrepute," Paterno admitted in a *Sports Illustrated* interview. Players quit. Two were suspended for drinking on campus. Another was caught driving drunk after having a big game. Running back Leo McClelland, who was called "Hollywood" by his teammates because of his colorful bragging, quit the team because he believed he wasn't playing enough. (McClelland was one of the few players to feel Paterno's sarcastic wrath in his autobiography: "Leo McClelland, who had the habit of spreading the unconfirmed news that he was a Heisman candidate, was overcome by some affront or another and quit the team in a huff.") Another player was suspended for a week after getting in a fight. Two players showed up late for a bowl game breakfast and were sent home. Another player entered a private home for reasons he never could make clear and narrowly avoided being shot.

Paterno himself had a lapse of judgment. Every Friday night before games, especially in the early years of his coaching, he would have an off-the-record session with the media. He might offer a few state secrets about strategy; sportswriters might tell him a college football rumor they had heard. Mostly, though, the conversations had nothing to do with football. They would argue about politics, books, movies, how to raise children. "Joe probably looked forward to those meetings more than we did," longtime Philadelphia writer Bill Lyon said. "His whole family, with his parents, they were raised on give and take. Disagree, but don't be disagreeable.

"He'd let his hair down. He'd have a Jack Daniel's. . . . There was a writer, Ralph Bernstein, God rest his soul, what a crusty old curmudgeon. But we loved him. There was a presidential election, it was either just beginning or just over, and Joe was going on. And Ralph interjected and said, 'You may know football, but you don't know shit about politics.' And Joe said, 'You know what, Ralph? You may be right.' "

The gatherings were like that. And, of course, it was all off the record. That was key. After Paterno got famous, he was constantly searching for places where he could be himself, where he didn't have to watch what he said. This was why he loved going on the annual coaches' trips put on by his friend, Nike CEO Phil Knight. On those trips, there were no autograph seekers, no photographers, and, best of all, no reporters. One year, after a tough season, Paterno decided he wasn't going on the trip. "Okay," Sue told him, "but I don't know how you'll fix your meals, because I'm going." He went. "He needed those escapes," Sue said. "They were so hard to find."

The Friday-night gatherings with sportswriters was one of those escapes. Then, suddenly, they were not. "So Joe," one of the writers asked, "when will you leave coaching and go into politics?"

"What, and leave coaching to the [Barry] Switzers and [Jackie] Sherrills?" Paterno asked back.

There was laughter in the room. It was typical of the Friday-night vibe: loose, off the cuff, a little bit cutting. Oklahoma's Barry Switzer and Pitt's Jackie Sherrill were believed by many to be running programs that featured a variety of cheating. Paterno meant this as jocular talk in a backroom that smelled of smoke and whiskey. It took on a very different meaning when his quote appeared in the newspaper. Coaches are not supposed to publicly attack other coaches. Sherrill was so outraged that he and Paterno got into an argument on the field before the Pitt–Penn State game that ended with Sherrill promising that his team would pound Penn State. (It did). More than the individual dynamics, though, was how the comment made Paterno look. He sounded smug and sanctimonious, two bad traits he would admit fighting all his life. "Is he too pious?" his brother, George, wondered aloud in *Sports Illustrated*, then answered his own question: "Absolutely."

"What are you going to do?" Paterno said of his comment being published. "That should never have gotten out. Somebody betrayed the trust there, and I never did trust the media as much after that. But, I did say it. And, at least in part, I meant it."

This incident would have a lasting impact on his life. His relationship with sportswriters was frayed. He boycotted the Friday-night gatherings for a while and threatened to stop them altogether, though he eventually relented. Even when he began showing up at the gatherings again, however, he was never as unguarded. His mistrust of the media would only grow, and perhaps nobody felt more unhappy about that than Paterno himself. "It's a shame," he said. "I enjoyed it more back then."

As for the two coaches Paterno mentioned, it took him a long time to mend fences with Sherrill, who he viewed as the symbol of what was wrong with college coaching. But in a twist of fate, Sherrill became one of Paterno's most supportive friends during the difficult years of the early 2000s.

Paterno's relationship with Switzer was more complicated. He called Switzer immediately after the quote was printed to apologize and explain the context of what was said. (He did not call Sherrill.) Switzer forgave him, or said that he did. Paterno grew to like Switzer, so much so that he wrote the foreword to Switzer's book *Bootlegger's Boy*. The two would enjoy each other's company. But in the end, after former assistant coach Jerry Sandusky was arrested for child molestation and Paterno was fired from Penn State, Switzer was more outspoken about it than any other coach. Paterno had said, and would say until his last day, that he had been fooled, that he had not been told the complete story and did not know about Sandusky's crimes against children. Switzer insisted, "Everyone on that staff had to know."

TO PATERNO, THE 1979 SEASON felt like one long, uninterrupted nightmare. Their 8-4 record was a disappointment for a team that had almost won the national championship the year before. Players kept getting in trouble, and opposing coaches who Paterno believed cheated their hearts out were now celebrating his troubles. Paterno became grumpier, less patient, less enthusiastic about everything. Sue tried to jolt him out of it: "The Alabama game is over!" she shouted at him one evening after she had grown tired of his moping. He tried to energize himself.

But this time his energy would not return; the void was bigger than the Alabama game. Paterno had stopped so rarely to think about the big things. His motto, the one his players heard him say a hundred times every season — "Take care of the little things, and the big things will take care of themselves" — that was how Paterno lived. *Be on time. Work the problem. Concentrate on the moment. Do what you think is right.* But now he was fifty-two, and the Alabama loss and tough season prompted him to stop and look around. What had he done with his life? He saw expectations he could never meet, praise he didn't deserve, whispered doubts that he too harbored about his abilities.

When the 1979 season ended, Paterno went home to Brooklyn. He had a hard decision to make, and he wanted to make it where he grew up. He walked around his old neighborhood for ten days. He always tended to do his best thinking when walking. It was his solitary time; when friends or family members asked if he wanted company on his walks, he almost always said no. Anyone who watched him when he was in one of his moods would see a man walking at a brisk and steady pace, his head up, eyes locked on a target far ahead. "Sometimes, it was like he went into a trance," his daughter Mary Kay recalled.

For the first and perhaps only time in his life, Paterno thought about giving up football. He thought about going into politics. He thought about becoming more involved in college administration. He thought about trying something completely new. Of this time he would remember feeling confusion and uncertainty, two emotions he had rarely felt before.

This had been building for a while. Two years earlier, in 1977, on the day before Penn State played Syracuse, Joe and Sue's eleven-year-old son, David, hurt himself falling off a trampoline at school. He landed on his head. Joe rushed to the scene. The ambulance was already there, and Joe rode to the hospital with his son.

Sue was in a van with seven other mothers on Interstate 80 heading for Syracuse when a police car pulled up alongside. The officer said through a megaphone, "Follow me back to the station. I have an emergency message for one of you." Each of the women feared the emergency was for her, but Sue had a premonition: "I thought, 'It's David. They want me.'" When the van reached the police station, her fears were confirmed. She rushed in and called the hospital. She talked to Joe.

"He fractured his skull," Joe said in a broken voice. "You have to get here fast. I don't know how much time you have."

Sue blacked out.

The next week was hell. Joe stayed in the hospital room while Penn State played Syracuse. It was the only time in his life when he did not care if his team won. It looked like David might not survive, and then it looked like he would live but would never be the same. After that the news never seemed to get better. David was in a coma. Sue and Joe took turns staying with him and talking to him, then wandering off to cry and pray. "I never thought he wasn't going to make it," Sue recalled. "I would not allow that thought." Joe admitted he could not stay quite so positive. One week after the accident, David woke up. "I need your prayers," he told them.

"You've had everybody's prayers," Sue said.

"I know," David said. Behind Sue was a calendar that showed it was October 21. David said, "Today's Jay's birthday."

"Well," Sue would say thirty-five years later with tears in her eyes, "I can cry whenever I think of that moment."

David would struggle but recover, and Joe would always say that the incident gave him a deeper appreciation for what really matters in life. "You know, people call me a complicated guy or whatever. I'm not really complicated. I like a challenge, the harder the better. I like to wake up every morning and think, 'Okay, how in the heck are we going to beat Michigan? And how am I going to get Billy to put more effort into his classes? And how am I going to convince Tommy that he's got to practice harder because he's selling himself short?'

"That's what I love. You asked me if I ever thought about giving it up. Yeah, sure, many, many times. But never for very long. A few minutes here or there. 'Ah, wouldn't it be nice to spend more time at the beach?' But not seriously."

After 1979, he thought seriously about quitting. He asked people he trusted if he should give up coaching; he'd been at it for thirty years. His brother told him that it might be a good time to try something new. Father Bermingham, the priest who had translated Virgil with him at Brooklyn Prep, advised, "Follow your heart."

When his visit to Brooklyn was over, Paterno had decided: he had to coach. The previous year had been a test; he had made mistakes; he had wallowed in self-pity after the Alabama loss. He had grown to dislike his players after a few of them messed up. ("We're not as bad as you think we are," one player told him.) He had doubted himself, ignored his instincts, perhaps taken a few too many chances. "I went to New York knowing something had to change," he said. "And I came back thinking, 'I'm a football coach. That's who I am. I just have to be a better one.' "

Shortly after he returned, he had an interview with sportswriter Douglas Looney for *Sports Illustrated*. At the end of the article, which was as balanced as anything that had been written about him, Paterno talked about a note he had gotten from another coach after one of the hundreds of articles lionizing him had been published. The note was four simple words: "You're not that good."

"I'm not that good," Paterno repeated.

The *Sports Illustrated* article ended with these two rather celebratory lines: "Hear ye, then, that Joe Paterno is not a saint. But he'll do 'till one comes along." That was exactly the sort of thing Paterno did not want to hear. He wished the story had ended with "You're not that good," the closest thing to *Memento mori* a football coach was likely to get.

Paterno and his team at halftime of a game *(Penn State University Archives, Pennsylvania State University Libraries)*

{ *Intermezzo* }

The plain uniforms, like so many fixtures of Penn State football, became a cherished tradition. White and blue. That's it. No "Penn State." No "Nittany Lions." No players' names, of course. No stars. No patterns. No logos. The players wore a white helmet with a single navy-blue stripe down the middle, and even that stripe was sometimes considered too showy. And black shoes. Always black shoes.

When he was sixteen, Paterno's high school football coach, Zev Graham, took him to the 1943 World Series and pointed out how elegant the Yankees looked in their immaculate and simple pinstriped uniforms. Then Graham pointed to the Cardinals players, who wore sloppy-looking wrinkled uniforms with two red birds sitting on a bat. "Now," Zev said, "guess who is going to win the World Series." The Yankees, of course. (The Cardinals had beaten the Yankees the year before, however. Paterno laughed when asked what Penn State uniforms would have looked like had Zev Graham taken him to that World Series instead.) Paterno took the message to heart. He wanted his team's uniforms to be the plainest and simplest in college football. He thought that simple uniforms would represent class, like those Yankee pinstripes. One of the thrills of his life was when Yankee great Joe DiMaggio himself told Paterno how much he liked Penn State's uniforms.

"The other team knew what they were in for when they saw those plain white uniforms," said Bob White, captain of the 1986 Penn State team. "They knew, 'It ain't gonna be easy.' . . . That's what I liked about that. It represented what this country was built on, which is the blue-collarness, the iron workers, the steel workers, not all that fancy stuff all over your uniforms and helmets."

In time, Penn State's uniforms became about as famous in college football as Script Ohio at Ohio State, Rocky Top at Tennessee, Touchdown Jesus at Notre Dame. The uniforms would be called a symbol of Penn State football: unadorned, no frills, blandness in the face of a "look at me" generation. But perhaps more than anything they were a testament to Joe Paterno's stubbornness. He refused to change them. When he allowed a small Nike swoosh to be added to the breast, it was big news in Pennsylvania; some said it was like spray-painting the Sistine Chapel. Paterno liked consistency, liked for today to be a whole lot like yesterday. He lived in the same house, drove the same car, walked to work the same way. He never quite forgave the Catholic Church for going away from the Latin Mass, not because he knew Latin but because it was a change. "I have trouble accepting that what's right on one day, especially in matters relating to eternity, is suddenly not right or not necessary the next day," he wrote in his autobiography. He would teach his quarterbacks to run the same play, again and again, until the defense stopped it. Don't change, he said, until you have to change.

Lou Bartek, a former player, said, "When you first get there you don't really like the uniforms. . . . But after a while you figure out something about them. They are forever. When you turn on a television, and you see those uniforms, nobody has to tell you what team you're watching. That look is forever."

Everything Paterno did felt as if he meant it to last forever. Every drill, every meeting, every practice, every speech was governed by how things have always been. The players always got dressed for home games in the football building. They got on the buses that took them to the stadium on exactly the same route. The first bus would take the offense, with the starting quarterback sitting in the left front seat and Paterno sitting in the right front seat. The defense would get on the second bus. The young players who wouldn't play much would get on the third bus. The starters would walk off the bus first. Always.

In practice, the color of a player's uniform depended on his place on the team. A freshman wore a white uniform if on offense, an orange one if on defense. He would find out he had moved up—or down—based on the color of the uniform hanging in his locker. Third-team offense wore gold; third-team defense wore maroon. Second-team offense wore green; second-team defense wore red. If you made it up to first team, you wore blue: light blue on offense, navy blue on defense. For many players, the moment they remembered best from college was not a certain play, not an exchange with Paterno, not anything at all on the field. It was the first time they looked into their locker and saw a blue uniform hanging there.

For forty-six years, Paterno called them the same names when he was angry (boobs, fatheads, con artists, hotshots, hot dogs, goofballs, knuckleheads) and offered the same guarded praise when he was pleased ("Do it like that on Saturday!" "That wasn't the worst I've ever seen!"). For forty-six years, he ran some of the shortest practices in college football—almost never more than two hours—but those practices were scripted to the second, and identical from season to season. For forty-six years, he threatened to throw players off the team if they didn't shape up in the classroom or on the field. For forty-six years, he kept the same general rules about everything big and small: no earrings, no facial hair, jackets and ties when traveling, and a bizarre rule about wearing socks to class. The marvel of Paterno's coaching was his ability to stop time, to make 2011 feel like 1986, 1978, 1969. Players periodically came back to campus and talked about how Paterno had changed, had softened, how he didn't yell quite as loudly and didn't seem quite as fearsome. But if they were honest with themselves, they would have admitted that it wasn't Paterno who had changed.

"Has anybody told you about the Coke breaks?" former player Rodger Puz asked. Puz lived a full life after college; he was a petroleum engineer, then he went to law school, graduated cum laude, and became a prominent lawyer in Pittsburgh. He never forgot those Coke breaks. While the players practiced in the scorching heat of August, Paterno would have the team managers bring out six-ounce glass bottles of Coca-Cola and put them on a bed of crushed ice, where all the players could see them. This was before coaches understood (or particularly cared about) the importance of keeping athletes hydrated. Going for a long time without water was viewed as a way to toughen up the players.

"You would see those Cokes over there," recalled former star wide receiver Kenny Jackson, "and, man, I can't even tell you how much you wanted one. It was like the most important thing in the entire world. You're hot, you're sweaty, you're stinking, and there were those Cokes, man. If somebody had said to you at that moment, 'I'll give you a million dollars or I'll give you a Coke,' you'd take the Coke."

Just when the players thought they would collapse from thirst, Paterno would blow his whistle and yell, "Okay, Coke break!" Players ran full-speed for the Coca-Cola. "It was like a commercial," Jackson said. (Ironically, Penn State became an exclusive Pepsi school a few years later.) They drank those Cokes as fast as possible because they had only two and a half minutes before break was over.

"He'd give you about two seconds to drink that Coke," Jackson remembered.

"We would chug those things down," Puz said. "And for the rest of practice, you would hear players belching all over the field."

"Burping like crazy," Jackson said.

"You'd be running around and you could hear the Coke bubbling inside you," Puz said.

"I'm telling you, it was the greatest thing ever invented," Jackson said. "Oh, Joe had his tricks, boy. You need to tell Joe to get that back. Coke breaks help you. I never wanted anything in my life more than I wanted one of those Cokes at practice."

When I asked Paterno about Coke breaks, he shrugged. "Guys remember that stuff?" Then he smiled and said, "I always told them, 'You'll be surprised, when you get older, what you remember and what you don't.' But Coke breaks? Geez."

Paterno enjoys watching his star quarterback, Todd Blackledge, answer reporters' questions *(Penn State University Archives, Pennsylvania State University Libraries)*

Mountaintop

The strange part was how calm Paterno felt as he stood on the sidelines of the Penn State–Pitt game in late November 1981 — strange for a couple of reasons. First, of course, Paterno never felt calm. He did not like calm; he thrived on tension. Even in the summer, when there was nothing to do, when he sat in the sun at the beach house in Avalon, New Jersey, read books, listened to waves roll on the shore, he wasn't exactly calm. "No, it's not easy for me to turn off my mind," he admitted. After a few days at the beach, he would invariably be ready to go home, back to his office and back to work.

The second reason calm seemed out of place, though, was more compelling: Penn State was losing to Pittsburgh 14–0. It was the last regular-season game of a wonderful but ultimately unsatisfying 1981 season. Penn State had been ranked No. 1 in America when they lost at Miami on Halloween Day. Two weeks later, they were beat up by Bear Bryant's Alabama team again. (Paterno faced Bryant four times; Alabama and the Bear won all four games.)

Now Penn State was losing at Pitt by two touchdowns. Led by future Hall of Fame quarterback Dan Marino, Pitt was ranked No. 1 in the country. Still, somehow, Paterno felt calm. Absurdly calm. He walked up and down the sidelines and he did not scream. Players remembered him saying, "Okay, guys. We'll be fine. We're better than they are. Let's just take care of business. We'll be okay, it's all going to work out."

Things did work out for Penn State. Paterno and defensive coordinator Jerry Sandusky shifted the defense into a bewildering zone that confused Marino. He had thrown two quick touchdown passes, but after that he threw four interceptions. Paterno also unleashed the offense, breaking away from the conservative style he had made famous. He allowed his promising quarterback Todd Blackledge to take chances and throw downfield to talented receivers like Kenny Jackson. The two combined on two long touchdown passes. Penn State won 48–14. Paterno was sure it was a sign.

"When I was being recruited by Penn State," Jackson said, "everybody told me, 'Man, you're a good receiver, why do you want to go there? He ain't gonna throw you the ball, man.' But Joe told me, he said, 'People don't realize it, but we're going to throw the ball a lot.' And he did."

Paterno seemed to understand, in that moment on the sideline, that his team was on the brink of being something special. Even after returning from his visit to Brooklyn, his attention had been drifting. Penn State asked him to become athletic director as well as head coach, apparently to take advantage of his fund-raising talents, and to the surprise of family and friends he took the job. "I know people think I took it because I was power-hungry. But it really wasn't that. I thought I could help."

He kept the job for two years, and mostly disliked it. He thought the best thing the job did was give him a new appreciation for women's sports. He had come into the job with a primitive view of women's sports (and, perhaps, women in general): "I honestly didn't think women really wanted to compete." Over time he grew to feel differently. "I was kind of a Neanderthal about all that—at least that's what my daughters told me. But then I watched some of our women's teams play, and I thought, 'These young women are great athletes and they play with great passion.' They made me a better person, I think."

It is paradoxical, perhaps, that the most far-reaching move Paterno made as athletic director was to hire women's basketball coach Rene Portland. She had been a star player at Immaculata College just after Title IX had changed the landscape for women's athletics, and Paterno was impressed with her intensity and sense of purpose. She reminded him a bit of himself. Portland was a hugely successful coach for Penn State; she won more than six hundred games and took Penn State to twenty-one NCAA tournaments.

But she was also staunchly and publicly antihomosexual. She was quoted in a *Chicago Sun Times* newspaper story saying, "I will not have it [homosexuality] in my program." In 2005, a player named Jennifer Harris filed a federal lawsuit accusing Portland of cutting her from the team because of her perceived sexual orientation. The lawsuit was eventually settled, and Portland resigned. This, of course, was decades after Paterno had given up the athletic director's job, but there were those, especially at the end of his life, who said that he should have used his power to put a stop to any discrimination happening on the women's basketball team.

"What power are these people talking about?" Paterno asked. "I didn't stick my nose in other people's programs." His son Jay recalled a conversation he'd had with his father about Portland just after her resignation. Joe told him, "I really don't know anything about it.

I don't want anyone telling me how to run my program, why should I tell anyone else how to run theirs?" When Jay said he would not want one of his own daughters discriminated against or treated badly, he remembered Joe agreeing: "You're right. Everybody deserves a chance. If that was happening, that was wrong."

But what Paterno really learned from his time as athletic director was that he didn't want to be athletic director. He liked to coach. He was good at other things when inspired: charming the media, energizing the alumni, giving speeches, building business plans, seeing widespread possibilities, and nobody was better at raising money for Penn State. Those things did not bring him joy the way coaching did. There were several attempts to get him to jump into politics, but he would always say that he did not feel qualified. His reluctance probably had little to do with qualifications; it was all about desire. Coaching was the thing that jolted him out of bed in the middle of the night to scribble notes. Coaching was what woke him up in the morning, always before the alarm, and inspired him throughout the day. He loved it, all of it, the preparation, the game plans, the teaching, the sense of purpose, the competition, and, at the end, the confirmation of a job well done.

"It might sound like a cliché, but I think Dad always saw coaching as four-dimensional chess," Scott Paterno said. "That's chess where the pieces constantly change in strength. So one year, he would think, 'Okay, we have a weak left tackle, how can we work around that?' And the next year he would think, 'Okay, our linebackers are good, but our defensive line is young, how can we build a great defense?' And then he could take his plan, put it into action, and change young men's lives along the way. That's what drove him."

As he calmly stood on the sideline of that Pitt game knowing, absolutely knowing, that his team was going to win, a lot of things clicked for him. He quit the athletic director job within a couple of months and passed it to his longtime friend Jim Tarman. He reworked his offense away from a stale and conservative power game into a modern, fast-paced passing attack built around players' speed. And he thought,

"You know what? Next year, we're going to win the national championship."

THERE WERE OTHER COACHES—BEAR BRYANT at the lead, but also Woody Hayes, Vince Lombardi, Jimmy Johnson, and Bill Parcells— who inspired and frightened players with their passion and demanding expectations. They gave raucous speeches. They poured out their emotions. They found ways, in the words of onetime Alabama coach Bill Curry, to "reach inside your chest, massage your heart so that it pumped twice as hard, and make you feel like you could do anything in the world."

Paterno was not like that. Now and again he would give an emotional pregame speech. Now and again he would galvanize his players with a few choice words on the sideline. Mostly, though, Paterno believed that the hard work of coaching and playing happened during the week, during practice. There, on the practice field, he raged and encouraged and insulted them. He seemed inescapable to his players; there was something almost supernatural about it.

"I still dream about it," said Mark Battaglia, the starting center on the 1982 team. "He would be very, very vocal, very involved. . . . He had an uncanny ability on the practice field to see you from a very long distance away and run over and start yelling at you with his high-pitched voice."

"He just saw all the little things," 1982 co-captain Pete Speros said. "You'd jump offsides in practice and he'd let you have it for twenty minutes."

"Sometimes, you'd lose sight of him," said Rodger Puz, "and you would not intentionally ease up, but maybe you'd lose a little concentration. Invariably, from two football fields away, you'd hear that high-pitched yell: 'Hey, Puz! That's lousy! That's terrible! You're the worst player we've ever had here!' "

"He would get in your face," said Mike Suter, who had a moment in that 1982 season that Penn State fans will never forget. "He would shout, 'This is how you make a tackle!' You would hear stories about other coaches being up in a tower. I never saw Joe doing that."

On the practice field, his cutting comments and high standards and obsession with time created a football whirlwind. The players were almost never on the field for more than two hours. "Joe knows that football is not the most important thing," Paterno's longtime assistant Fran Ganter said in a television feature that followed Penn State through a week of preparation. "It just isn't. And so he would say, all the time, 'We've got to get those guys off the field so they can study and be college students.' " Paterno believed that his team spent less time on the field practicing than any major football program. That was by design.

But that time was precious, so much so that coaches would spend much of their week begging for an extra two minutes to work on something. Defensive coordinator Jerry Sandusky would plead for three more minutes to work on goal-line defense. Ganter would plead for an extra minute to work on the screen play. Paterno loved being the controller of time, and he rarely gave his coaches anything extra; if he did, he would demand a few seconds in barter. "Get it done in the time you have," he told them. The players ran from drill to drill—nothing set off Paterno like seeing someone just standing around and waiting—and were expected to concentrate throughout. There were no excuses for lapses. "You're wasting my time!" he would shout, and for him that was breaking the Eleventh Commandment: "Thou shalt not waste my time."

Tuesdays were for hitting: the players called them "Bloody Tuesdays." Wednesdays allowed for slightly less violent play and refinement; Paterno worried constantly that the coaches were working on too many things. Simplify. Always simplify. Thursdays were without violence; this was the time to reach for perfection. Fridays were for rest. And every second of those practices was to be treated with respect. "I remember they'd post a practice," Suter said, "and they'd have a time like 4:07 to 4:15 for individual drills."

Penn State practices stopped for nothing. Paterno closed them to reporters, not only because he wanted secrets kept but also because he did not want anyone to see him scream at his players. He had little sympathy for injuries, perhaps because until the end of his life he had so little concern for his own pain. "I got hurt once," recalled Jack Curry, a receiver on Paterno's first team, "and I took so much abuse for it I swore I'd never get hurt again."

"If you had something wrong with your leg, a broken hand, a pinched nerve, if you were sick, that didn't get you out of practice," a 1982 player, Lou Bartek, remembered. If someone was hurt badly enough that he couldn't practice on the field, Paterno would have him stand on the sideline wearing a giant red X on his jersey. "You felt like you were a casualty of war or something with the Red Cross," Kenny Jackson said. "You didn't want to be over there."

"Oh yeah, listen, I was tough," Paterno admitted. "It wasn't 'nice guy Paterno' out there. The thing I believed was that players didn't know how good they could be. They didn't understand their own limitations. I thought it was our job as coaches not to make them as good as they thought they could be but to make them a lot better than that. That meant playing through pain. It meant never letting up. It meant demanding more from them than anybody ever had before. I wasn't interested in them liking me."

For the most part, they didn't like him, certainly not while they were playing for him. "There were times I wanted to scream at him," tight end Mike McCloskey told columnist Bill Lyon in 1982. "And there were times I wanted to punch him out."

After hearing from scores of former players, a clear "Stages of Paterno" chart built in my mind. Not everyone went through all the stages. Some never grew to like Paterno; some liked him even when being yelled at. But in large part, the Stages of Paterno might look something like this:

During recruiting process: Parents like Paterno; players ambivalent but respectful.
During college: Players despise Paterno.

Immediately after graduation: Players respect what Paterno has done for them but are mostly glad that the experience is over and they can go on to real life.

Later in life: Players find they think about him every day, remember lessons he taught, believe that in large part he made them into the people they became, and have grown to love him.

This, not incidentally, is similar to the feelings many sons have toward their fathers.

EVERY YEAR PATERNO ORDERED A fresh blue line to be painted in front of the football practice fields. That blue line represented a separation. He would tell the players that when they crossed the blue line, nothing mattered except football. Nothing. Not family. Not school. Not girlfriends. Not problems. Nothing. He would tell them there was nothing they could do about those other parts of their life when practicing football, so they were to put them all away. This, he said, was what discipline was about. He would also tell them that they should draw blue lines throughout their life: when in class they should not be thinking about football; when on a date they should not be thinking about class or football; when helping a friend they should paint a blue line around the scene and focus on the moment.

Paterno considered the blue line something close to holy.

"When you'd cross back over the blue line," Pete Speros explained, "he'd come up to you and ask how your family was doing. You'd say, 'Wait a minute, a few minutes ago you just ridiculed and embarrassed me.' . . . That's the attitude that he took, and we all got molded to it. It was effective, really effective. But you'd leave a lot of practices shaking your head."

THE GAMES WERE DIFFERENT. PATERNO did not want to overmanage the games. He would say, "Practice is for the coaches. Games are for the players." He did not want a team of robots that would do only what they were programmed to do. He did not even want players calling him Coach Paterno; he demanded they call him Joe. A linebacker from Brooklyn, Greg Buttle, remembered asking Paterno something in practice: "Coach Paterno, can I do it this way?"

"No, Player Buttle," Paterno responded. "Do it the way we talked about."

No, Paterno did not want to control games. He believed the coaches were supposed to teach players how to play football at the highest level. Few things made him happier than seeing a player anticipate an opportunity, freelance away from what he was taught, and make a game-turning play. He believed the greatest thrill of coaching was when discipline joined inspiration. "I always believed you have to give players that freedom," he said. "I can't say I was thrilled if a player tried for something and cost us a big play. Still, my thought was, you prepare them to play, and then you let them play. I believe you can't be a great team if you have players who are afraid to make a mistake."

In Paterno's mind, it was this fearlessness that made the 1982 team so special. That team certainly had great talent. Curt Warner was a once-in-a-generation running back; Paterno compared him to all-time greats Lenny Moore and Gale Sayers, and Warner would have a marvelous pro football career. Quarterback Todd Blackledge finished sixth in the Heisman Trophy voting. Receiver Kenny Jackson had breathtaking speed and was the fourth pick in the 1984 NFL draft. The defense was loaded with terrific players, like linebacker Scott Radecic, defensive end Walker Lee Ashley, and safety Mark Robinson.

He'd had teams with more physical talent. What made this team special, he insisted, was that he could count on them. He knew that someone on this team would find a way to make a winning key play.

The team was also lucky. In the fourth week of the season the Nittany Lions played second-ranked Nebraska at dusk in Beaver Stadium. This was before the stadium had lights, and CBS, which was broadcasting the game, brought portable lights because of the late start. Nebraska led 24–21 in the final seconds. Penn State had played somewhat sloppily (two touchdowns were called back because of penalties), but they got the ball back with a minute and eighteen seconds. They haltingly moved the ball up the field and then faced a fourth down and 11. Blackledge's strong pass to Jackson got the first down. On the next play, Blackledge threw a 15-yard pass to Mike Mc-Closkey that moved the ball to the Nebraska 2-yard line with just a few seconds left.

The replay shows that McCloskey caught the ball out of bounds. Paterno saw the film later and conceded the fact. The referees had missed the call. Missed calls are part of football, part of sports, but in later years Paterno would get touchier about missed calls. When reminded that his 1982 team was greatly aided by a couple of bad calls, he smiled and said, "Yeah, it's human nature to forget the ones they called for you."

With four seconds left in the game, Blackledge threw a low pass in the end zone to a tight end named Kirk Bowman, who players on the team openly called "Stone Hands." Bowman made a tough catch, and Penn State beat Nebraska.

THE NEXT GAME DEFINED PENN State's season. It was the last time Paterno's team faced an Alabama team coached by Bear Bryant, and Penn State fell apart; there's no other way to describe it. Blackledge threw four interceptions. The Nittany Lions suffered four sacks, lost a fumble, and had two punts blocked. Penn State lost by three touchdowns.

But two season-turning things happened that day, two things that spoke to Paterno's coaching style. The first, curiously, involved one of the biggest mistakes not only of that year but of any Penn State year. Mike Suter was a hardworking backup defensive back (he had an interception that day) and one of the key blockers on special teams. With the game still in doubt, Suter backed up into Penn State punter Ralph Giacomarro and blocked his own team's punt with his butt. Penn State probably would not have won the game, but Suter's play was so freaky and embarrassing that it seemed to be all anybody talked about afterward. Suter never forgot how Paterno responded: "I remember walking off to the sidelines and Joe looking at me with his arms out, like 'What the . . . ' And then in the locker room reporters talking to me. I said I wasn't sure what happened.

"The next day, in the film room, Joe was not happy with our play. He talked about a lot of plays that went wrong. But mine wasn't pointed out any more than any other. . . . Joe never really talked to me about it, except he came up before the Syracuse game [the next week] and said, 'I took you off the punt team this week. I didn't want you hanging your head. Play a solid game at safety and show who you are.' "

That was vintage Paterno. He would tear players to shreds, make them feel as low as they ever had in their lives over the tiniest mistakes during practice. But he seemed to know when they needed him to back off and be supportive. When Suter got home after the game, he'd heard from his brother that an announcer on a new sports television network, ESPN, had called him "the loneliest man in college football." But he didn't feel lonely. His teammates rallied around him. And Paterno, undoubtedly knowing how badly Suter felt about the play and how much he wanted to atone for it, stood behind him. When asked about his college career, Suter replied, "Playing for Joe Paterno? Are you kidding me? It was awesome."

The other thing that turned the season around involved another player who was not a starter. His name was Joel Coles, a gifted running back who had the misfortune of being at Penn State at the same time as the more gifted Curt Warner. That meant Coles hardly played. "Would I come back, knowing how it turned out?" he asked Bill Lyon after the season ended. "No, I can't say that I would."

But after the Alabama game, Coles stepped forward and gave a speech everyone in the locker room remembered thirty years later. He shouted that they still had six games left, and they still had a chance to show everyone the greatness of their team.

"He gave one of the most inspirational, emotional, spirited motivational speeches," Mark Battaglia said. "It helped galvanize us. He said we could do one of two things, and we were going to do the one and finish the season. And it was a critical turning point."

"If Joel doesn't step up there and give that speech," Paterno would say, "I don't think we go on to do what we did. In fact, I know we don't." This, at heart, was what Paterno believed coaching was about. Joel Coles was disappointed; he thought he was going to be a big college football star, and it hadn't worked out for him. But Paterno told him—told all of them—that the important thing is not what happens to you, but how you react to what happens. In that moment, Coles saw what he had to do, spoke out, spoke from the heart, and though life isn't like the movies and stirring speeches don't always lead to victory, it is true that the Nittany Lions won every game for the rest of the regular season, and no team finished within a touchdown of them. The amazing run of dominance led Penn State back to New Orleans and the Sugar Bowl, where they would play for the national championship, just as they had three years earlier against Alabama. This time, they would face Georgia and a near-mythical running back named Herschel Walker.

WHEN HERSCHEL WALKER WAS A young boy in Wrightsville, Georgia (slogan: "The Friendliest Town in Georgia!"), he did not do much of anything. His father asked him, "What do you like to do?"

"Watch TV," Herschel said.

His father made a deal with him: he could watch television, but during the commercials he had to exercise. Herschel agreed, and so during the commercials he did push-ups and sit-ups and went outside and ran sprints. Though it was said that he never lifted weights, he was soon the biggest, strongest, and fastest football player in all of Georgia. In his first padded practice at the University of Georgia, the legend goes, a senior intending to teach the kid a lesson rushed in to unload a hit on the hyped freshman. The senior woke up woozy a few minutes later. The first time Walker carried the ball in an actual game for Georgia, he broke four tackles and scored a touchdown against Tennessee. "My God," Georgia's legendary broadcaster Larry Munson croaked, "a freshman!"

College football had never seen anything quite like Herschel Walker. He was faster than anyone out there. He was stronger than anyone out there. Georgia's offense, like Penn State's offense in 1973 with Cappelletti, was two-dimensional: sometimes Walker ran left, and sometimes Walker ran right. Yet that, along with a great defense, was enough to make Georgia the 1980 national champion. In the bowl game, Walker dislocated his shoulder in the first quarter against Notre Dame. "Pain is sort of in your mind," he said. He had the shoulder popped back in and ran for 150 yards in the victory.

This was the force of nature Penn State faced in 1982. Georgia had not lost a game. Walker had won the Heisman Trophy. Early in the year, he had gained more than a hundred yards against Brigham Young and South Carolina even though he played with a broken thumb in both games.

The players would say that they saw something a little bit different in Paterno in the weeks leading into the Georgia game. He worked them harder than normal. A freshman running back named Steve Smith (who would become a team captain and would go on to a nine-year NFL career) had the honor of playing Herschel Walker in practice, and the Penn State defenders hit him so hard and often that, at some point, Smith said, "I don't want to be Herschel Walker anymore."

For the game, Paterno and his thirty-eight-year-old defensive coordinator Jerry Sandusky unveiled what they called the "Magic Defense": the plan was for the defense to change formations on every play and leave the Georgia offensive linemen wondering whom they were supposed to block. The goal, in essence, was to stop Herschel Walker. Of course, this was the goal of every team that played Georgia, but Paterno was willing to go further than other teams. He would leave openings down the field and dare Georgia to throw the ball. He would have his defenders sell out on almost every play and hit Walker with everything they had. "We want to make Herschel Walker mighty sore," Penn State defensive end Walker Lee Ashley said before the game.

"Talk is cheap," Herschel responded.

This was more than talk. In the end, Walker rushed for 107 yards, which was his lowest total for any game where he got more than twenty carries, and he got twenty-eight carries in this game. His longest run was just 12 yards; he'd had longer runs in every game he'd played, except for the one that broke his thumb. He was essentially stifled. The Magic Defense worked exactly as planned.

Except for Georgia's quarterback John Lastinger. Paterno dared him to throw for a simple reason: "We thought there was no way they could beat us throwing the ball." Lastinger had averaged fewer than seven completions per game the entire season. But for this game, he found his touch. Penn State led 20–3 when Lastinger began leading Georgia back. He threw one touchdown pass, saved another drive with a big third-down completion, and suddenly Georgia trailed by only 3.

There were two key plays that sealed the game for Penn State. One of them is probably the most famous play in Penn State history; it happened in the fourth quarter, and ABC broadcaster Keith Jackson called it: "Now, Blackledge is gonna put it up on first down . . . he's going for the bundle . . . Garrity! Touchdown!" That was a 47-yard touchdown pass from Blackledge to a former walk-on named Gregg Garrity, who caught the ball as he dived into the end zone. A photo of Garrity holding the football in his left hand with his arms up in the air in the touchdown signal would be on the cover of *Sports Illustrated* that week. "No. 1 at Last!" was the headline above his head.

That touchdown gave Penn State a seemingly comfortable 27–17 lead. But it wasn't comfortable enough. Lastinger had a little more magic left. He drove Georgia in for another touchdown, completing the drive with a 9-yard pass to tight end Clarence Kay. There were still almost four minutes left. The Magic Defense had frustrated Herschel Walker, but Georgia was still in position to win.

Penn State got the ball back, and on third down and 3 to go, a time-out was called. There was still enough time left that a punt could lead to defeat. Blackledge came to the sideline and wanted to throw it. Paterno would remember other coaches saying that they should play the percentages and run the ball. It was not exactly the situation he had faced against Bear Bryant and Alabama three years earlier, but it was close enough. Blackledge was looking at his coach, and Paterno saw something in Blackledge: confidence. The kid was sure he could make the first down.

"Throw it!" Paterno ordered. "Just make sure you throw it far enough. Let's win this thing."

Blackledge's rather dull 6-yard sideline pass to Garrity would not be replayed again and again in Pennsylvania, but it was the play that sealed the victory. Penn State won. Though Paterno had believed (and always would believe) his previous three undefeated teams should have been national champions, this team was his first to actually be called national champion.

At two in the morning, Paterno left the celebration party to go to bed. "I didn't sleep a wink," he said. Instead he stared at the ceiling and tried, for just a few happy moments, to reminisce, to think about all that had happened, all those great players he had coached, all the people whom he had come to know along the way. It didn't come easily to him; looking back never did. He also spent a few minutes thinking about his father, who had worked his way through law school, who had died almost thirty years earlier, who had wondered why his oldest son had become a football coach when he might have been president of the United States.

"Pop," Joe Paterno remembered thinking, "I think we did it the right way."

FIVE THOUSAND PEOPLE WAITED FOR them at the airport in Harrisburg when the team plane landed. This thrilled Paterno, and he said a few words of thanks. He did not know that this crowd was only the beginning. The team got on a bus and began the ride back along

U.S. Route 322 to State College. In the dark, in the cold, people lined the road to wave and blow kisses to the Penn State bus. Parents held up their small children. Cars were parked along the side of the road, and horns blared.

A fire truck met them outside of Harrisburg, its siren blaring, lights flashing, and still there were people along the road, and more people pounding their car horns. A few minutes later, the fire truck from the next town picked them up. They went through Dauphin and Newport, Millerstown and Thompsontown and Mifflintown and Lewistown, Port Royal and Burnham and Reedsville. And the fire trucks kept meeting them at every county line, the sheriffs kept escorting them through every town, the people kept waving.

Inside the bus, Paterno blinked back tears. He would say that this was the most humbling moment, the moment he realized the impact his football team had on people. For one hundred miles on a road in south central Pennsylvania, Joe Paterno felt as if he would live forever.

Less than a month later, Bear Bryant, just four weeks after retiring as Alabama football coach, died of a massive heart attack at sixty-nine. For the rest of his life, Paterno kept a version in his files of the Heartsill Wilson poem Bryant read in his last public appearance:

This is the beginning of a new day
God has given me this day to use as I will
I can waste it or use it for good
What I do today is very important because I am
Exchanging a day of my life for it
When tomorrow comes, this day will be gone forever
Leaving something in its place I have traded for it
I want it to be a gain, not loss—good, not evil
Success, not failure, in order that I
Shall not forget the price I paid for it.

Two Callings

Joe Paterno could get testy whenever someone called his 1982 team his first national championship team. He believed his undefeated teams in 1968, 1969, and 1973 all had a claim on the title. He even had mixed emotions when his 1982 team was finally awarded the title. That same year, Southern Methodist, led by the great running back Eric Dickerson and several other future NFL stars, finished the season unbeaten (with one tie). Paterno admitted that SMU had its own right to the title, and, as he often had before, he lobbied for a playoff that would decide the championship more fairly.

Still, however he may have felt about it, winning a national championship had moved Paterno into a different level in the sporting public's mind, and he knew it. He had an even higher pulpit now, and people were even more eager to listen to him. In 1973, when he had his first splash of national stardom, he had spoken about the pursuit of excellence and not allowing the world to break your spirit. Now he had something else he wanted to say.

A few weeks after Penn State beat Georgia, Paterno was invited to speak to the Penn State Board of Trustees. They likely wanted him to just say a few inspiring words and accept their congratulations. But Paterno had other ideas. He had decided that Penn State was underachieving as a university. He had grown tired of watching the school raise so little money and have what he considered such small ambitions. Fund-raising became his first mission.

Paterno was never shy or reluctant about asking for money, perhaps in part because of his own mixed feelings about money. One of his favorite opening lines to potential donors was "How much money do you need?" It was a question he often asked himself. "I'm not opposed to making money, believe me. But I think the only reason to have money is to do some good with it." He and Sue were relentless fund-raisers. They would not only chair fund-raising projects and personally entertain donors in their home, but they would invariably ask for significantly more money than expected. Business leaders around State College described what they called the "Paterno moment," when, for example, a group announced that they were trying to raise three million dollars, and Paterno would shout from his chair, "No! Ten million!"

When Penn State was trying to build a spiritual center on campus— it would become one of the largest in America and the place where Joe Paterno's funeral was held—the Paternos gave a significant personal donation. More important, they convinced one of the richest men in the state, Frank Pasquerilla, to donate more money than he had intended. "My mom at one point basically told Frank, 'You're not leaving this house until we get the last million for this,' " Scott Paterno recalled. The money was secured, and the Pasquerilla Spiritual Center was built.

This kind of story was repeated often. One businessman recalled a conversation he had with his wife in which he told her, "I have to go over to Joe and Sue's house, so we might need to refinance the house when I get back." Years later, one of Paterno's grandchildren told his grandmother how uncomfortable he was asking for money for the Pennsylvania Special Olympics. Incredulous, Sue asked him, "Are you sure you're a Paterno?"

Paterno had no misgivings about going into the board of trustees meeting and demanding that they raise a lot more money. It was time to make Penn State a world-class academic institution: "We have never been more united, more proud, and maybe it's unfortunate that it takes a No. 1 football team to do that. . . . It bothers me to see Penn State football No. 1, then, a few weeks later, to pick up a newspaper and find a report that many of our academic departments are not rated up there with the leading institutions in the country."

To Paterno, the way to make Penn State a great academic institution was obvious: they needed to recruit brilliant, aggressive, and vibrant teachers. "We have some," he said. "We don't have enough of them." Then they needed to recruit the most promising and dazzling students, "the star students that star professors get excited about." And the key was to raise money, more money, to endow chairs, to build science and computer labs, to fund scholarships, to build the nation's best library. He was particularly passionate about the library: "Without a great library, we can't be a great university." Over the next twenty years, he and Sue would donate millions of dollars and raise millions more to build a world-class library that would be called the Paterno Library.

In challenging the board of trustees, and later challenging the faculty itself, Paterno was typically blunt. He praised some departments and called others lousy; he praised some professors and called others lazy. He said they needed to raise seven to ten million dollars over the next few months, while the opportunity was there. "I think we can be more than we are," he insisted, "and make students better than they think they are."

There it was, Paterno's philosophy in a sentence: *Be more than we are, and make students better than they think they are.* The speech sent a jolt through Penn State. Some board members were offended and thought Paterno was out of line. They thought he came across as sanctimonious and self-righteous—the usual Paterno complaints. But others were energized and inspired; they too believed Penn State was a great underachiever. The school had as many alumni as any university in the country and yet did not have a powerful fund-raising engine in place. In 1983, an energetic new president named Bryce Jordan would take Paterno's vision and amplify it; he announced a $200 million fund-raising campaign to help make Penn State a great institution. Paterno's close friend and Merrill Lynch CEO Bill Schreyer chaired the campaign and several like it in the future. And, of course, Paterno was front and center.

"I never understood the unwillingness to ask for money for good causes," Paterno would say. "I would always ask: 'Do you want this to be a great university or don't you? Do you want to help make this a better world or don't you?' How much money does one man need, anyway? It seems to me that if you are going to fight for something, you have to fight."

In 2010, Penn State launched its most ambitious fund-raising campaign: to raise two billion dollars. In 2012, even after a shocking scandal, Penn State ranked in the top twenty-five nationally among universities in fund-raising efforts.

THE SECOND MISSION PATERNO CHAMPIONED in the afterglow of his national championship was more controversial. It involved race. Paterno believed that colleges owed their athletes (especially high-profile athletes like football players) an excellent education that would give them their best chance to live remarkable lives. If the school failed to provide that level of education, he said, they were failing the students, failing the school's mission, and failing society.

Paterno wanted tougher academic standards for football players. It sickened him that schools accepted great athletes who did not display the high school grades or necessary ambition to succeed in college, and then used them up for football. He understood the temptation, for he battled with his own competitive nature. He was strongly opposed to freshman eligibility, for instance, because he thought freshmen were rarely ready physically or emotionally for the intense life of a being a college football player. They needed a year to acclimate themselves, he insisted. But as strongly as he felt about it, he too played freshmen: not playing them would devastate his recruiting efforts and put his team at a severe, perhaps even insurmountable disadvantage. In the early days, he admitted, he "was too weak to fight that battle."

But in 1983, he decided to take on the battle for tougher standards. He backed a proposal by the NCAA called Proposition 48, which required incoming freshmen to meet a threshold high school grade point average and standardized test scores in order to be eligible to participate in college sports. Paterno was also in favor of Proposition 49B, which stated that players who did not meet those academic thresholds could still get athletic scholarships but could not play or practice with the team for a year, giving them time to raise their grades. As Paterno saw it, the propositions made freshmen ineligible for their own good.

As usual, Paterno's forcefulness on the issue infuriated some people. The bulk of the athletes who would be affected by Prop 48 were African American, and Paterno argued that the system had "raped" black athletes for far too long: "We can't afford to do that to another generation." When several presidents of mostly black universities spoke out against Prop 48—their main argument being that the standardized tests were racially biased—Paterno told a large audience at the NCAA Convention he was surprised to see "black leaders standing here and selling the black students down the river, selling them short." This, of course, added more heat to the argument.

"I deeply resent your statement about 'black leaders selling their students down the river,'" Charles Lyons Jr., chancellor of Fayetteville State University, wrote to Paterno. "Many have spent their entire professional careers giving opportunities to low income and deprived black youngsters. But for them and the institutions which they head, these youngsters would forever languish and perish on the scrap heap of humanity."

Paterno felt chastened by Lyons's letter—"I have a big mouth," he would say with regret—and tried to tone down his rhetoric. But he did not scale back his argument. He believed he was right. He believed that schools had a responsibility to teach, challenge, motivate, and graduate athletes, especially those who came from the most deprived environments. He also believed that talented young athletes were selling themselves short if not challenged and inspired. He was willing to fight for this cause.

In the end, Proposition 48 passed, but not before the fight turned nasty for Paterno. Penn State, like other rural schools, had always had a very small percentage of African American students. Some people said that Paterno supported Prop 48 because he did not recruit many black athletes. Penn State's all-time football great Lenny Moore was quoted as saying that the football team had racial problems and that Paterno himself had not done enough to recruit more black athletes or hire more black coaches. Moore later claimed he had been misquoted; in his autobiography he wrote that the story belonged in the "Misquote Hall of Fame." He insisted that his issues were with the school and not the football team, that Paterno was a good and fair man, vigilant and color-blind. At the time, Paterno was actually having more success recruiting African Americans—and graduating them at a high rate—than at any point in his career. The two men stayed friends, and Paterno wrote the foreword to Moore's book, *All Things Being Equal*. But the quote still made all the papers.

"You know what matters?" Paterno said years later. "Doing what you believe is right. It doesn't matter what they say about you. It really doesn't. Yeah, sure, some of the things people say hurt, especially if you don't think they are true. But nothing good ever got done without criticism."

"I'll tell you what," said Bob White, a linebacker, 1986 team captain, and one of the great success stories of Paterno's career, "the world is filled with people who will tell you that you can't do something. The world doesn't have enough Joe Paternos, who tell you that you can."

Joe and Sue Paterno ride in a parade through State College *(Penn State University Archives, Pennsylvania State University Libraries)*

Evil and Good

Joe Paterno never seemed happier than when he was designing something new. He loved the bursts of inspiration. They woke him from the deepest sleep and compelled him to grab one of the lead pencils he always kept by his bed and start writing. ("Lord, I hated those pencils," Sue said. "They left marks all over the bed.") Those bursts of inspiration prompted him to excuse himself in the middle of social gatherings and race back to his office, where he scribbled feverishly. Those bursts of inspiration were a reason he kept coaching long after he had accomplished so much. He did not know how to live without those moments of electricity.

Perhaps the greatest burst of inspiration of his coaching life, greater even than his invention of a new defense back in 1967, happened at the end of the 1986 football season. It was a vision he shared with his defensive coordinator, Jerry Sandusky. Together they decided that the way to win the biggest college football game ever played was to walk into the bullfight wearing bright red.

MORE PEOPLE WATCHED PENN STATE play Miami on television in the January 2, 1987, Fiesta Bowl than watched any other college football game ever played. There were logistical reasons for this: it was the only game played on a Friday night in winter, a good television-watching night. "*Miami Vice* and *Crime Story* will not be seen tonight so we can bring you this special presentation of the Fiesta Bowl" was how NBC introduced the game. The game was an anomaly: there were rarely games played after New Year's Day. And the game had a biting clarity: this was a true national championship game. Miami was ranked No. 1. Penn State was ranked No. 2. Neither team had lost a game all season.

More than anything, this game was pure cinema, with villains and heroes, Axis and Allies, Darth Vader and Luke Skywalker, evil and good. Of course, it wasn't really good against evil; it never is except in the movies and professional wrestling. But this game was close enough.

Penn State was supposed to represent the good. The Nittany Lions had finished the regular season 11–0 for the second straight year. In the 1985 season, they finished the regular season No. 1 but lost to Oklahoma in the Orange Bowl. "We were the better team," linebacker Trey Bauer declared, echoing the thoughts of his teammates. Their undefeated record in 1986 impressed few across the country: they played just one ranked team, a Bearless Alabama they beat 23–3; the rest of the schedule was bland; and the games were too close. They almost lost to Cincinnati, they almost lost to Maryland, and they almost lost to a subpar Notre Dame team.

The offense was led by an affable and much maligned quarterback named John Shaffer, who wasn't especially fast and couldn't throw particularly well but had a knack for being on the winning side—a quarterback right out of the Joe Paterno–Chuck Burkhart mold. All year, it seemed, the offense always did just enough. Paterno thought that was largely because of Shaffer. From the seventh grade through his senior year in college, Shaffer's teams won every game he started except for the one against Oklahoma. When Shaffer graduated, he played for the Dallas Cowboys, but after only a short while he asked to be released. He had won enough football games. He went to work on Wall Street instead.

The team's core was its defense, particularly its linebackers. Penn State was already known as "Linebacker U," but this was especially true in 1986. Seven linebackers on that team were drafted into the NFL, another had a long and successful professional career in Canada, and a ninth was perhaps the team's most vocal leader. That was Trey Bauer.

It was Bauer, as much as anyone, who inspired the flash of insight in the minds of Paterno and Sandusky. Miami was one of the most talented teams in the history of college football. The offense featured the 1986 Heisman Trophy winner, quarterback Vinny Testaverde; three future NFL wide receivers, including future NFL Hall of Famer Michael Irvin; and Alonzo Highsmith, a running back who would be picked third in the NFL draft. The defense was equally talented, overloaded with future pro stars, but it was the Miami offense that got Paterno and Sandusky thinking.

"Can we handle it?" Paterno remembered asking.

"Beats me," Sandusky replied.

TREY BAUER HAD PLAYED HIGH school football for his father, Charlie, in Paramus, New Jersey. He was an Ohio State fan growing up, but he ruled out playing for the Buckeyes after getting into a rip-roaring argument with the recruiting coordinator and then hanging up on the guy. It was a long story. With Bauer, there were a lot of long stories. He showed up at State College a year after he attended a camp there. He liked the campus and told Paterno he was coming. Paterno asked about going to New Jersey to visit his parents. Bauer responded, "Why? They're not the ones coming here. I am."

In his freshman year, Bauer was thrown out of study hall, and even thirty years later he claimed it wasn't his fault. It was another long story. Paterno didn't see it that way. Bauer's hair was long; he had a habit of getting into fights; he was a pain in the neck. After the study hall incident, Bauer showed up ten minutes late for a team meeting. "Bauer, I've had it with you," Paterno shouted at him. "Call your parents. You will never play a down at Penn State. I will do anything I can to help you transfer to another school, but you're done here."

Bauer was stunned. He called home and got his mother and father on the phone. He told them what Paterno had said. Charlie Bauer, a Paterno fan through and through, said, "I'd throw you off the team too. You're a pain in the ass, your hair's too long, and you're a punk." Meanwhile Bauer's mother was crying and saying, "No, Charlie, don't say that." Nobody knew what to do. Finally Bauer made a decision. "I'm not leaving," he told his parents.

"What?" his father said.

"I'm not leaving. I don't want to leave."

And that's exactly what Bauer told Paterno. Paterno seemed at a loss. He told Bauer, "You're never going to play here." And Bauer replied, "Well, I'm not leaving." He cut his hair. He worked hard in class. He straightened up his act, at least somewhat. He kept showing up and always on time. And Paterno, without ever saying anything about it, made Bauer one of his leaders.

"I know that's what Joe wanted me to do," Bauer said. "But I can't say it was a test. He was going to throw me off the team. He was sick of me. But I think he also knew where my heart was. . . . From that point on, there was something unspoken between us. He knew that I wasn't going anywhere. And I knew that he knew."

• • •

WITH BAUER'S LEADERSHIP AND TOUGHNESS, and with a group of defensive players who played together as well as any Paterno team, the two coaches decided to try something even more extreme than the Magic Defense they used against Georgia. In the month or so of preparation before the bowl game, they devised a defense to attack the one glaring flaw they saw in Miami's offense: arrogance.

For four weeks, Sandusky taught his players to back up. It was not a natural movement for them. The defense had been built around toughness and fury. Shane Conlan was an attacking linebacker; defensive back Ray Isom launched himself at receivers; Bob White and Mike Russo took on two and three blockers at a time. Now the coaches were asking them to pull back, to give way. Paterno and Sandusky rarely agreed; they did not like each other. Paterno often fired Sandusky, and Sandusky often quit, and the two men clashed so violently in team meetings that other coaches expected a fight to break out.

But every now again, like before the 1983 Sugar Bowl against Georgia, their goals and judgments meshed. They decided that the way to beat Miami was to bait them into destroying themselves. Paterno gave the order, and Sandusky put it into motion. The two men, for one month at the end of 1986, worked together better than they ever had before and certainly ever would again. One person close to the program said, "I know this sounds bitter, but I think that's the last game Jerry Sandusky really coached."

For that one game, they were of one mind.

"What if they don't fall for it?" Paterno asked Sandusky.

"Beats me," Sandusky said.

PATERNO ALSO TOLD SHANE CONLAN that he would never play another down at Penn State. But in Conlan's case, it was a near miracle that he ended up at Penn State in the first place. He was a skinny kid from a tiny school in a tiny hamlet called Frewsburg in upstate New York. He played running back, mostly. Nobody recruited him. Then, in one of those crazy acts of providence that seemed to happen in Paterno's life, an eight-millimeter film of Conlan playing in high school ended up in the office of Penn State's assistant defensive coach, Tom Bradley. "It was so grainy you could hardly see anything," Bradley recalled. "And what you did see was bad football. I mean bad. Go into any restaurant and pick eleven people and we could beat this team. But I saw Shane playing, and he was tough. And I had this feeling about him."

Bradley called Conlan's coach, Tom Sharp, and asked him who else was recruiting him. "Nobody," Sharp said. That was discouraging. But Sharp asked Bradley to come watch Conlan play in a basketball game. So Bradley drove up to Frewsburg ("I'm thinking, I must be nuts!"); he knew he had arrived when he saw the barn with "Welcome to Frewsburg" painted on it. Conlan fouled out in the third quarter of the game, and Bradley thought, "Well, he is aggressive."

Bradley told Paterno he had a good feeling about Conlan and wanted to bring him in.

"You're going to have to coach him," Paterno said.

"I know," Bradley agreed.

"You better be right," Paterno warned.

During a practice in Conlan's freshman year—he had been moved to linebacker—he was covering teammate Kevin Baugh, who pulled one of those stunts that work on freshmen: Baugh pretended that he had pulled a hamstring. When Conlan asked, "Hey, are you okay?" Baugh ran right by him and scored a touchdown. The next thing Conlan heard was that familiar high-pitched voice yelling, "You stink, Conlan! You hear me? You will never play here! You're a quitter! You stink! Get out of my practice!"

But Bradley's instincts were on target. Shane Conlan was a remarkable football player. First, he was a great athlete: "People never really understood just how fast and strong Shane was," Trey Bauer would say. Second, he had a great mind for football: "Shane was always where he was supposed to be," Paterno said. Third, he was tough. That came from his father, Dan. Conlan never complained. In fact, Conlan hardly ever even talked.

"If you're lucky," Paterno said, "you get to coach a guy like Shane Conlan once in your life."

THE DAYS LEADING UP TO the 1987 Fiesta Bowl were mayhem. Miami coach Jimmy Johnson had arrived in Phoenix ahead of his players, which allowed them to hatch a plan to show the nation just how serious they were about this game: they came off the plane wearing army fatigues. Penn State players, of course, wore jackets and ties. *Sports Illustrated* had just named Paterno Sportsman of the Year—only the second coach, after UCLA's basketball legend John Wooden, to be so honored—and sportswriter Rick Reilly's story painted the now fully formed portrait of Saint Joe. "Over the last three decades," Reilly wrote, "nobody has stayed truer to the game and at the same time truer to himself than Joseph Vincent Paterno, Joe Pa to Penn State worshipers—a man so patently stubborn that he refuses to give up on the notion that if you hack away at enough windmills, a few of the suckers will fall."

The narrative, good versus evil, had been put into motion.

"Look, they weren't bad guys," Trey Bauer insisted. "It was more like the inmates were running the asylum. They were just doing whatever they wanted. They were so talented, I think they figured it didn't matter what they did—they were going to destroy us anyway."

Jimmy Johnson seemed to have the same attitude. In his first press conference, he casually referred to Paterno as "Saint Joe" and at one point during the week said with a wink, "Everybody respects Joe's image . . . and nobody would dare say anything bad about it." Johnson seemed to think the army fatigues stunt was beneficial to his team's unity. "We have a oneness I've never seen before," he announced.

Five days before the game, both teams gathered for a steak fry; they were supposed to present little skits to poke fun at each other. Penn State went first, led by punter John Bruno. He made fun of Jimmy Johnson's hair in a bit that included a giant can of hairspray. He also made a joke that was in poor taste, about how Penn State had ideal race relations, so much so that they even let the black player eat at the training table with the white players once a week.

There would be some disagreement about the impact of Bruno's jokes. A few news reports at the time suggested Miami's players were actually more offended by the hairspray joke than the racial one. Miami players and others later claimed that they were reacting to the training table joke. But it seems likely Bruno's jokes had nothing to do with what followed. When it was time for the Hurricanes to do their skit, Miami's Jerome Brown tore off his clothes to reveal the army fatigues underneath—confirmation that what was about to happen wasn't a spur-of-the-moment decision but had been planned—and shouted, "We're not here for you all to make monkeys of us. We're here to make war. Did the Japanese sit down with Pearl Harbor before they bombed them? Let's go!" With that the Miami players walked out, all of them now wearing fatigues. Johnson and the other Miami coaches just watched.

John Bruno would cut some of the tension with the best line of the night—"Hey, didn't the Japanese lose that one?"—but the scene was chaotic. "Are you kidding me?" said Bauer. "Who was in charge? I mean, we had too much respect for Joe to walk out to the bathroom much less walk out of the place."

Paterno was privately outraged by the scene. "Combat fatigues?" he wrote in his autobiography. "Why not hang bayonets and hand grenades on their belts too?" But he was also thrilled. The trap was set. It was clear the Miami coaches and players did not just want to beat Penn State; they wanted to destroy and embarrass Penn State. And those were exactly the ambitions Paterno was hoping for.

"They left after they ate, right?" Paterno joked with reporters. "Typical football players." Quietly he told his players not to comment on the walkout. They would have plenty to say once the game began.

FOOTBALL COACHES HAVE AN ARCHETYPE in their minds, a player who represents the kind of athlete they love to coach. It could be a quarterback who can run and throw and adjust to whatever the opposing defense offers. Paterno was lucky enough to have guys like that; Todd Blackledge, Chuck Fusina, Kerry Collins, and Michael Robinson come to mind. He also had quarterbacks who had a knack for winning, like John Shaffer. He was blessed that way.

But it might not be a quarterback. It might be a linebacker who is tough as sandpaper, who makes tackle after tackle and, in the biggest moment, finds ways to force the fumble or tip the pass or make the interception that wins the game. Paterno was doubly blessed there. The list of wonderful linebackers at Linebacker U is long: Jack Ham, Lance Mehl, Shane Conlan, Brandon Short, and, well, you could keep going for a while.

Then again, the archetype could be a running back, someone who just loves running the ball, again and again, never tiring, never wilting, a runner who pounds forward and finds a way to drive into the end zone and will, every now and again, break a long run that destroys the other team's spirit. In this Paterno was triply blessed. The list of astonishing and impassioned runners at Penn State is even longer than the list of linebackers: Charlie Pittman, Franco Harris, Lydell Mitchell, Curt Warner, D. J. Dozier, Blair Thomas, Ki-Jana Carter, Larry Johnson, and, of course, John Cappelletti.

Over forty-six years Paterno would coach brilliant players at all positions, and those young men would be inspired by different muses, driven by different demons, motivated by different methods. As Paterno said about Lydell Mitchell and Franco Harris, who played for him at the same time, "They were different. Lydell would run through a wall for you. Franco would walk to the wall and feel for cracks."

Still, if Paterno had the perfect player in mind, the player who represented what it was all about for him as a coach, the player might have been Bob White. He grew up in Haines City, Florida, where migrant workers harvested citrus and the Ringling Brothers had stationed their theme park, Circus World. He never knew his father, and he worked in the citrus groves and tobacco fields to help his mother and grandmother keep going. His middle school basketball coach, Bob

Eisenberg, saw a bright future for Bobby White. He was an extraordinary young athlete, but more than that, he had a kind of wisdom that was uncommon for a young man. Eisenberg was from McKeesport, in the heart of Pittsburgh, and he thought Bobby would have a better chance up north. "My mother was against it," White recalled. "But she knew it was a good chance."

White moved to McKeesport and lived with a social worker for a while, then a school librarian. He developed into an extraordinary football player. He was big and strong and fast, but what separated him was that he played with this quiet rage. "If it was Bobby's responsibility to control the A-gap," Trey Bauer said, referring to the gap of space between the offense's center and left guard, "it wouldn't matter if the whole place caught fire. He was going to control the A-gap."

More than a hundred schools recruited White. He remembered that they promised him dreams: he would be a starter right away; he would be an All-American; he would make millions in the NFL. But Bob Eisenberg was right about White's uncommon sense. He did not fall for dreams. White wanted to play for Joe Paterno.

Paterno was skeptical. He loved the young man's spirit, but he did not think White could succeed as a student at Penn State. In his autobiography he wrote, "Here was a kid who had never read a whole book!" White would say that was an exaggeration, but only a slight one. He had not grown up in an environment of reading, to say the least. But when he wanted something, he fought to get it. He spurned big offers, under-the-table promises, guaranteed fame. He wanted to play for Joe Paterno.

"I'll make you a deal," Paterno said: he would take White on, but only if he agreed to be personally tutored by Sue Paterno. White happily agreed. Together Sue and Bob read *Huckleberry Finn*, *Moby-Dick*, and *A Tale of Two Cities*, classic junior high and high school books about which White said, "Honestly, I had never heard of them." He struggled with his classes at first, but he was smart and he was driven, and in time he graduated with a degree in administration of justice. Not long after that, he got his master's degree in counselor education. He was also captain of the 1986 Penn State football team.

On the first play of the Penn State–Miami game, Penn State quarterback John Shaffer was sacked for a 14-yard loss. Two plays later, he was sacked again. This was how it would go all day. Penn State's offense had no chance to move the ball against Miami's brilliant and ferocious defense. "Years later, I watched a tape of the game," Trey Bauer recalled. "And I said, right in the middle, 'We have no chance to win this game.' And I *played* in that game."

Paterno was unconcerned. He had suspected that his offense would struggle against Miami; he had told his offensive coordinator Fran Ganter that the offense's main job was to avoid turning over the ball. The real question in his mind was whether Miami's offense would fall for Penn State's ploy. It didn't look good at first. Miami took the ball and drove down the field. Quarterback Vinny Testaverde completed a pass to Michael Irvin. He completed another to Charles Henry. He completed a 10-yarder to Alonzo Highsmith.

Then Paterno saw the first sign that the plan would work. On third down and 2 at the Penn State 28, Testaverde threw a long pass into the end zone that was incomplete. That made it fourth down, and Miami was in field goal range. But they were not interested in kicking field goals. The Hurricanes had worn battle fatigues; they had walked out of dinner; they had compared themselves to the Japanese bombing Pearl Harbor. All season long they had gotten in various kinds of trouble off the field. They had come to Arizona to score touchdowns and win big and show everyone in America that they were invincible. They went for it on fourth down, and Charles Henry dropped a pass over the middle to give the ball back to Penn State.

"You have to understand something about Joe," Bauer said. "He didn't care how much we won by. Ever. He didn't care what the game looked like. He didn't care who got the credit. He didn't care what anybody said about it. All he cared about was playing to win—one point, seven points, thirty points, absolutely no difference to him."

This was at the heart of the Paterno plan engineered by Sandusky: Penn State wanted to win; Miami wanted to destroy. So the Penn State defense would back up, back up, let Testaverde see the field, let the receivers catch passes, let Alonzo Highsmith gain yards. But they would never give Testaverde the same defensive look. When the receivers caught those passes, the Penn State defenders would hit with such force that receivers would think twice about catching another. And as for Highsmith, Paterno gambled that Miami would be too impatient and single-minded to run the ball every time. "If Miami had given Highsmith the ball forty times," said Bauer, "we wouldn't have known what to do. But they didn't. And Joe knew they wouldn't."

The second time the Hurricanes had the ball, they were driving down the field again when Testaverde completed a pass to Irvin over the middle. Ray Isom, Penn State's short but powerful safety, rushed in, pounded Irvin, and forced a fumble. It was one of a couple of huge hits Isom had in the game. Irvin was shell-shocked by the hit. He would drop five or six passes in the game before it was over. After the game, he would claim the ball was slippery.

The third time the Hurricanes had the ball, they were driving again. But on third down, Testaverde grew impatient—not for the last time—and threw the ball downfield, where it was intercepted by defensive back Duffy Cobbs. The first quarter was over. Miami had not scored. The intensity was overwhelming; both teams felt it. They screamed at each other and cursed at each other and a couple of fights almost broke out. At one point, a Miami player hit Shaffer late in what Paterno called "the worst cheap shot I've ever seen." But his plan was working. Frustration was building on the Miami sideline.

Miami did score a touchdown in the second quarter when Shaffer fumbled deep in Penn State territory. Paterno groaned. As he had told coach Fran Ganter, the offense had to hold on to to the ball or the plan could not work. But Shaffer promptly led the team on a long scoring drive to tie the game. He completed two critical third-down passes—two of only five completions he would make all night—and he ran for the touchdown himself after faking a pass. The score was 7–7. NBC's Bob Costas spent halftime on television interviewing President Ronald Reagan.

In the Penn State locker room, Paterno told his team that the plan had gone brilliantly; if not for the fumble, it would have been perfect. He knew that Miami's players and coaches were fully ensnared in their own pride. He knew, absolutely knew, that the Miami players were angry, baffled, and determined to come out in the second half and end this nonsense. And this was exactly how the plan worked. They would come out even more impatient and distracted. Penn State had pounded and confused the Hurricanes into a state of panic, and the Nittany Lions had dozens and dozens of new looks to unveil in the second half.

When Miami got the ball at the start of the second half, Paterno got his confirmation. Highsmith dropped a pass. Irvin dropped a pass. The next time Miami got the ball, Testaverde tried to throw a bomb once, then got sacked trying to throw another. The next time, Testaverde slipped and threw a pass that Shane Conlan intercepted.

It was like hypnosis. Though Highsmith was running free—he would gain 119 yards—and though the game was tied, Johnson and the other Miami coaches refused to give him the ball. They were still going for the knockout. On the first play of the fourth quarter, Testaverde threw another interception, this time to Penn State linebacker Pete Giftopoulos.

Miami did manage a field goal in the fourth quarter, on a drive built around two long Highsmith runs, to take a 10–7 lead. But on their next possession, they were again throwing downfield, and again Testaverde's pass was intercepted, again by Conlan, who ran the ball all the way to the Miami 5-yard line. Penn State offensive lineman Keith Radecic recovered a fumbled snap, and D. J. Dozier scored on a 6-yard run. It seemed impossible to just about everyone watching. Penn State led 14–10.

Miami's panic increased: their next series ended with a fumble.

The one after that ended when Testaverde's deep pass fell incomplete. Finally, it came down to the last series of the game. This was where the Paterno–Sandusky plan reached its limit. "We knew," Paterno said, "that at some point we would have to stand up. Miami was too good. We knew they would have one great drive in them. The question was: Could we stop them when they made that drive?"

Miami made that drive. Well, first, Trey Bauer dropped a sure interception. "We had to win that game twice," he muttered later. On fourth down from deep in their own territory, Testaverde completed a pass to Brian Blades, who shook off his defender and raced 30 yards. For an instant, it looked like he might score. Ray Isom was outraged at linebacker Eddie Johnson, who had reverted to his usual instincts and had gone for the interception. "What are you doing?" Isom shouted at Johnson.

"Ray, stop yelling, call a play!" Conlan yelled at Isom.

"Everybody focus!" Bauer yelled at all of them.

Miami moved the ball to the Penn State 5-yard line with less than a minute remaining. On the next play, Penn State's defense was a bit confused, and a couple of receivers broke open, but just as Testaverde was about to throw, Penn State's Tim Johnson came rushing from the blind side, grabbed the bottom of Testaverde's helmet and pulled him hard to the ground. The ball was at the 13-yard line. There were twenty-five seconds left.

TREY BAUER KEPT A PHOTOGRAPH of the moment in his office. It was a photograph of the sideline, with Miami just a few yards away from the end zone and time running out. There they were—Bauer and Sandusky and defensive assistant Jim Williams and Paterno—and they were faced with perhaps the toughest call of their lives. They had to keep Miami out of the end zone. Sandusky was at a loss. He stuttered and looked around nervously. He had no idea what to do.

That's when Paterno walked over. "What are you guys running?" he asked.

"We don't know," Bauer answered.

Paterno looked at him, at Sandusky, nodded, and walked away.

"It was the only time—the only time—I ever saw him at a loss for words," Bauer said. "I look back and think about it, and I think it was the ultimate sign of trust. The play didn't really matter. He just thought: 'You'll find a way.' "

On third down, Testaverde threw a panicked pass as he was falling backward that fell incomplete. That led to fourth down. Testaverde dropped back, looked left, and threw into a crowd of Penn State players. It was the last confused pass of a broken quarterback. Any of a number of Penn State players might have intercepted the ball, but it was Pete Giftopoulos who actually did. He ran awkwardly for a few steps. "Get down!" Bauer and Isom and Conlan all yelled at him at the same time, though Giftopoulos really couldn't hear anything.

Then Giftopoulos fell to the ground slowly, awkwardly, like a child trying to hide under his bed during a thunderstorm. And Penn State fans rushed onto the field.

JEROME BROWN, THE MIAMI PLAYER who stripped down to fatigues and shouted about the Japanese and Pearl Harbor, went into the Penn State locker room after the game to congratulate his opponents. He called Penn State a great team. Just five years later he died in a car wreck. John Bruno, the Penn State punter who joked about Japan losing the war, died of cancer that same year.

The game lived on. Miami players, many of them, would always insist that they should have won the game. "The better team did not win," running back Melvin Bratton said in the immediate aftermath, and that would be a theme. Many years later, an ESPN documentary about Miami football took it for granted that Miami was indeed a much better team than Penn State and would have won easily if not for its seven turnovers.

"Yeah," Bob White said twenty-five years later, "and if a frog had wings he wouldn't have to hop around on his butt all day either."

Trey Bauer said, "I think the fact that so many of them still think they should have won tells me they still don't get it. They didn't just make mistakes. We forced them into making mistakes. I said after the game, and I still believe it, 'If we play them ten times, we win nine of them.' You know why? Because we knew how to win. And Joe would have figured out a way."

Rhythms

J oe Paterno set his clock to the rhythms of college football. Those
rhythms lifted him and dropped him, thrilled and frustrated
him. His teams hit spectacular peaks at fairly regular intervals:
they were great in 1969, again in 1973, and again in 1978. They won
national championships in 1982 and 1986. It seemed like every four
years or so, a special group of seniors would take hold, a group of
juniors and sophomores and even a few freshmen would mesh their
talents, the breaks would bounce right, and the team would win week
after week. Paterno would tell recruits that if they came to Penn State,
they would be part of at least one magical team that had a chance at a
national championship.

The autumns in between magical teams varied. Some impetuous
freshmen did not become talented sophomores; some talented sophomores did not become skilled juniors; some skilled juniors did not become senior leaders. Sometimes the breaks broke bad. In 1988, Penn
State finished 5-6, its first losing record since Paterno became head
coach. He turned sixty-two that year, and so, of course, the talk was of
time passing by the old man. Paterno had dealt with much skepticism
and doubt throughout his life, but this was the first time that such talk
clanged at a high volume, and he didn't like it. He told friends that

he was determined to have one more great team, one more national champion. In 1991 Penn State finished the year ranked third in the nation. In 1992, they finished 7-5 and Paterno admitted that he and the coaches had lost control of that team. Again people shouted that Paterno had lost his stuff. He turned sixty-six that year.

Penn State started playing football in the Big Ten Conference in 1993. The school had officially joined the conference in 1990, after a contentious and uneasy negotiation. On the surface, the marriage made a lot of sense. For the conference, Penn State brought football prestige and the power media markets of Philadelphia and Pittsburgh, not to mention New York. For Penn State, the Big Ten brought stability and shelter. Paterno had been one of the first to understand that college football was becoming too expensive for a school to go it independently. A conference could negotiate big money deals with television networks. A conference could work out long-term relationships with bowl games. Paterno had tried in the late 1970s to spearhead an eastern conference featuring Syracuse, Pittsburgh, and others, but the talks had fallen apart. (Paterno had raw feelings about those failed negotiations; the Nittany Lions even stopped playing longtime rival Pittsburgh after 2000.) By the late 1980s, Paterno realized that because of the costs, the day of the college football independent was over. He was right: Before long, football powers like Florida State and Miami had joined conferences—only Notre Dame, with its national appeal, could go it alone. Paterno and Penn State administrators decided that the Big Ten, with its strong academic standing and sports prowess, would be a good fit and would raise the entire athletic department and the rest of the school.

But while it looked good on the surface, there were a lot of reasons it was not a good fit. Remote State College made any road trip for other Big Ten schools difficult. Indiana's basketball coach (and Paterno's longtime friend) Bob Knight griped, "It's a camping trip up there." Although Paterno believed the Big Ten could be good for his football team—could help with recruiting and push them to play better football by consistently playing better teams—he knew that the conference was set in its ways and might make decisions that were contrary to Penn State's best interests.

Still, a number of people, Paterno among them, decided that Penn State should be in the Big Ten. It was a sloppy process. First, there were secret dealings among the Big Ten presidents and athletic directors. There was an awkward "invitation in principle." There was some loud skepticism from some of the Big Ten athletic directors and coaches. There was fierce voting by the school presidents and the outcome was uncertain until after the final negotiations. Then came the actual invitation. And even after the invitation, several coaches and administrators in the Big Ten complained about it. "Perhaps if we had to do it all over again," Big Ten Commissioner Jim Delany said, "we'd use a different process."

Paterno would sometimes regret joining the Big Ten. He did believe the conference challenged Penn State in good ways—the beautiful Bryce Jordan Center was built in large part to give Penn State a basketball arena good enough for Big Ten play—but he also thought that the other schools in the conference did not share many of Penn State's interests. Some of his many notes contain the question "Get out of Big 10?"

PATERNO HAD ONE MORE UNDEFEATED team and one more losing battle with the college football polls. The 1994 team was unlike any in the school's history. The offense was unstoppable; a reasonable case can be made that it was the greatest college football offense ever. Paterno had built a reputation, one he took more than a small measure of pride in, as a conservative offensive thinker. For years, Joe Paterno golf balls were sold in State College with the slogan (which Paterno loved) "Like the Penn State offense, three out of four are guaranteed to go up the middle." It was a bit of a myth—Penn State's 1982 national championship team had a fast-paced and high-scoring offense—but it was mostly true.

The 1994 offense was so overloaded with speed and skill and

the ability to make big plays that Paterno simply gave in to a daring and attacking offensive strategy. Running back Ki-Jana Carter had a staggering combination of power and speed; he ran for more than 1,500 yards, scored twenty-three touchdowns, finished second in the Heisman Trophy voting, and was the first pick in the NFL draft. Quarterback Kerry Collins was six-foot-five and had such a strong arm that two Major League Baseball teams drafted him as a potential pitcher. Collins finished fourth in the Heisman Trophy balloting and was the fifth pick in the NFL draft. Tight end Kyle Brady was an All-American and a top-ten NFL pick. Wide receiver Bobby Engram was an All-American and would win the Biletnikoff Award as the nation's best receiver. It was an embarrassment of riches. All year, Penn State never scored fewer than 30 points in a game. They scored 61 on Iowa, 63 against Ohio State on homecoming, and 59 against Michigan State. It looked nothing, absolutely nothing, like a typical Paterno team. "He didn't adapt for 1994," boasted All-American offensive lineman Jeff Hartings. "Honestly, we were just that good."

They were that good—certainly on offense—and by late October they were ranked No. 1 and seemed destined to win Paterno's third national championship. But three strange circumstances conspired to move Penn State down in the rankings.

First, the defense was not good. Trey Bauer loved telling players on the 1994 team that they could not beat his 1986 champions because they "couldn't stop anybody." Paterno was not happy about this, and he knew who was mostly responsible: Defensive Coordinator Jerry Sandusky. In 1993, Paterno wrote what the family would sometimes call the "Why I Hate Jerry Sandusky Memo." In it Paterno complained that Sandusky had stopped recruiting, seemed constantly distracted, had lost his energy for coaching, and was more interested in his charity, The Second Mile. "He would gripe about Jerry all the time," one family member said.

The defensive issues were not an especially big deal in 1994 because the offense was so good. They gave up 27 points to Rutgers. So what? They scored 55. The week after their homecoming destruction of Ohio State, however, the defensive lapses did matter, at least aesthetically. Penn State led Indiana by 21 points late in the game. In the last two minutes, led by a backup quarterback, Indiana scored two touchdowns, the second on the last play of the game. Indiana added a 2-point conversion on that final touchdown to make the final score look extremely close: 35–29.

"The Indiana people looked like they won it," Paterno joked after the game, but it was no joke. The sportswriters and coaches who voted in the polls were not all aware of the details, they simply saw that Penn State had beaten a weak Indiana team by a mere 6 points. Penn State dropped to No. 2, behind Nebraska.

The second factor involved Nebraska and its respected coach Tom Osborne. He had never won a national championship. He had come close in 1983 with a team many, even then, called the best in college football history. But his team had lost to Miami in the Orange Bowl when Osborne went for a 2-point play at the end rather than settling for a tie. He and Paterno were friends, and they shared some of the same philosophies of coaching: "I think, I hope, that Joe and I tried to remember what's really important," Osborne said. "You can really influence football players. A kid might sleep through history class, but he won't sleep through football practice. He is invested. And so you have a chance to help develop his character. It's a responsibility, one I tried to take very seriously, and I know Joe took it very seriously too."

Osborne was well-liked by coaches and sportswriters. So, in large part, was Paterno, but he had already won two national championships. Sentiment was rooting for Osborne and Nebraska.

The third factor was that Penn State had just joined the Big Ten, which meant the Nittany Lions were now tied into the conference's bowl agreeements. If they had still been an independent, they could have played Nebraska and settled things once and for all. But the Big Ten champion went to the Rose Bowl, and that's where Penn State went to face a good but not great Oregon team. Nebraska went to the Orange Bowl to play a very good Miami team. As one Penn State player said, "We could have won the Rose Bowl 100–0 and it wouldn't have mattered."

Penn State beat Oregon convincingly but not overwhelmingly in the Rose Bowl, 38–20, and finished the year undefeated. Nebraska beat Miami and won the national championship. Paterno's emotions were mixed. He was happy for Osborne, but he also felt sure his team would have beaten Nebraska. (For his part, Osborne felt sure his team would have beaten Penn State: "I wish we could have played that game.") Paterno again railed against the system and again talked about a playoff. He was sixty-eight years old with a near-flawless record and was once more on top of the college football world.

"Step down then?" Paterno would ask near the end of his life. "After 1994? Are you kidding me? Why? I never even thought about it."

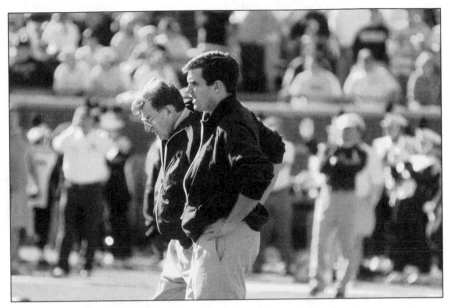

Joe Paterno and his son and assistant coach, Jay, look on during a game *(Jason Sipes/Altoona Mirror)*

Jay

T he five Paterno kids grew up with different relationships to
football, but everybody understood that it was Joseph Paterno Jr., the son everyone called Jay, who lived for the game.
The girls, Diana and Mary Kay, were the oldest and were raised in
a time before Joe became a legend and an icon. Their lives were
interwoven with the by-products of the coaching life. They prepared
food for the various gatherings and cleaned up afterward and helped
Sue entertain recruits and their families. They played with the young
siblings of the recruits and of the biggest donors. They were taught
to live frugally. Once, Mary Kay remembered, someone tried to convince her father to join a country club so the kids could use the pool.

"What are they, big shots?" Joe snapped back. "They can swim in the neighborhood pool like everyone else." And, of course, they prayed every week for the team and for their father.

David, born third, was very different from his father; from a young age his mind revolved around the physics of things, turning him inescapably into an engineer. Everyone in the family recalled David at Disney World explaining how every one of the rides worked. ("I don't want to know! I want the magic!" Sue pleaded.) David was very different from Joe, who struggled with the mechanics of turning on a vacuum cleaner.

Scott, the youngest, had the toughest relationship with Joe. "Until I was twenty-three or twenty-four, I couldn't stand my father," he confessed. Perhaps it was because the two were so alike; they argued constantly. "You could expect that if the two of us were sitting at a table, it was going to end up with yelling."

When Scott was sixteen, he was sent to the Kiski School, an all-boys boarding school in Saltsburg, about two hours from State College. Scott remembered his father driving him there and the line Joe gave him when they arrived: "One of us is moving out, and the mortgage is in my name." It turned out that Kiski was ideal for Scott, so much so that he named a son after Jack Pidgeon, the tough-as-nails headmaster. The son-father relationship changed dramatically after Scott went to college. "My dad obviously understood college kids," Scott said. "That was his life. So when I got to college, every trick I tried to play, every stunt I tried to pull, he'd already seen it a thousand times. After going through that phase, we just started to talk." When he told his father he was considering law school, Joe was thrilled; finally, there would be a lawyer in the family, a tribute to Angelo. They found their connection through politics and history (especially Abraham Lincoln). Football didn't fit into their conversations. Scott was a fanatical Penn State football fan—the family made him sit in a separate part of the stadium because he was so loud and passionate—but whenever he tried to bring up football with his father, Joe would say, "Ahhh, I already have enough people telling me what to do."

No, football talk was for Jay. When Jay was three or four, he used to draw numbers on Lincoln Logs and pretend they were football players. He would line them in up formations and design plays for them to run. He soaked himself in football. Around the neighborhood, kids would play two-on-two football, and Jay kept meticulous stats on the games. When anyone at the house asked Sue a football question, she would rustle up Jay, who would explain exactly why the pulling guard got caught up or why the linebacker was not in the right position to defend the play. From his earliest moments of consciousness, Jay could remember having only one dream: to coach football at Penn State. He had many skills, and he was smart and driven. At one point Joe wanted Jay to become a lawyer. At another, he wanted Jay to think about politics. He thought Jay could be a great writer if he put his mind to it.

But Joe recognized the same passions in his son that had marked his own life. Jay was a backup quarterback at Penn State in the late 1980s. He became a graduate assistant coach at Virginia. He was a wide receivers coach at Connecticut and then quarterbacks coach at James Madison, where he was so highly thought of that coach Rip Scherer wanted to bring him to Memphis as his offensive coordinator in 1995.

But that was the year a spot opened up for a recruiting coordinator at Penn State. Joe, who would never be too open about his thinking behind the choice, hired Jay. Did he hope that someday Jay would replace him as coach? It's hard to imagine a father not thinking along those lines, but Joe insisted that wasn't in his mind. "Are you kidding me?" he scoffed. "You think I would want Jay to have to deal with that?" He thought the Paterno name hurt Jay more than it helped him. "Jay's a good coach, a darned good coach. And I think a lot of people refuse to see that because his name is Paterno. I would sometimes tell Jay, 'You should go coach somewhere else, where people will give you a fair chance,' because I don't think he always got that fair chance. But Jay's tough."

"I didn't want to coach anywhere else," Jay explained. "I wanted to coach for the best coach and the best program in the country. That was Joe Paterno and Penn State."

Jay and Joe would coach together for the better part of seventeen seasons. Jay proved to be an easy target for critics during the tough years—a simple way to get at the old man—and there would be many tough years. One of the jokes that made its way around town was that they really wanted Oe Paterno coaching—that is, "Joe" without the "Jay." There were a lot of jokes and a lot of shots at Joe's son.

"I'll tell you something Joe taught me," said Jay. He always called his father "Joe" when the subject was coaching or football. "He taught me that the critics come out when you're losing, and they go into hiding when you're winning. That's because, deep down, they're cowards.

"Joe could not stand cowards. He would say all the time, 'Do what you think is right. And if you're wrong, stand up and face it.' All the people who said stuff about me, they don't matter. I got to coach with a great man. And he happened to be my father."

ACT IV:
WHAT COMES AFTER

It's not enough to be fair. You must *appear* to be fair.

—JOE PATERNO

{ *Aria* }

Joe Paterno
coaches' staff meeting
May 26, 1998 (reconstructed from Paterno's notes)

We are going to have to do everything better than we have been doing things. And I know we have to do a better job than we did last year. We are not ahead of anybody. There are people (Purdue, Michigan State, etc.) who are catching up to us. Wisconsin, Iowa, and Northwestern are even with us. And Michigan and Ohio State may be pulling away now that their coaching staffs have not only become more stable, but they are much more confident.

It's my job as the head coach to see that we do a better job, and that's what we are going to do.

We face stiffer competition, and we are making financial commitments to facilities THAT DEMAND that we GET BETTER. Plus facilities which present opportunities to MAKE GREAT THINGS HAPPEN FOR THIS PROGRAM.

And I intend to make sure that great things do happen.

And to do that I think we have to talk about a new

direction, or at least guidelines that I think will make us a more focused and more productive staff. And I believe this has been a problem for me and for some of you.

Our structure cannot be static but dynamic. Things are changing all the time. Here's what I want to talk about.

A. *When someone is talking, especially me, PAY ATTENTION. That means no reading, signing letters, drawing up cards and no side conversations. We've been having too much "We never said that" or "I didn't hear that."*

B. *We have to have an open exchange, BUT we don't need unnecessary and prolonged attempts to win a point.*

C. *We have to understand there will be differences and respect each other's views.*

D. *Don't sulk if your idea gets outvoted or I turn it down.*

E. *Don't think that you are the only one who should or can make suggestions or be critical of your coaching area.*

F. *As for myself, I may present some "way-out" ideas to get some reaction or to stimulate some discussion (and to make sure we don't have "yes men"). I may even change sides in a discussion.*

G. *Everybody needs to show strong interest in EVERYTHING that we do. We should be ready to learn from each other and help each other. I intend to sit in on as many meetings as possible.*

I've talked about this before, but let me say it again. When dealing with the press be careful to emphasize, "We are young, eager, coachable, but we have a long way to go." TRY NOT TO BE QUOTABLE.

And don't turn your head if you see a player not abiding by our rules. I'm talking about earrings, beards, studies, appearance, attitude. . . . These things equal the "Penn State

Way." *Players must believe that there are rules that make Penn State special—unique.*

And remember: Team morale, team attitude, this is my concern. I want input and suggestions from you. But I have to set the tone.

Joe Paterno the year he turned eighty *(Jason Sipes/Altoona Mirror)*

The Filthiest Word

Deep in a file Paterno labeled "Speeches, Clippings, Etc." was a single sheet of paper that perhaps explained the last dozen years of his coaching life better than anything else. Paterno's files were a beautiful blend of order and chaos. He wrote countless notes on graph paper, stapled them together, and added sticky notes to them. He kept detailed notes for every major speech he gave, staff meeting he held, and big talk he gave the squad. He would sometimes go back to these notes, but more often he did not. He just liked to know that they were there, in the files, in case he faced a similar problem or challenge in the future.

Paterno loved breaking down concepts into simple and pithy expressions. To him, this was what coaching and teaching was about: simplifying things, then simplifying them some more, and then simplifying them again. This was why he loved Hemingway's writing. Hemingway wrote declarative sentences. Punchy. He drank his coffee and it was good. Paterno enjoyed playing with words. One time he wanted to tell his team that they should not say anything bad about opponents before games. Why? It's not classy. He wrote down the words "Be classy." But "Be classy" would not move nineteen- and twenty-year-old men. It just wasn't interesting or true enough. "You have to tell them why," he thought.

Why not say anything bad about opponents? Because talk is cheap. He wrote that down: TALK IS CHEAP. But this is a cliché. What does it mean to say that talk is cheap?

TALK WILL NOT WIN GAMES.

There it was; this was closer to the point. Talk doesn't help a team win. But was this true? Paterno was not sure. "One thing about kids," Paterno always said. "You can't fool them." The truth seemed to be that sometimes a little talk could get into opponents' heads, make them nervous, distract them. Paterno could not deny this. He had another thought.

TALK WILL NOT BEAT GOOD TEAMS.

Ah, now he had it. Talk might help beat the lousy teams. But so what? Talk won't matter against the best teams, the teams Penn State had to beat in order to get to where the players wanted to go, to move them up to No. 1 and put them in position to win a national championship. Yes, this was the point. Finally, he wrote down the sentence that he told the team:

TALK DOESN'T BEAT GOOD TEAMS; TALK ONLY BEATS SOMEBODY YOU WERE GOING TO BEAT ANYWAY.

The files were filled with such Paternoisms, hundreds of them, thousands of them. Here are a few from just one note from around 2000:

Tradition is not a gift. It's a challenge.
Everybody, every play, go to the ball.
Think about getting up WHILE you're falling down.
Big plays don't happen; you have to make them happen.
It's all about creating an opportunity for victory.
My father always said that nobody gets carried out of the ring;
　　one person just gets tired of getting up.

The files, though, were much more than just Paterno's musings. He obsessively clipped things he read and liked. He underlined his favorite parts. Here is a line from the poet Robert Frost that he liked: "I never feel more at home in America than at a ballgame, be it in park or in sandlot. Beyond this I know not. And dare not." He wrote down this quote from Albert Einstein: "Great minds have always encountered violent opposition from mediocre minds." There was a story in *Reader's Digest* about lessons to be learned from Christopher Columbus: Never give up; be a lifelong learner; do your homework; believe in your own destiny. There was basketball coach John Wooden's pyramid of success (personalized for Paterno by Wooden himself), with this quote at the top: "Success is peace of mind which is a direct result of self-satisfaction in knowing you did your best to become the best that you are capable of becoming." Paterno seemed to constantly be looking for inspiration, for something that could get him to see football and competition and life from a slightly different angle.

Paterno had been talking publicly about retiring from coaching since the early 1970s. For a time, he seemed interested in politics. At one time, he considered playing a larger role in cleaning up college athletics. Maybe these were serious considerations, maybe they were not, but he talked about them a lot.

"Four more years," he said when he was in his fifties.

"Five more years," he said when he was in his sixties.

For a while, the writers and fans took such talk seriously. He seemed like the kind of well-rounded person who would let go of coaching at some point and spend the later years of his life traveling with Sue, reading on the beach, perhaps writing books and enjoying life as a grandfather and elder statesman. Paterno liked to think of himself that way too, at least at first. When he told writers in the mid-1970s that he wasn't going to be an old coach, they believed him. In the mid-1980s, he again said he wouldn't coach much longer. Some people still believed him. By the mid-1990s, he said that he would leave soon. "I don't think I want to go over 75," he told the *St. Louis Post Dispatch* in a question-and-answer session. "I think that would be a mistake." By then, nobody believed him, least of all Paterno himself.

It became clear to him, and to those around him, that being a football coach was more than just what Paterno did. He *was* a football coach. The man who always said that football was only a small part of life began to tell people that he did not have any other interests. "What am I going to do in retirement? I don't golf. I don't fish. I don't garden. What am I going to do?"

He began to tell reporters the ominous story of Bear Bryant, who had died so soon after he retired from coaching. Paterno made it sound like he feared the same fate. He got touchy whenever anyone asked him about it. His former star player and sometime nemesis Matt Millen would always remember an exchange he had with Paterno.

"Joe, it isn't any of my business," Millen said. "But maybe it's time you thought about grooming a successor and maybe easing out of coaching."

"You're right, Millen," Paterno snapped. "It isn't any of your business."

Some of the people who knew Paterno best thought his refusal to retire spoke to some of his greatest attributes (fearlessness, certainty, relentlessness), others to some of his greatest flaws (stubbornness, unwillingness to face reality, the need to be in charge). Maybe it was both. Paterno turned seventy in 1996, and he kept on going. PBS did a special on ageless wonders in 1998, and Paterno was a big part of it. At the end of the decade, he signed on for five more years. When the Penn State president made it clear that it was time to move on, he fought back and stayed on even longer. He coached through pain, through terrible seasons, and through controversy. He coached until he was eighty, and he kept on going. His hearing went. His mobility went. His energy went. But his mind stayed sharp, his memory too, and he kept on going even when his age had become a national punch line. He coached right up to the scandal that led to his firing and the cancer that led to his death.

Why did he keep coaching? There are no shortage of theories. Ego? A loss of perspective? Or was it simply that he was human? "Joe refused to admit he was getting old," one friend said. "Isn't that the most human thing of all?"

In Paterno's files, among all the letters, outlines, charts, photographs, quotes, regulations, theories, apologies, and regrets, there was one piece of paper that stood out, a poorly copied page of a book. Across the top was written the name "Hemingway." Paterno's literary hero. The name was underlined twice. Below was a series of paragraphs from the book A. E. Hotchner wrote about his friend Ernest Hemingway. In the middle of the page were three sentences Paterno had underlined:

> *I remembered Ernest once telling me, "The worst death for anyone is to lose the center of his being, the thing he really is. Retirement is the filthiest word in the language. Whether by choice or by fate, to retire from what you do—and what you do makes you what you are—is to back up into the grave."*

Sandusky

The two men despised each other from the start. This was well-known among those who knew Joe Paterno and Jerry Sandusky, but at the end it seemed like nobody wanted to mention it. The news reports would assume they were the best of friends or, at the very least, colleagues who respected each other. The truth was more complicated. Paterno thought Sandusky was a glory-hound who had stopped coaching with any zeal years before he finally retired. And Sandusky, according to people who knew him well, thought Paterno a stick in the mud and deeply resented him for blocking his path to be Penn State's head coach.

These bitter feelings had built to a crescendo over the years, as they sometimes do with longtime colleagues. But the two men were never close; their personalities would not allow it. Sandusky despised meetings, was not especially interested in details, and had no enthusiasm at the end of his career for recruiting or the detailed organizational parts of the job—which, of course, made him Paterno's polar opposite. Sandusky and his wife, Dottie, were severe teetotalers, and the Paternos drank socially; this alone was enough to keep Sandusky from coming to the Paternos' house, even for recruiting functions. But more than that, the two men had so little in common. Paterno was, of course, buttoned up, high-strung, and ordered. Sandusky, in the words of Penn State's marketing guru Guido D'Elia and many others, was "a knucklehead." He liked practical jokes and messing around, knocking a guy's hat off his head, making prank calls, sneaking up behind people to startle them. When President George H. W. Bush named Sandusky's charity, The Second Mile, one of his Thousand Points of Light, Sandusky grabbed the microphone during the press conference and shouted, "It's about time, George!"

The two men clashed for many years. Sandusky played football at Penn State, and Paterno hired him as a full-time assistant coach in 1969, when Sandusky was just twenty-five. At one of the first practices before the season, Sandusky was supposed to be on the field but was instead joking around with some players. Paterno screamed at him to get on the field and did not think more about it in the moment. Later, when Paterno watched film of the practice, he saw Sandusky running onto the field waving his arms like a bird and shouting, "The breakdown coach is on his way! The breakdown coach is on his way!" It was ridiculous. Paterno called in Sandusky, screamed at him at length, called him a complete goofball. But he did not fire him. He still thought the young man might develop into a good coach.

Over time, for all of their personal differences, Paterno did come to admire Sandusky's coaching on the field. He coached the defensive line for a year, linebackers for a few more, then Paterno promoted him to defensive coordinator in 1977. When he was focused, Sandusky was a force of nature around the players; he connected to them in ways Paterno never could. He joked with them, hugged them, taunted them, and often inspired them. The players, most of them, loved him for that. Paterno was, in so many ways, a stern father figure: brilliant but distant, caring but judgmental, loving but cold. He was the piercing voice of conscience that squealed whenever they made a mistake or got too comfortable. *"You are the worst player we've ever had at Penn State!"*

Player after player would talk about how they came to appreciate Paterno only after they left school, when they could see things from a

distance. But Sandusky's coaching was something the players understood and felt in the moment. He was like a big brother teasing them,
pushing them, grabbing them, reminding them that they could be
great. He often sympathized with them after Paterno had been especially cruel. "Hey," he would tell the players, "nobody's taken more
abuse than I have."

Paterno and Sandusky understood that, in tandem, they could lift
each other up professionally. That didn't change the personal chem-
istry. They did not talk outside of the office. They complained about
each other incessantly. Paterno tried to hide his distaste for Sandusky
publicly but was not always successful. He referred to Sandusky spe-
cifically only once in his autobiography, the same number of times he
talked about the Brooklyn Dodgers pitcher Sandy Koufax. Sandusky,
meanwhile, offered reporters funny but biting quotes about Paterno,
like the time he mocked Paterno for always griping that defensive
players need to have their hands up when running after the quarterback: "What else would they do? Have their hands down?" Looking
back, many of the stories published about Paterno, even the most
glowing, contain a slightly caustic quote from Sandusky. After a while,
whenever an anonymous source took a shot at Paterno, well, Paterno
just assumed it was Sandusky. There were a lot of signs like that. Most
of them were written off publicly as the trivial conflicts between men
who have worked together for a very long time.

Behind the scenes, though, their dislike for each other was not
hidden or insignificant. "I would be in meetings," said Christian Marrone, who came to Penn State as a player, got hurt, and then served
on the coaching staff, "and they were openly hostile toward each
other the entire time. Joe would say something, Jerry would roll his
eyes, Joe would scream something, it was crazy." Player after player
told similar stories of near fights they saw on the sidelines between the
two coaches. Reporters closest to the program noticed the tension too.
"You know, they really didn't like each other," said Rich Scarcella of
the *Reading (Pennsylvania) Eagle*, the dean of Penn State reporters, at
the end of Paterno's life. "I was shocked by that at first, when I was on

the beat. I knew that Joe and Jerry had masterminded that 1986 championship game, knew that they had worked together for a long time. But it was clear that even though those guys had a healthy respect for each other, they could not really stand each other."

As the years went on, that thin line of respect that had kept their relationship operating began to fade. Paterno thought Sandusky's energy for coaching decreased considerably after the 1987 triumph over Miami. He grumbled to people that Sandusky was getting too full of himself. In Paterno's mind, an earlier coach, Dan Radakovich, was the real coaching genius who made Penn State into "Linebacker U," the ideal place for linebackers to play. He thought Sandusky was taking way too much credit. More to the point, Sandusky's defense wasn't stopping anybody. Even during the undefeated 1994 season, Paterno thought the defense was way too soft. The Nittany Lions gave up 21 points a game on average—too many, in Paterno's book—and had gone undefeated only because the offense was so great. The defense was worse the next year. Paterno's frustrations bubbled. He complained to friends that he did not know what to do about Sandusky. He began writing little notes to himself, things he wanted to say to Sandusky in meetings:

- Why is it you are the only one who, when a meeting starts, wants to know when it will end?
- Jerry, we ARE going to tighten up the ship.
- I knew I should have been worried when Jerry said Wisconsin got impatient running the ball against us. We have to stop people.

There was something else: The Second Mile. Sandusky had started The Second Mile charity for children in 1977. He was forceful about his Christian faith; the name of the charity was inspired by Jesus' Sermon on the Mount: "You have heard that it was said, 'An eye for an eye, and a tooth for a tooth.' But I tell you not to resist an evil person. But whoever slaps you on your right cheek, turn the other to him also. If anyone wants to sue you and take away your tunic, let him have your cloak also. And whoever compels you to go one mile, go with him two."

The charity's stated purpose was to help troubled children, a worthy cause that seemed to obsess Sandusky and his wife. Unable to have children of their own, they adopted six children. In 2002 Jerry and Dottie Sandusky received the Angels in Adoption award (later rescinded) from the Congressional Coalition on Adoption. They took in so many foster children that even their closest friends could not keep track of them all. Children constantly surrounded Sandusky, so much so that they became part of his persona. Nobody at Penn State, and certainly not Paterno, knew who these children were. They could be Second Mile kids; they could be foster kids; they could be adopted kids. This would seem much more sinister later, when a Pennsylvania grand jury indicted Sandusky for child molestation and released a presentment with details so graphic and grotesque that they would shock a nation. But at the time, people saw only Sandusky's charity. "He would bring around new kids, and you would just say, 'I guess those are his new foster kids,' " D'Elia explained, and his words were echoed by dozens of people I interviewed. "And—this is terrible to say now, but it's true—you just didn't think anything more about it. Everybody just thought Jerry was this great guy."

Paterno respected Sandusky's efforts on behalf of children. In the foreword to a self-published book Sandusky wrote about coaching linebackers, Paterno wrote nice things about him. Reporters quoted Paterno praising Sandusky, and he made a few half-hearted gestures of support for the charity. But when you scratched just below the surface, it was not difficult to see how Paterno felt about The Second Mile. When Sandusky painstakingly relived the early financial struggles of The Second Mile in his ominously titled book *Touched*, the absence of Paterno's name and support is unmistakable. One of Paterno's financial advisors said, "I could be wrong, but I don't think he ever gave a dime to The Second Mile, certainly not in the later years." Sandusky conceded as much in a detailed interview with Ron

Bracken of the *Centre (County) Daily Times* in April 2000: "Joe gave me the opportunity to coach. And he gave me the opportunity—or maybe I should say he didn't stop me—to start The Second Mile." In *Touched*, where he thanked dozens of people for the work they did building up The Second Mile, he did not mention Paterno.

Paterno would say again and again that he did not see anything perverse in Sandusky's dealings with children. His problem with The Second Mile was much simpler: the kids annoyed the hell out of him. There's really no other way to say it. Paterno had compartmentalized his own life, putting work and family in separate categories, so that there wasn't much crossover. Football was sacred. Practice was sacred. Family was sacred. Paterno had drawn his famous blue line around every element of his life. He did not want kids around when there was work to do. And Sandusky brought the kids around. He worked on The Second Mile constantly. Paterno and other Penn State officials with knowledge said Sandusky would often use Penn State letterhead and mailing capabilities to promote the charity (which drove Paterno crazy in a different way; he would not even let his own children use Penn State pencils at home).

These were problems that drove Paterno to distraction. He did not want to fire Sandusky; he had never publicly fired a coach. He felt loyalty to Sandusky for all his successes. He also understood the politics. Because of the team's defensive success, his gregarious personality, and The Second Mile, Sandusky was almost as prominent in the Penn State community as he was. Paterno turned seventy in 1996. Rip Engle had retired at fifty-nine, Bear Bryant at sixty-nine, and Vince Lombardi had quit the Green Bay Packers at fifty-four. Sandusky was seventeen years younger than Paterno. If a vote had been taken in 1997 to name the next Penn State coach, Sandusky probably would have won in a landslide. There were many who thought that change was long overdue.

Paterno felt certain that Sandusky did not have the work ethic, maturity, or dedication to be the next head coach. And besides, Paterno did not want to retire. Sandusky never said anything about it publicly, but he did tell a friend that Paterno had promised him the job when he retired, and then would not retire. Sandusky felt betrayed. Paterno told his family that Sandusky had stopped caring about coaching. Paterno felt betrayed. The animosity between the two men grew to the point where, according to three different coaches, change was inevitable.

AT THIS POINT, WE MUST swim in murkier waters. In spring of 1998, according to a Pennsylvania grand jury presentment, Sandusky met with one of the many boys he knew from The Second Mile and brought him to Holuba Hall, the indoor practice facility on campus where the football team trained. The boy was identified as "Victim 6" in the presentment. Sandusky and the boy worked out together, and the boy told investigators that Sandusky did some things that made him feel uncomfortable. Victim 6 said that Sandusky put his hand on his knee, wrestled with him on a mat in Holuba Hall, and handed him shorts to put on even though the boy was already wearing shorts. Then, Victim 6 said, Sandusky insisted that they shower, even though the boy did not feel sweaty. In the shower, Sandusky allegedly grabbed the boy, picked him up, and said, "I'm going to squeeze your guts out."

When the boy got home, he told his mother what had happened. She was shocked and enraged that Sandusky had showered with her son and reported the incident to Penn State University police, who had jurisdiction over the campus. The investigation led to a hundred-page police report and at least two recorded conversations between Sandusky and the boy's mother on or around May 13 and May 19; the latter included a haunting quote from Sandusky: "I was wrong. I wish I could get forgiveness. I know I won't get it from you. I wish I was dead." Sandusky was questioned directly by detectives and told not to shower with young boys. The case was closed by Centre Country District Attorney Ray Gricar (who disappeared years later under mysterious circumstances, sparking many conspiracy theories). Sandusky was also investigated by Centre County Child and Youth Services, but, for reasons that are not clear, the agency did not indicate the report, which would have put Sandusky's name on the Pennsylvania State-wide Central Register of child abusers.

In 2011, Sandusky was charged with more than fifty counts of sexual abuse of children. In 2012, he was convicted of forty-five counts.

In his grand jury testimony, Paterno stated that he did not recall hearing about the 1998 incident, but he admitted that rumors about Sandusky could have been discussed in his presence. In the last months of his life, he sounded more sure that he was never told about the 1998 incident. Sally Jenkins of the *Washington Post* interviewed Paterno a week before he died and wrote, "Paterno insists he was completely unaware of a 1998 police investigation into a report from a Second Mile mother that Sandusky had inappropriately touched her son in a shower." This denial matches what Paterno told me.

"I don't want to say Jerry was the last guy I would ever expect something like that from," he said, "because I don't want to exaggerate. But he would have been one of the last guys I would have expected it from. Jerry was a man's man, you know, a tough guy. This is not exactly my field of expertise, but I certainly never thought anything like that about Jerry." As we will see, the truth is cloudier than that. In the months after Paterno died, some evidence surfaced that he had been told something about the 1998 incident, though what he was told remained unclear.

There is reason to believe that, whatever Paterno was told, it did not make much of an impact on him. The coaches' meeting that leads this section was held on May 26, 1998—precisely at the time Sandusky was being investigated—and his detailed and pointed notes make no mention of any investigation. Also, by the late 1990s, he had explored numerous options for removing Sandusky from his coaching staff. He tried to start a football program at one of Penn State's satellite campuses with Sandusky as head coach; it didn't pan out. He tried to find Sandusky a job in athletic administration; Sandusky refused to consider it. If Paterno did know the details of the 1998 investigation, he might have used it as a way to get rid of Sandusky. He did not. The fact is, Sandusky coached with Penn State for two more seasons, the second of those being one of the most frustrating and infuriating of Joe Paterno's coaching life.

WHEN SANDUSKY SUDDENLY DECIDED TO retire in 1999, it surprised many people. From the outside, he seemed to be at the top of his game. He was fifty-five years old, decorated as a coach, celebrated as a humanitarian, beloved by Penn State fans and players alike. His retirement would later be used as circumstantial evidence that Paterno, knowing about the 1998 incident, quietly pushed him out.

Some evidence, however, points to the contrary. The notes Paterno wrote to himself leading up to the retirement did not contain any reference to the 1998 investigation. These files could have been censored, of course, but there were so many private notes in the files that it seems unlikely. Multiple sources, including Sue Paterno and several Penn State administrators, confirmed that Paterno made several attempts to move Sandusky into another job before the 1998 incident occurred. "Jerry was the second most famous coach in Pennsylvania," Sue said. "And the perception was that he was a great coach. Joe knew that if he tried too hard to push Jerry out, there would be an uproar."

In May 1999, when Paterno was seventy-two, the school announced a special retirement program in which employees could get a large percentage of their retirement package early. Sandusky showed interest. He was fifty-five and had grown tired of waiting for Paterno to retire. He went to see Paterno, and the discussion did not go well. Paterno would say he unloaded on Sandusky about his dwindling work ethic, his divided attention, and his lack of effort as a defensive strategist. He told Sandusky he would not be the next head coach at Penn State. Sandusky mentioned the early retirement package, and Paterno suggested it might be a good time for him to take it. Both men later said that the 1998 incident was never discussed.

Paterno said of the meeting, "I told Jerry he wasn't going to be the next coach. I think that disappointed him a lot, and he was angry and hurt. I can't really blame him for that, but it was the decision I made. He decided to retire."

Sandusky did take the retirement package, but he had a series of demands, another sign that the 1998 investigation was not the reason for the retirement. It's hard to imagine his being in a position to negotiate if that was the case. He negotiated his deal almost entirely with Athletic Director Tim Curley. The Lancaster, Pennsylvania, newspaper, the *New Era*, reported in 1999, "Interestingly, Sandusky said he never informed Paterno of his decision. Instead, he went to Penn State athletic director Tim Curley. . . . In fact, Sandusky and Paterno didn't confer on the subject very much at all, even before a decision was made. 'We talked some, but I didn't talk to him that much about it,' Sandusky said."

Sandusky wanted to maintain an office on campus and access to various athletic operations. This was something several other coaches had been granted on their retirement. But he had other, more formidable demands, the big one being the chance to coach the Penn State defense for the 1999 season. It was obvious why he wanted this: the 1999 defense was one of the most talented in the school's history. Sandusky still aspired to be a head coach, and he knew that coaching this defense could make him an attractive prospect to other schools. Paterno's concession on this is harder to figure; he would say before he died that he thought Sandusky had earned the right to coach the 1999 team because of his many years of service. In other words, he acquiesced out of loyalty. Undoubtedly, Paterno was also being practical; Sandusky retired in May, and it would have been disruptive to replace a defensive coordinator so late in the year. Whatever his reasons, Paterno allowed Sandusky to coach the 1999 season, something else that seems unlikely had he been conscious of Sandusky's secret life. But even for reasons having solely to do with football, letting Sandusky coach was a decision Paterno would deeply regret.

• • •

THE 1999 SEASON, SO FULL of promise at the start, developed into a disaster. Paterno had long believed that the Penn State program tracked through peaks and valleys. He saw the 1999 team as potentially his last great peak. The defense was anchored by defensive end Courtney Brown and linebacker LaVar Arrington, who would make history by becoming the No. 1 and No. 2 picks in the 2000 NFL draft. (This was just the third time in the sixty-four year history of the draft that the top two picks had come from the same school.) There were future NFL stars all over the roster. That team was bursting with talent, so much so that *Sports Illustrated* ranked Penn State the preseason No. 1 team in America. "Joe knows this can be a special year," an unnamed player told the magazine's Tim Layden, "and doesn't want anything to mess it up."

The tension between Paterno and Sandusky gurgled just below the surface. At the team's Media Day in August, the defensive players said they wanted a photo taken with Sandusky. As Paterno walked out of range, Sandusky barked out, "I've waited thirty years for that." He laughed. Paterno did not.

Still, with so much talent, and with the hope that Sandusky would refocus in his final year, Paterno felt optimistic. Penn State opened the season by destroying fourth-ranked Arizona 41–7. A week later, even Paterno's best efforts at sportsmanship could not prevent his team from scoring 70 points against Akron. As November began, Penn State was 9-0 and had defeated four teams ranked in the top twenty. But Paterno sensed there was something wrong. The defense was not dominant; they had not put together a shutout, and with this kind of talent, Paterno thought, this team should be pitching shutouts. The defense gave up 23 points to Miami, which had an excellent offense, but then gave up 24 to Indiana and 25 to Purdue. Reporters made clear in their stories that Paterno was edgier than usual.

On November 6, Penn State played Minnesota. It was Paterno's

400th game as head coach. It was also Penn State's homecoming. There were almost 97,000 people in the stands. Minnesota was coached by Glen Mason, who idolized Paterno so intensely that he began wearing ties on the sidelines to be like Joe. It seemed like a nice setup for Penn State, but the game did not go as expected. With less than two minutes left, Penn State led 23–21 and had the ball on the Minnesota 33-yard line on fourth down. Paterno could have had his kicker try a 50-yard field goal (the wind would have been at kicker Travis Forney's back), but he didn't feel good about the chances. He decided—and he never wavered from the rightness of this decision—that the best chance he had to win the game was to punt the ball and make Minnesota drive the length of the field against the most talented defense in America. "I didn't think they could do it," he said.

Minnesota did do it. The Gophers stumbled down the field, over-coming a sack by Arrington and a crushing hit by David Fleischhauer. They found themselves facing fourth down and 16 on the Penn State 40-yard line. Minnesota quarterback Billy Cockerham flung the ball downfield, all the way to the Penn State 13. The ball might have been tipped by Penn State's Derek Fox; it definitely deflected off Minnesota receiver Ron Johnson. Then, somehow, the ball was caught by an-other Minnesota receiver, Arland Bruce. When asked after the game if the play involved luck or skill, Cockerham did not hesitate. "Luck," he said. Three plays later, just before the clock expired, Minnesota's Dan Nystrom kicked the field goal that beat Penn State.

The press pounded Paterno for not having tried the field goal. "Young athletes can make mistakes under pressure and so can veteran coaches," Joe Lapointe wrote in the New York Times. "In his 400th game as coach of Penn State today, Joe Paterno made a difficult decision that might have cost his team a chance for a national cham-pionship." Other reporters followed suit. Closer to home, the Daily Collegian published a column blasting Paterno for not having tried a field goal.

But Paterno, as self-critical as he was, did not blame himself for this loss. In his mind, he had done exactly the right thing: he had relied on what was supposed to be a great defense, a defense that would never allow a team to drive the length of the field in the final minutes, lucky play or not. "It wasn't just Jerry," Paterno would say. "It was all us coaches. That should have been a great defense. And it wasn't."

Things got worse. A week later, again at home, this time on Senior Day against Michigan, Penn State built a 27–17 lead with less than ten minutes left. Once again Paterno felt sure that his defense would not blow the lead. Once again, he was wrong. Michigan's young quarterback, Tom Brady, scored a touchdown and threw for another to give Michigan a 31–27 victory. Again the press blamed the offense, which was indeed anemic (Penn State had just 7 yards rushing for the game) and sloppy (they lost three fumbles). Even LaVar Arrington seemed to suggest that the offense could have helped out more. "It seemed like we were out there a lot," he told reporters.

Again, though, Paterno's fury focused on the defensive failures. How could the team win when it gave up 31 points? When Penn State lost again the next week—this time a 35–28 embarrassment to Michigan State, with the Spartans' T. J. Duckett scoring four touchdowns— the collapse was complete. Years later, Paterno would call 1999 his worst coaching job. "We let those kids down," he admitted. When I asked him if Sandusky deserved the lion's share of the blame, he shrugged. "We all deserve the blame."

Penn State played Texas A&M in the Alamo Bowl, and for this game the team was motivated. Penn State won 24–0. This kind of dominant defensive performance only made Paterno angrier; it suggested what the season might have been. When the game ended, the players gave Sandusky the game ball. "Man, it was like a Hollywood script," Arrington told reporters.

"Will you miss Joe Paterno?" *Sports Illustrated*'s Jack McCallum asked Sandusky.

"Well, not exactly," he replied.

• • •

WHEN THE SEASON ENDED, THERE were various celebrations for Sandusky. Paterno was conspicuously absent. He released a statement on the day Sandusky's retirement was announced: "We can't say enough about what he has brought to the football program as an exceptional coach, a fine player and a person of great character and integrity." But he did not answer questions, and he did not say much publicly about Sandusky. He did not even offer the expected nice comment about Sandusky for Jack McCallum's *Sports Illustrated* story. At the team banquet, Paterno usually called up the seniors individually and said something about them, but this time he told Guido D'Elia that he would rather not. D'Elia recalled, "He told me, 'We let those players down. We did a terrible job coaching them. I can't stand up there and just act like it's a celebration.' "

Paterno appeared briefly at Sandusky's retirement celebration in April; he left early, claiming a "prior commitment." Shortly afterward, at Penn State's Media Day, he unloaded on Sandusky's coaching deficiencies, while carefully not using his name:

- People don't realize that we have not been a good defensive team since we've been in the Big Ten.
- My biggest concern is for us to get back to where we're a good defensive team.
- You win by forcing turnovers, not getting stupid penalties, and the team that plays tough, hard-nosed defense ends up winning most of the time.
- If we're going to be a better football team, we can't be seventieth [nationally] defensively.

And perhaps most pointed:

- We've got to improve on defense. We've got to do things better as a coordinated defense than we did at times last year.

That word, *coordinated*, was the direct hit. Sandusky, after all, had been defensive coordinator. Paterno was so eager to eliminate Sandusky's fingerprints from the team that he got rid of the defensive coordinator title and instead called Tom Bradley assistant coach in charge of defense and cornerbacks. He later regretted making his feelings about Sandusky so public, and he tried to clear the air a bit by telling reporter Gordie Jones of the Lancaster (Pennsylvania) *Intelligencer*, "Jerry did a great job." However, even in that story, he could not keep himself from saying that the team had to recruit better because Sandusky had "not done a lot of recruiting in recent years."

By then, Sandusky and Penn State Athletic Director Tim Curley had worked out the final details of a retirement package, which included professor emeritus status, access to athletic facilities (including the locker rooms), an office near the football building, a parking pass, and access to Penn State email. Paterno was not directly involved in the negotiations, and he would say at the end of his life that he was opposed to allowing Sandusky access to the football program, simply because he did not want the potential for distraction. When I told Paterno that people would find it hard to believe that he could not have influenced Sandusky's retirement package, he said, "People like to give me too much power. That's Tim's department. I told Tim how I felt. He worked out the deal as he saw fit."

Through the years, Paterno worked with a lot of coaches. Some retired. Some left for jobs at other schools. Some, like longtime offensive coordinator Fran Ganter, found jobs in athletic administration. It was business. In Paterno's mind, Jerry Sandusky was no longer his concern.

Joe Paterno at a rally in State College for Adam Taliaferro *(Penn State University Archives, Pennsylvania State University Libraries)*

Adam

aterno felt sure that with Sandusky off the staff and with a few changes, everything would feel new and exciting again. Everyone talked about how energetic he seemed as the 2000 season started. He tinkered with everything. He had the players' sheet of rules and regulations rewritten so that it was a little bit stricter but also a little bit fresher. (Paterno added, "As they said in *The Lion King*: *Remember who you are.*") He worked hard to be more active in practice, to challenge coaches more, to do anything to eliminate the bad taste of the 1999 season.

But the 2000 season turned out to be the worst of Paterno's career. It crashed before it even began. In May, Penn State quarterback Rashard Casey and a friend were arrested for aggravated assault against an off-duty police officer outside a bar in Hoboken, New Jersey. What made matters worse was that it appeared to be a racial incident; Casey was black, and the police officer, who was white, was with a black woman. Casey went to see Paterno in his office. "Rashard looked me in the eye and said, 'Coach, I didn't do anything,'" Paterno recalled. "I knew Rashard. I knew what was in his heart. And I believed him."

Paterno announced that he would not discipline Casey and would start him in the first game of the season. This set off a firestorm, with columnists across the country calling Paterno a hypocrite and a sellout. "Just a guess," a Pittsburgh columnist wrote. "If the Penn State long snapper had been charged with assault, he would have been kicked off the team." Most of the stories that criticized Paterno's decision to play Casey also mentioned that Paterno was only seven victories away from passing Bear Bryant for most victories by a Division I-A coach. "People rush to judgment and they want to believe the worst," Paterno responded.

At the end of the season, it was announced that Casey would not be indicted. In time, he would be awarded a settlement in his own lawsuit against the Hoboken Police Department for malicious prosecution and violation of his civil rights. Paterno had been right; Casey was not guilty. "May they burn in First Amendment Hell!" Casey's lawyer Dennis McAlvey said of all the people who had convicted Casey in the press. Paterno did not say anything at all. By then few Penn State football fans even cared.

The reason few cared: Penn State kept losing. The Nittany Lions began the season ranked twenty-second in the country, but in their first game they got pounded by Southern California. Then, in perhaps the most shocking loss of the entire Paterno era, they lost to Toledo 24–6. In retrospect the loss was not so shocking: Toledo was a very good team, probably better than Penn State. But at the time it suggested a colossal shift in college football. Penn State was supposed to destroy teams like Toledo. After the game, Penn State running back Larry Johnson (son of assistant coach Larry Johnson Sr.) did something perhaps even more shocking than the loss: he ripped the coaching staff. "Everything we do is too predictable," he told reporters. "Everybody knows what we are doing. The system has been around too long. We've got coaches who have been here for thirty years, twenty years, it seems like things never change."

Penn State lost again two weeks later, to Pitt, and suddenly there was a lot of talk about Paterno's age. He was seventy-three. His team looked out of sorts. He was still six victories away from passing Bear Bryant's record, and many people thought that record was what motivated him. His son Jay thought he knew better: "The people who think that Joe cares about the wins record just don't understand what makes him tick."

Paterno downplayed his age and the slow start. "I work harder at coaching today than I have ever worked in my life," he told the *New York Times*, one of several news organizations that sent someone to State College to find out what was going on with Penn State football. When asked on his weekly radio show how he maintained his composure through the tough start, he answered, "I guess I'm philosophical." Paterno figured if he just kept pushing and demanding and insisting, things would get back to normal. It had always worked before.

ADAM TALIAFERRO WAS A BRIGHT and talented freshman who grew up outside of Philadelphia. His story is familiar to anyone who follows Penn State football because it is the story of so many of Paterno's players: he was recruited by numerous schools, by flamboyant and charismatic coaches, but he was drawn to Penn State by Paterno's honesty. "Coach Paterno didn't make me any guarantees. He didn't tell me, 'You will start as a freshman' or 'You will be an All-American.' Other coaches said that stuff. But he just told me that Penn State was a good place for me, that I was more than a football player, that I could do anything and that he would always help me."

The Taliaferro path was like hundreds of others. Paterno was as hard on him as he was on every freshman, telling him on more than one occasion that he was useless and not Penn State material. "Play like that," Paterno told him once, "and I'll send you back to New Jersey."

As mentioned, one of the great dilemmas of Paterno's coaching life was how to handle freshmen. He believed deeply that freshmen were not ready physically (in most cases) or emotionally (in all cases) to play college football. Yet he played freshmen. He would say he had little choice if he wanted Penn State to be competitive. And he did want that very much. "I've been a hypocrite about that my whole life," he said. "I always knew that it was wrong to play freshmen. But I did it. True, I did it less than most people. But I still did it."

He did do it less than most. For years, other coaches would tell eager high school seniors, *You don't want to go to Penn State. They don't play freshmen.* But as time went on, Paterno played freshmen more and more. He knew that playing freshmen was the new reality of college football, and he did not deny that he was making another concession for success. The last great coaching surge of his life would be powered by freshmen.

But before that, in 2000, he played freshman Adam Taliaferro. "It was actually a bit surprising," Taliaferro said. "I really didn't think I would get a chance to play much as a freshman." Taliaferro had shown a great sense of the game, a great feel for what to do in confusing moments on the field, and this was what mattered most to Paterno. Before the 2000 season, he had given his players a score sheet that showed exactly how he and the other coaches would grade them. It looked like this:

Attitude (10 points). This means behavior off the field, class attendance, grades, appearance, maturity, respect for teammates and other people, and being on time for meetings and appointments.

Athletic ability (10 points). This is a tough one. . . . Remember, if you have the essential quality—attitude—our evaluation of your athletic ability will be based just on that and nothing else.

Speed (8 points). No explanation needed.

Toughness (8 points). It isn't only physical, but also mental toughness.

Durability (8 points). If you cannot practice or you cannot stay healthy, you really don't have much of a chance to be a significant part of a great team. This is not to say that there are not legitimate injuries, but I do mean to say that some people are more prone to injuries than others.

Character (6 points). Are you a good person, an honest person, a moral person? Are you dependable and responsible?

Strength (8 points). Obvious.

Coachable (6 points). We all can get better and some people are not as good as they think they are. Better techniques don't come easily and as a result some people rationalize they don't need to work to improve.

Experience (2 points). I only give this 2 points because . . . we are going to play the best players on this year's squad, not the best on last year's.

TALIAFERRO SCORED HIGH ON EVERYTHING except experience. He was tough, fast, coachable, and, more than anything, had a marvelous attitude. "Adam Taliaferro would have been a pro," said Paterno. "I have no doubt in my mind."

Then came the Ohio State game. It was a gray, rainy day. Penn State was overmatched. Taliaferro was in the game with less than two minutes left—Ohio State had a 38–6 lead at the time—and he set himself to tackle tailback Jerry Westbrooks. Taliaferro's helmet hit Westbrooks's knee, and Taliaferro fell. His helmet crashed to the turf. His body rolled over. He had no feeling from the neck down. Paterno ran onto the field, looked at Taliaferro's face, and though he had seen injured players a thousand times, he was shocked by what he saw. Trainers carried Taliaferro off the field on a stretcher. Players on both sides prayed. The look on Taliaferro's face stayed with Joe Paterno for the rest of his life: "Seeing the fear in Adam's eyes was the worst moment I've ever had on the football field." Jay Paterno would say he saw his father cry twice, once when his mother, Florence, died in 1989, and the second time when he saw Adam paralyzed on the football field.

"I remember we had a long walk home after a game," Jay Paterno said. "This was after Adam. And Joe told me that every player we have, someone—maybe a parent, grandparent, but someone—poured their life and soul into that young man. They are handing that young man off to us. They are giving us their treasure. And it's our job to make sure we give them back that young man intact.

"I think he felt like he had failed to protect Adam Taliaferro. Of course, he knew that football is a dangerous game and that people get hurt; Adam wasn't the first player to have a serious injury. But I think with Adam being a freshman and this great kid, the way the injury happened, it really hit him hard."

Adam's story would have a happy ending, with Paterno playing a lead role in it, but the rest of the season went badly. Penn State finished 5-7, its worst record under Paterno to that point, and he did not want to talk with me about it. "It's in the past," he said. His friends believed that the season had diminished him. "I think Joe looked at what happened to Adam," said Guido D'Elia, "and he thought, 'What am I doing with my life?' " But Paterno said he never once considered retiring: "No, no, no. Absolutely not. What good would walking away do? No, the only time I ever really thought about walking away was after the 1979 season. After that, whenever we had lows—and we had a lot of them—I would view it as a challenge." He told *Sports Illustrated*'s Rick Reilly at the end of that dreadful 2000 season, "Every time I'd get to thinking, 'Man, this isn't worth it,' I realized how important it is. . . . I knew they needed me. And I needed them."

● ● ●

PATERNO WAS NOT THE SAME. His energy level was visibly lower, his crankiness harsher. His relationship with the media had been deteriorating for years, but at this point it collapsed altogether. He had long thought that sportswriters had moved out of the business of writing about sports and into the business of controversy. He thought that the twenty-four-hour appetite of the Internet and talk radio made reporters sloppier and more interested in being first than being right. "I feel bad saying this, but I just don't trust reporters," he said.

The feeling from some reporters was mutual. Many of these, especially the younger ones who did not remember a more genial Paterno (and it seemed they were all so young), thought he had become a bully and had lost touch.

"I think it is true that he didn't like the way many reporters were doing their jobs, and I agree with him to a point," one of Paterno's friends said. "But I think it's also true that Joe changed. He became more insular. He wasn't interested in having a relationship with reporters like he did when he was younger. He didn't see the value in it anymore. He saw the media as a nuisance or worse. And he treated some of the reporters badly. I think that hurt him in the end."

Except for coaching, Paterno began to see almost every demand on his time as a nuisance. He slowed his recruiting travel; he rarely showed up in parents' living rooms, where he had always been one of the great recruiting closers in college football history. He mostly stopped traveling around the region to give speeches, and he mostly stopped trying to charm donors and Penn State board members. He was seventy-four years old. He wanted to be left alone to coach his football team.

ON A SATURDAY MORNING AT the beginning of February 2001, Paterno got a phone call from a graduate assistant named Mike

McQueary. Everything surrounding this incident would become a point of contention, even the date. Originally, prosecutors—and McQueary himself—seemed convinced the call was made in March 2002. Later, based on various clues uncovered during the investigation, the date was moved back to February 10, 2001. Paterno never claimed to know the date. His memory of the entire incident was fuzzy.

If we assume the date was February 10, 2001, it was the day Paterno went to Pittsburgh to be inducted into the Pittsburgh Sports Hall of Fame. The city of Pittsburgh did not love Joe Paterno, because he had extinguished the Penn State–Pittsburgh rivalry by refusing to play the game after 2000. He was hoping to diffuse some of the tension with his speech. He was also preparing for the annual coaches' trip sponsored by Nike, perhaps the highlight of his and Sue's year. The trip was the following week.

Mike McQueary grew up in State College and played quarterback for Paterno. The football dream was infused in him by his father, John. The *Pittsburgh Post-Gazette* would tell this story: When Mike was born in 1974, John raced to the phone, called the Notre Dame football office, and told the coach, Ara Parseghian (or his secretary; John could not remember), that Notre Dame's 1992 starting quarterback had just entered the world. John and the family were hurt when Notre Dame chose to recruit another Pennsylvania high school quarterback, Ron Powlus, instead of Mike. But then Joe Paterno came to the house, and even though John had carefully crafted a strategy for picking a school, complete with color-coded charts, Mike was so awed he couldn't help himself. "Coach Paterno," he said, "I'd really like to commit to Penn State."

He was a team captain his senior year, set a school record for most passing yards in a game, and then he kicked around for a while in pro football, chasing that goal all the way to Scotland, where he played quarterback for the Scottish Claymores. When that dream fizzled out, he came back to Penn State to be a graduate assistant coach. He wanted desperately to coach full time. Later, in a letter to Paterno, he wrote, "I will someday be a head coach of a program. I know that and believe it to be true. . . . You might say, 'I will it to happen every day.' "

Mike McQueary claimed that when he called Paterno on February 10, 2001, Paterno told him, "If this is about a job, don't bother coming over because there are no openings." Paterno did not remember saying that, but the details do fit the date; the day before, it had been announced in the papers that receivers coach Kenny Jackson had left Penn State to take a job with the Pittsburgh Steelers. McQueary said it was not about a job. He had something important to tell him. Paterno invited him to the house.

Paterno remembered McQueary's nervousness more vividly than anything else. He remembered telling McQueary more than once to calm down as they sat at the kitchen table. McQueary had a hard time catching his breath. Though the conversation they had that morning would become critically important in the Jerry Sandusky investigation, both Paterno and McQueary had trouble remembering what was said. So, again, it is necessary to delve into that foggy world of memory and perspective.

McQueary's later confusion about the date is illustrative. When questioned by the police and the Pennsylvania grand jury almost a decade later, he was openly uncertain about the year. The one thing he did seem certain about was that the incident had occurred the Friday before Penn State's spring break. However, even that memory was faulty; the date that prosecutors eventually settled on—February 9, 2001—was three weeks before spring break.

Paterno and McQueary agreed that they discussed these details: On Friday night, McQueary had gone to the Lasch Football Building to drop off a pair of sneakers in his locker and pick up a few recruiting movies to watch at home. As he walked into the building, he heard two or three disturbing slapping sounds, sounds he thought were sexual. He also thought he heard the shower running, which was odd for a Friday night in February. He went to his locker, dropped off the shoes, and then he saw Jerry Sandusky and a young boy naked in the shower together.

Paterno remembered that even to extract this much information from McQueary that day was difficult. What struck Paterno most was just how edgy and uncomfortable McQueary was.

Here was what Paterno said about that conversation when I interviewed him in late November 2011:

Q: Did Mike say that he saw anything?
Paterno: I think he said he didn't really see anything. He said he might have seen something in a mirror.
Q: A mirror?
Paterno: Yeah, like the bathroom mirror. But he told me he wasn't sure he saw anything. He just said the whole thing made him uncomfortable.
Q: What did you think he saw?
Paterno: I didn't know. I thought he saw them horsing around. Maybe he thought he saw some fondling. I don't know about any of this stuff. But I could tell it made Mike very upset.
Q: What did you say to him?
Paterno: I told him he didn't have to tell me anything else. I told him he did the right thing bringing it to me, and that now it was my job to get him together with the right people for him to report it.
Q: Did you consider calling the police?
Paterno: To be honest with you, I didn't. This isn't my field. I didn't know what to do. I had not seen anything. Jerry didn't work for me anymore. I didn't have anything to do with him. I tried to look through the Penn State guidelines to see what I was supposed to do. It said that I was supposed to call Tim [Curley]. So I called him.
Q: That day?
Paterno: I'm pretty sure I called him that day. I know it was a

weekend, so I can't be a hundred percent sure, but I do
think I called him that day.

Q: And what did you say?

Paterno: I said, "I think there may be a problem here. You
need to get to the bottom of this."

This was nearly the same story Paterno told on several separate occasions, including in a short appearance to the Pennsylvania grand jury. There were times he was not as sure about when he called Curley—he could not recall for the grand jury if he had called at all over the weekend—and his memory of the actual conversation with McQueary was always blurry.

Q: Were you shocked?

Paterno: I wasn't really even sure what it was. Mike didn't give
me any details. I could just tell he was upset.

Q: Had you heard any rumors at all about Jerry Sandusky
[showering with boys]?

Paterno: Absolutely not. Maybe people talked about it, I don't
know. But I didn't hear anything.

Q: Did you think about investigating yourself?

Paterno: I wouldn't know how to investigate something like
this. I don't know anything about it. [Jerry] didn't work for
me. I had a meeting with Tim, and Gary [Schultz] might
have been there, and I told them what Mike had told me.
And they said they would get to the bottom of it. I trusted
Tim would take care of it. He's a good administrator. He
had negotiated the retirement deal with Jerry, and he was
still in contact with Jerry. Tim's a good person. I expected
him to handle it right.

Q: Did you ever follow up?

Paterno: No. I trusted Tim.

Q: Do you regret that?

Paterno: I did what I thought was the right thing. . . . If what they're saying about Jerry is true, I think we all wish we would have done more.

Paterno was almost eighty-five years old when I conducted this interview. He was going through both radiation and chemotherapy for lung cancer, and he was exhausted. It was more than ten years after the McQueary conversation. This is not to excuse or explain any contradictions or failures of memory, but to fairly set the stage. He never wavered from saying he wanted the truth to come out. After Paterno died, numerous Penn State interoffice emails were uncovered during the Sandusky investigation. None of the emails were written by or to Paterno—he did not have an email account—but at least three of the emails suggested that Paterno had missed key details.

First, the emails indicated he was told something about the 1998 incident. Two emails—both written by Athletic Director Tim Curley to school vice president Gary Schultz—suggest that Curley himself alerted Paterno to the investigation. On May 5, 1998, Curley wrote: "I have touched base with the Coach. Keep us posted. Thanks." And in a follow-up email, Curley wrote: "Coach is anxious to know where it stands." Neither of these emails say what Paterno was told about the investigation itself. Paterno was told that the investigation was closed by the State College District Attorney.

Second, it appears, based on another interoffice email, that Paterno was consulted about the 2001 incident, at least unofficially. In life, Paterno was probably criticized by admirers and supporters more for not following up than for any other nonaction. In a series of emails between Curley, Schultz, and president Graham Spanier, it is made clear that the three met without Paterno on Sunday, February 25, to discuss how to handle the Sandusky accusation. An email from Schultz to Curley after that meeting read: "Tim, I'm assuming that you've got the ball to (1) talk with the subject ASAP regarding the future appropriate use of the University facility; (2) contact the Chair of the Charitable Org and (3) contact the Dept of Welfare."

Two days later, Curley wrote that he wanted to have a meeting.

"After giving it more thought and talking it over with Joe yesterday—I am uncomfortable with what we agreed were the next steps. I am having trouble with going to everyone but the person involved." Curley then recommended meeting directly with Sandusky, to alert him to their knowledge of the first incident and to "indicate we feel there is a problem, and we want to assist the individual to get professional help." He went on to write: "We feel a responsibility at some point to inform his organization and maybe the other one about the incident." ("His organization" meant The Second Mile. It is possible "the other one" meant child services.)

When news of this email broke, the general media takeaway from this email chain was that Paterno had convinced Curley to back off reporting Sandusky and to handle this in-house. Others familiar with the emails believed instead that Paterno had demanded they confront Sandusky. It is entirely possible, with those opinions based only on a short email, that both explanations are wrong. Paterno had not talked about any follow-up meeting at all, and he died before the emails were discovered.

It is beyond the scope of this book to look at the role of anyone but Paterno in this harrowing affair, but it is certain that no one, Paterno included, was aware enough, courageous enough, or decent enough to stop a man who would be found guilty of forty-five counts of child molestation. Jerry Sandusky committed heinous crimes against children, and—as Paterno himself said—many people in and around State College would have deep regrets. Nobody—not the president of the school, not the athletic director, not the legendary coach—reported the incident to the police, and this would haunt a community, shatter the reputation of a great American university, and darken the legacy of the coach who made it his life's goal to strive for success with honor.

TEN AND A HALF YEARS after that conversation between Paterno and McQueary, a more complete and sinister picture appeared, and it appeared suddenly and brutally. The Pennsylvania grand jury released a presentment that charged Jerry Sandusky with forty counts of child abuse (later the total was fifty counts). The presentment was graphic and grotesque and included numerous charges of Sandusky indecently fondling, performing oral sex on, hugging, and kissing young boys who were involved in his charity, The Second Mile. Some of these alleged crimes happened on the Penn State campus. It was as revolting a document as most people will read in their lives, the most stomach-turning Paterno had ever read.

In the presentment, the story was this: On Friday, March 1, 2002 (later changed to Friday, February 9, 2001), at about 10 P.M., McQueary went to the Lasch Building. When he got there, he heard those rhythmic slapping sounds he described to Paterno. As he put his sneakers in the locker, he looked into the shower and saw a boy about ten years old with his hands up against the wall who was "being subjected to anal intercourse by a naked Sandusky." The next morning McQueary "went to Paterno's home, where he reported what he had seen."

The presentment, as such things do, made black and white what was a smoggy gray. When questioned, McQueary admitted that he did not see anything very clearly. He also said under oath that "out of respect," he had not used graphic terms and had not gone into much detail with Paterno. In this their memories coincided: Paterno said what McQueary told him was not even close in specifics or in brutality to what was in the presentment.

There is strong evidence that McQueary was much less certain about what he saw in the aftermath of the incident. According to testimony, that Friday night, after he left the Lasch Building, he went to his father's house to ask for advice. The two of them talked at some length, and then they called over a family friend, Dr. Jonathan Dranov. Dranov, a prominent doctor in the community, told Paterno family investigators in 2011, and a Pennsylvania jury in 2012, that McQueary said he heard some "sexual sounds" but could offer no more detail. Dranov said that three times he pressed McQueary to describe what he actually saw, and three times McQueary said that he did not see anything in the shower. Dranov conceded that McQueary might have been holding back; he too remembered just how upset McQueary was, which was why he kept pressing the issue. But at the end of the conversation McQueary continued to say that he did not see any act but that he heard those noises.

Dranov said McQueary's visual description was of a naked young boy in the doorway of the shower. McQueary then said he saw an arm pull the boy back out of the way, and seconds later Sandusky walked around the corner with a towel wrapped around his waist. Dranov and the McQuearys agreed that Mike had not seen enough to go to the police, and Dranov recommended that McQueary go to Paterno on that Saturday morning. Dranov conceded all those years later that, though the incident sounded bad, Sandusky's reputation as a community icon was still intact. He said he had never heard any rumors about Sandusky and that what McQueary had seen led to the possibility of a misunderstanding and "an innocent explanation."

Paterno would later say that if McQueary had told him he saw Sandusky raping a young boy, "We would have gone to the police right then and there, no questions asked." Whatever McQueary actually said that morning, Paterno heard something vague. He clearly did not want to think too much about it. He was seventy-five years old, from another time, and he would say he simply did not comprehend the potential gravity of the situation.

This must be said again: Paterno did not like Sandusky. Paterno had not wanted Sandusky to have access to the Lasch Building in the first place. He had pushed Sandusky out. Paterno did not feel like he should be involved for another reason: He knew that many fans and people in State College viewed Sandusky as the guy who should be coaching Penn State; he did not feel that he was in a position to get involved. He tried to make this clear to the grand jury: "Obviously, I was in a little bit of a dilemma since Mr. Sandusky was not working for me anymore." This reticence to publicly charge his former assistant and possible rival with molesting a child based on the agitated recollections of an assistant coach was something he had trouble explaining. He had gone by the book, word for word. He reported the conversation to Curley. This was what the law required him to do, and he did it. The Freeh report—and the public—concluded that it was not nearly enough.

THE 2001 SEASON PROVED TO be another painful one, though it began with joy. Paterno had spent every available moment with Adam Taliaferro in the hospital. He was there when they told Adam that a vertebra in his neck had burst and that his spinal cord had been bruised. He was there when doctors told Adam he had a 3 percent chance of walking again. And he was there when Adam said that he wanted to lead the team out of the tunnel to start the next season— and he would lead the team while walking.

"He was so positive," Taliaferro recalled. "He made me believe that I could do anything." In time, Taliaferro would graduate from Penn State, go to law school, and become a lawyer, and Paterno was with him at every step, pushing him, inspiring him, writing letters of recommendation for him. After Paterno died, Taliaferro successfully ran for a spot on the Penn State Board of Trustees, where he intended to keep alive Joe Paterno's vision for the school.

And at the start of the 2001 season, Taliaferro led the team out of the tunnel. He walked, even jogged, while the crowd in Beaver Stadium, the first crowd of 100,000 in Penn State history, cheered and cried. It was a beautiful beginning.

Then Penn State lost four games in a row, the worst start and longest losing streak of Paterno's career. The nation was watching closely. After planes crashed into the World Trade Center on September 11, Americans wanted something to celebrate. Paterno was supposed to lead that celebration. He started the season only two victories away from passing Bear Bryant. But the team kept losing. "As angry as I am right now, all I feel like doing is punching a wall," Paterno said after the team was crushed by Wisconsin.

"I don't think I'm too old," he told the *New York Times* after a 20–0 loss to Michigan.

"It's the late winter of Joe Paterno's coaching career, and what a cold time it has become," Ivan Maisel wrote in *Sports Illustrated*.

Paterno read books for strength. He read *Moby-Dick* again, and Michael Shaara's classic Civil War novel, *The Killer Angels*, and *The Red Badge of Courage*. He was looking for tales of triumph over adversity. In the fifth game of the season, Penn State beat Northwestern 38–35, and Paterno tied Bear Bryant's record. A week later, the Nittany Lions beat Ohio State at home in front of more than 108,000 people for the emotional victory that pushed Paterno past Bryant to the top of the all-time victories list. The word "finally" was in the headline in most newspapers.

"You know, every once in a while, people say 'You ought to get out of it,' " he told reporters after the game, a classic bit of understated Paterno humor since that was all anyone had said to him for months. "I think about it, and I think about how much it means to me, and the great moments I've had. I don't want to get out of it."

The team played better the rest of the season, but not a lot better. They finished with a losing record for the second year in a row.

EVERYBODY SEEMED TO HAVE A theory about why Paterno's team stopped winning. His age, of course, was the most prominent of these. He turned seventy-five after the 2001 season, and it was written again and again that the game had passed him by. There was talk that the move to the Big Ten prevented Penn State from ever being a national power again; the competition had grown too tough. There was talk about how Paterno's basic football philosophy—*Play great defense. Hold on to the football. Make fewer mistakes than your opponent*—could not win in the new reality of college football, where television and bowl connections and the money those generated drove the game.

But there was another prominent theory, one that would play a large role in the last decade of Paterno's life: that Paterno was simply not the same without Jerry Sandusky as his defensive coordinator.

"Most people don't realize how much Jerry meant," former star Brandon Short told *Sports Illustrated*. "He was just as much a part of Penn State as Joe Paterno is."

"Let us give credit to Jerry, not Joe, for all those wonderful years," a fan named Donald J. Smith wrote to the *Sunday News* of Lancaster, Pennsylvania. "No, I am afraid time has not passed by Joe Paterno. It has simply laid open before the world that Joe is an average coach who had some terrific assistants."

"I don't think people understand the impact Jerry Sandusky had," former player Mac Morrison told the *Seattle Times*. "He's not just an assistant coach. He has the best defensive mindset and defensive knowledge that I've ever known."

"The retirement of Jerry Sandusky removed a crucial pillar from the program's foundation," was the conclusion in the *Palm Beach Post*.

"The loss of longtime defensive coordinator Jerry Sandusky, who retired after the 1999 season, was a bigger blow than most people realized," argued the *Philadelphia Inquirer*.

"With each Penn State loss, the picture becomes more clear: Jerry Sandusky was the head football coach for the past twenty-five years, and Joe Paterno was apparently the director of marketing," an unnamed fan called in to the *Times Leader* in Wilkes-Barre, Pennsylvania.

And this in the *Bergen (New Jersey) Record*:

The defense, meanwhile, has not been as strong as years past, and some reason that the retirement two years ago of longtime defensive coordinator Jerry Sandusky was a turning point. At the University Creamery, the school's coffee house, Sandusky, like Paterno, has an ice cream named for him. Listed on the menu underneath the Peachy Paterno is the Sandusky Blitz, a banana and caramel swirl with chocolate-covered peanuts.

Victor Wills, a sophomore from Bethlehem, Pa., who works at the Creamery and plays the sousaphone in the marching band, said he wishes Sandusky would return, "So our defense will be the way it used to be and we'll be known again as 'Linebacker U.' "

These are only a few of the hundreds of things written and said about how Sandusky's retirement had exposed Joe Paterno. It would seem remarkable years later that, within a tight-knit community like State College, word of the 1998 investigation or McQueary's account had not leaked to someone in the media. But apparently, it had not. There was a powerful groundswell within the community to convince Paterno to retire, finally, and to bring Sandusky back as head coach. The sentiment was popular nationally too. So many who had admired Paterno, even grudgingly, were concerned that he was tarnishing his legacy by stumbling around as a coach when he could no longer compete.

Paterno refused to see it. He began to say things like "We're just a couple of plays away" and "We just need one or two breaks and we'll be back on top again." To many people, it sounded like Paterno was out of touch, but he believed it. "If I wake up one morning," he told an *Atlanta Constitution* reporter, "and believe the program would be better in someone else's hands, then it's over."

Paterno would live another decade after saying that. He would never believe that the program would be better in someone else's hands.

Joe Paterno hands the ball off to his brother, George, when they were teammates at Brown *(Penn State University Archives, Pennsylvania State University Libraries)*

Winter

George Paterno struggled with being Joe's younger brother. He had grown up in the same environment as Joe, going to Brooklyn Prep, playing football at Brown, serving in the army, but unlike Joe he never could find his life's center. "Joe is the doer," George would tell friends, "and I'm the dreamer." He worked as a football coach for a while. He was a police officer. He served as the radio color commentator of Penn State football, often criticizing his own brother on the air, which was a kick for everyone, including Joe. He enjoyed a drink and good company. He never married.

The brothers clashed often, as they had when they were young. But there was a deep connection that transcended friendship. George understood, in ways that few could, what drove Joe.

At the end of the 1992 season, for instance, Joe faced a difficult decision. He had a brilliant linebacker named Rich McKenzie on the team. McKenzie had been a star high school linebacker in Florida, the No. 1 high school linebacker in America, and he had gotten it into his head that great linebackers are supposed to go to Penn State. Paterno did not want him. McKenzie's grades were poor, his commitment to academics suspect. But McKenzie pleaded and Paterno made him a deal, similar to the deal he had made Bob White: if McKenzie would read three books over the summer and send book reports to Sue, and also agree to be tutored by Sue while in college, Paterno would give him a chance. McKenzie did the reports, and Paterno was impressed. For four years McKenzie teetered in his classes, always seemed on the brink of failing, but he managed to pull himself together. Paterno loved the kid. The whole family did. McKenzie even offered a toast at Jay Paterno's wedding. "This was a kid who, when he first got to Penn State, he couldn't even look you in the eye," Guido D'Elia said. "And by the time he left, he was a new man. He was ready to live a successful life. I don't want to overstate it, but Rich McKenzie was exactly the reason why Joe Paterno coached football."

In his senior year, however, McKenzie let things slide even more than usual. He thought he had failed a class, so he stopped going to practice for a while, and he stopped putting extra effort into his other schoolwork. Paterno warned him and warned him again, but McKenzie would not straighten up. At the end of the season, Penn State was invited to play in the Blockbuster Bowl near McKenzie's hometown of Fort Lauderdale. Paterno first decided he would not take McKenzie to the game, but Sue and Jay lobbied for him. "It's his hometown," Jay said. "All his friends will be there. He's been so great for Penn State." So Joe took him along, but he told McKenzie he would not play. "I've been fired," McKenzie told the media.

For all his bravado, Paterno was not sure benching McKenzie was the right thing to do. Yes, McKenzie had broken the rules and had to be punished; Paterno had always leaned to the side of the rules. But Paterno also understood that McKenzie had worked much harder than some of the other players to achieve as much as he had in school. None of it had been easy for him, and he had come so far. This game was in his hometown. Paterno wondered if benching the player was really fair.

Joe asked George to take a walk with him. Together they walked around Joe Robbie Stadium near Fort Lauderdale and talked about what to do. George told Joe he should play the kid. For one thing, the other players on the team were watching closely and would not think it fair if he didn't play McKenzie in his hometown in the last game of his college career. More to the point, though, George thought Penn State had no chance of winning without McKenzie. This bowl game was against Stanford and its brilliant coach, Bill Walsh. CBS was promoting the game as "the Genius versus the Legend." "I'm not sure which one I am," Paterno joked before the game. But to George it was no joke. He did not want to see his brother beaten by Walsh, leaving everyone to think he had been outcoached.

Joe listened carefully and finally said, "Ahhh, mind your own business."

He did not start McKenzie. He did allow him to play in a handful of plays in the second half, but that was after the game had been decided. Penn State lost 24–3, fulfilling George's fears. But the larger point was that Joe would listen to George, even when they disagreed. And there were not many people Joe Paterno listened to at the end. George wrote Joe a letter once about how his head was getting too big, and Joe took it to heart.

Paterno needed such balance. He feared getting too comfortable, being surrounded by yes men, being treated like some sort of icon rather than a real flesh-and-blood person. But even as he feared those things, they were happening. He had few close friends even in his younger days; it was not in his nature to open up. During the 2000 and 2001 seasons, when Penn State was losing and people were questioning his very ability as a coach, he would get encouraging calls from people all the time—and these calls made him crazy. He didn't need anybody to tell him that everything would work out. He didn't want anyone to tell him that. George was one of the few to understand this.

In 1997, George published a book, *Joe Paterno: The Coach from Byzantium*. It included some criticisms of Joe, and it created family friction. Joe insisted he did not care. Heck, he offered a quote for the back cover: "My brother tells me that the book is 80% good, 10% bad, and 10% his own personal observations. That's fine with me." Joe would always say he never read the book.

But Sue read the book, as did other family members. Most of the book *was* proud and supportive and admiring, but the negative stuff was what was played in the press. George seemed to buy into the idea that Sandusky's coaching genius was at the heart of Paterno's success. He made some unflattering remarks about Sue and her role in Paterno's coaching life, and at different times in the book, he called Joe sanctimonious, egotistical, self-centered, and forgetful of the virtues that made him successful in the first place. Everyone in the Paterno family found it appalling that George would write such a book while Joe was going through tough times. Some family members never could forgive him. "George was not in a very good place when he wrote that book," one close friend said. "He was very sick. He was in a lot of pain. And I think he lashed out. It caused a lot of pain, most of it to him."

"I don't mean this to sound negative," Scott Paterno said near the end of Joe's life, "but Uncle George was tough. He was tough. He was tough on my mom. He grew up in Brooklyn and had a different style from everyone else. He liked to have a couple of pops, and he had a drinking problem. He wasn't a mean drunk or anything like that. . . . He was the guy that would call Joe up and tell him off. There's nobody that does that anymore."

Joe felt deep regret about how George's life had turned out. Close to the end, George lived alone in New York. He was ill, and he was suffering. "I think he felt disappointed," Joe said. One of the thrills of

George's late life was appearing in a 1996 *Sports Illustrated* story titled "One Big Happy Valley Family." The story was positive and told of the fascinating relationship between the two brothers. But even this George wrote about with some sadness in his book:

> *The author kept implying that Joe and I are very different people. I convinced him we had the same ideals but used different methods in postulating and sharing them. Joe was a pragmatic idealist operating within the establishment, and I was the romantic idealist and dreamer operating out of the loop. The author decided I was an eccentric independent with a free spirit. I guess he's right. The article was well received and many people told me they identified with me and even though they were not famous either, they had productive and good lives. We all can't be heroes.*

At the beginning of 2002, Joe moved George back to State College and checked him into a hospital. He tried to bridge the gap. Some of Joe's children and grandchildren came to visit. George died in June of that year, and his death took a terrible toll on Joe, one he would not talk about publicly. "Their relationship was complicated," one friend said. "But when George died, I really believe, there was a void in Joe's life that nobody else could fill."

WHEN THE 2002 SEASON BEGAN, Paterno was surrounded by doubts. Reporters, alumni, and even longtime fans had come to believe that Paterno's time as a successful football coach had expired.

"I really don't care what people say," he told the *New York Times*. "I try to tell young coaches, the minute you start reacting to criticism, forget it. It affects your judgment and ability to make tough decisions. You lose your courage."

The team improved and won nine games in 2002, in large part due to the inspired running of Larry Johnson, who had so blatantly criticized the coaches two years earlier. Johnson was a powerful run-

ning back, but even more than talent and speed, his success origi-
nated in a deep rage that propelled him forward, a rage Paterno had
a hard time understanding. Paterno had called Johnson "high-strung"
and "impatient," and he kept him on the bench for three years. Johnson stewed as he waited for his chance to get on the field, and when
he got the opportunity he ran with a power that no Penn State runner,
not even John Cappelletti or Lydell Mitchell, had ever shown. He
blasted his way for 327 yards against Indiana. When he needed 264
yards against Michigan State to become the first Penn State running
back to rush for more than 2,000 yards, he got 279 in the first half.

Even during a modestly successful season—modest by Paterno's
high standards—there were signs that Paterno had lost his way. Penn
State began the season with three straight victories but then lost in
overtime to Iowa. As soon as the game ended, Paterno raced after one
of the officials, Dick Honig, grabbed him, and screamed about two
calls that he felt sure were missed. The image of seventy-five-year-old
Joe Paterno running after an official and grabbing him was striking; it
reminded some longtime college football observers of the sad scene at
the end of Woody Hayes's career, when he hit an opposing player at
the end of his last loss.

Paterno did not appreciate the comparison. He didn't hit anybody;
he didn't think he had done anything wrong. "Why should I regret
it?" he barked at reporters. "What did I do? I did not make contact
with him. . . . I was running into the locker room and grabbed him by
the shirt and said, 'Hey, Dick, you had two lousy calls.' "

Paterno had always demanded that his players treat the officials
with respect. He had always responded to missed calls with thoughtful irritation; he said that in life some calls go your way and some
don't. And although, yes, he privately grumbled to coaches and
friends about referees who he thought had cost him victories, he also
knew that through the years Penn State probably got more close calls
than most.

But suddenly that perspective had dissipated. He went public with his complaints. The Iowa incident was just the first. Two weeks after that, Penn State lost to Michigan in a devastatingly close game that may have been influenced by a close call that went against Penn State receiver Tony Johnson with just forty seconds left in the game. The officials ruled him out of bounds on a catch. The replays suggested he was in bounds, though there may have been some question about whether or not he had possession of the ball. It was probably a good catch. Paterno went mad. He had Tim Curley write a letter to the Big Ten demanding a full review. He publicly called into question the character of the officials by asking why three of them lived in Michigan. He even allowed a little referee effigy to be placed in front of his house; he would not say whether he put it there himself. He told reporters, "You've got a bunch of kids who are busting their butts to win a football game. . . . You owe it to them to make sure the game is won by the players."

It seemed so out of character for Paterno, who had managed, with few exceptions, to harness his competitive fury and act consistently with his belief that winning and losing weren't the most important things. Many across the nation wondered if he had lost his mind. "What's Up with Joe Pa?" *Sports Illustrated* asked. The *New York Times* wondered why Paterno was taking all the attention away from Larry Johnson, a legitimate Heisman Trophy candidate. (Johnson finished third in the Heisman voting, and there were those who thought Paterno should have worked harder to promote him.) "He knows better than anyone that no coach or argument should be bigger than his players," the *Times'* Joe Drape wrote.

Paterno seemed to realize that he had overstepped, and he backed off a little. But it was clear that something was different. He was testier. "I had known Joe well for more than forty years," one friend said, "and one day he called me into his office and just started screaming at me. He disagreed with something I had said, and he just tore into me. . . . Joe had always needed to be right. That was part of his personality. He used to joke about it. But I think as he got older, that part of him grew stronger. We all lose a bit of our patience when we get old—I certainly have. I think Joe lost some of his patience to listen to other points of view."

In the Capital One Bowl, Paterno's record-setting thirty-first bowl game, Penn State lost to Auburn 13–9, and there was much unhappiness afterward. Larry Johnson once again criticized the game plan. "We get so panicky and scared that we don't know the answer when it's right in front of our face," he griped to reporters. Paterno, meanwhile, criticized Johnson, something that had always been beneath him: "He fumbled the ball three times, he slipped a couple of times, dropped a screen pass. It wasn't one of his better games."

The larger story was that Paterno decided to play a defensive back named Anwar Phillips, who had been temporarily expelled from school while being investigated for allegedly sexually assaulting a woman. At the time of the bowl game there were no criminal charges, and though he was charged later, Phillips was acquitted. Paterno's playing Phillips was viewed as yet another sign that the architect of The Grand Experiment had lost his way. Even the school president, Graham Spanier, publicly declared that playing Phillips was a mistake, and he moved to create a rule that would prevent such things from happening in the future.

In time, Paterno would go to war with Judicial Affairs over what he viewed as the unfair singling out of his players. He would go to war with President Spanier as well.

Paterno works with quarterback Michael Robinson *(Jason Sipes/Altoona Mirror)*

To Be, or Not to Be

L ooking back, it is obvious that only a defiant legend could have survived Penn State's disastrous 2003 and 2004 seasons. The team lost more than they ever had under Joe Paterno: six games in a row in 2003, then six in a row again in 2004. Along with this, there was a conspicuous string of off-the-field incidents by players. There was obvious coaching confusion, including what seemed to be a basic clash over who was running the offense, a clash that involved Paterno's son Jay, who had become the quarterback coach. To outsiders, the program appeared to be in chaos. Paterno kept insisting that things were better than they looked and that the team was a play or two away from being winners again. These words did not comfort a panicked fan base.

The question of how Paterno survived those two calamitous years leads to a simple answer involving power, force of will, and stubbornness. But before getting there, there's a deeper question: Why? At the end of 2004, Paterno was seventy-seven, an age even he had conceded was too old to be coaching a major college football program. "I don't think I want to go over 75," he had told the writer Bill Conlin in 1998. "I think that would be a mistake." He had lost the energy to do so many of the things that a coach needed to do. He no longer traveled much to recruit; he had cut his speaking engagements to rarities; he almost never gave a one-on-one interview to a reporter; his practices, which had long been closed, now had the air of a secret government project. He would do charity functions reluctantly and usually only after Sue begged him.

So why go on? Why keep coaching? There is no shortage of theories, but no one can know the depths of another man's heart. Some took the most cynical view and believed that, despite his protests, Paterno wanted to finish his career with the record for most victories by a coach. Shortly after Paterno passed Bear Bryant on the all-time victories list, his friend and rival Bobby Bowden at Florida State passed Paterno. Paterno said repeatedly that the record didn't matter to him, which people close to him often confirmed, but many simply did not believe him.

Others, especially close friends and family, believed that Paterno kept coaching because he simply could not imagine another life. He could not imagine waking up in the morning without a thousand things to do, without a game plan to create, an opponent to defeat, and young men to teach. "His mind doesn't ever stop," his daughter Mary Kay explained. "It's like a joke in the family, that whenever he comes over, he will stay for a few minutes and then he will stand up and say, 'Okay, we better let these kids get some sleep.' He's got to go. He's got to work on something. If he's away for even a few minutes, he thinks of something he should be doing." "He can't even go on vacation," Guido D'Elia said. "He's there for three days and he's going stir crazy. He's got to get back to work."

Paterno reduced his explanation to this: he was afraid of dying, afraid, as Hemingway had said, of backing into the grave. He never forgot that Bear Bryant died so soon after he retired, and he believed the same thing could happen to him. "I'll know when it's time," he told friends and family, alumni and reporters, critics and sycophants and everyone else. But this was the riddle: How could he ever know it was time? How could he ever admit that he wasn't as strong, as quick, as full of life? How could he retire and face what comes after? "Old age should burn and rage at the close of day," he told me once, quoting Dylan Thomas.

There was something else too, something perhaps best summed up by his longtime friend and colleague Tim Curley: "I've never known anyone who loves a challenge more than Joe. When things are rough, he almost seems happier and more excited than when everything seems to be going well. I can remember during the roughest times, Joe would come into the office full of life and energy, like he was saying: 'Let's prove some people wrong today.' "

All around him in 2003 and 2004 (and the three years prior as well) was doubt. The newspapers were filled with anonymous quotes from donors and fans who said that it was time for Joe to go. That was the unofficial name of the campaign: "Joe Must Go." There were ads in the paper, letter campaigns to the school, secret meetings of rich and powerful people in the community, all sorts of efforts to convince Paterno to step down or, if that failed, to topple him. The more people tried, the more obstinate Paterno became. This, he admitted, was a function of his personality that he did not control well. He did not lose easily, and he did not lose well. He believed with every fiber of his being that he was the right man, the only man, to be head coach at Penn State. He understood that other people had a different opinion, and he knew they were wrong.

Bob Flounders, a reporter from the Harrisburg *Patriot-News*, asked Paterno at the end of the unsuccessful 2004 season if he deserved to be back. Paterno's response showed that Flounders's question had hit bone: "I really don't appreciate that question, to be honest with you. After fifty-five years to have somebody tell me that, I don't appreciate that."

No, Joe would not go. Jay Paterno would always remember being in the Beaver Stadium tunnel before a game, with 108,000 people screaming as the team prepared to run onto the field. Joe walked close to the entrance, the crowd grew even louder, and Joe turned back to his son, winked, and said, "Why would anybody give this up?"

The more they told him to go, the more Joe Paterno intended to stay.

THE 2003 SEASON WAS THE worst one yet. Paterno threw a player off the team after he allegedly struck a woman on campus. (The charges were later dropped.) He suspended a player for underage drinking and suspended another for driving under the influence. He cut another player from the team after a drunken-driving arrest and had a player expelled from school for allegedly assaulting his girlfriend. (He was convicted.) Other players got in trouble as well. Something rotten about Penn State football seemed to be in the news every day.

This was not exclusively a Penn State problem, of course. Every major college football program had off-the-field incidents, especially involving alcohol. "These are young kids—eighteen-, nineteen-, twenty-year-old kids," Paterno said. "They are aggressive young men. They make mistakes. What do we want to do, allow those mistakes to ruin them, or use those mistakes to teach them how to act?"

In 2004, Paterno believed he had to get tougher, had to impose discipline on his players. But no matter how tough he got, the off-field incidents kept showing up in the papers. There was a fight at an ice-skating rink involving three players. There was a bizarre bow-and-arrow incident involving two players; the charges were later dropped, but not before it became the talk of State College. Paterno thought—and never stopped thinking—that there were people trying to make a name for themselves by singling out his program and his players. In 2008, an investigation by ESPN's *Outside the Lines* reported that forty-six Penn State players had been charged with crimes between 2002 and 2008. Penn State's president, Graham Spanier, was quoted in the report saying that it was embarrassing. Paterno called the whole thing a witch hunt and later said that the report and others like it reflected something sad about society.

One afternoon in November 2011, while sitting at his kitchen table, Paterno offered a soliloquy on his role as football coach:

To so many people these guys are numbers. But I can honestly tell you, they were never numbers to me. I wanted every one of them to go on to live good and meaningful lives. We go into some rough places, and get some kids with rough edges. They grow up without fathers, without mothers, in places where most people wouldn't walk in bright daylight. Are they going to make some mistakes? Sure they are. And some of them are bad kids; there's nothing we can do for them. But most of them, they're not bad kids. They're good kids. They want to do good. They don't know how. They trip up. We can help them. We can make a difference in their lives.

You've got some people who want to catch them in the act, to punish them, to send them home. I'm just being honest about it. They don't care what happens to them after that. They see that a kid got arrested or that there was some kind of fight, and they immediately say, "Oh that's a bad kid. You should get rid of him. You should send him back where he came from." They don't even want to know what happened. I could make myself look good—hey, Tough Guy Paterno—if I cut them. But I couldn't do that. There are probably some kids I gave a second and third chance to who probably didn't deserve it. I've made mistakes. But I don't regret that. You know what I regret? I regret the kid I threw out too soon, the kid who I gave up on who I could have helped if I'd just stayed with him a little bit longer.

Let's not kid anybody, football players are targets, especially at a place like Penn State. They are in the public eye all the time. They make a mistake, and everybody knows about it. If they are falsely accused, everyone believes it because they're football players. I'm not condoning the bad things, and I threw plenty of kids off the team through the years. . . . But I always thought it was my job to coach them and to help them. I wasn't going to hurt them and give up on them just so I could look good in the paper or in some television report.

While the incidents of 2003 and 2004 made news, sparking "Happy Valley Not So Happy" stories across the country, Penn State kept losing. Most of the losses were close, which gave some credence to Paterno's enduring line about the team being only a play or two away from a victory. He again criticized officials after close losses. But as Paterno himself said, nobody at Penn State cared about moral victories or excuses. The losing told the only story anyone heard.

The losses came one after another, week after week: Minnesota, Wisconsin, Purdue, Iowa, Ohio State, Northwestern, all losses, all in a row in 2003. The talk Paterno had given to his coaching staff in 1998 about the other Big Ten schools catching up had come true. Perhaps because of a dip in their own recruiting, perhaps because of the parity of college football, Penn State was no more talented than the other schools. Every game would be close. Superior coaching and conditioning had led the Nittany Lions to so many close victories over the years. In the early 2000s they simply stopped winning those games.

An ad demanding that Paterno be fired was placed in the local paper. A "Joe Must Go" website was started. People chanted "Joe must go" at home games. Nobody, not even Paterno's biggest fans, would argue that he could turn the team around. The best anyone seemed able to say was, "Well, Joe Paterno has earned the right to leave on his own terms." Those weak defenses were soon drowned out. It seemed as though everybody agreed that the game had passed Paterno by, that he had to retire for the good of the program, his legacy, and the

Commonwealth of Pennsylvania. The only person who didn't agree was Joe Paterno.

He also seemed to be the only one who mattered.

The 2004 season was every bit as dreadful as 2003. Paterno shuffled his staff a bit, moving longtime coach and friend Fran Ganter into administration and hiring former Penn State quarterback Galen Hall as a new offensive coordinator. This raised more eyebrows; Hall had not coached college football for fifteen years, after being forced to resign as head coach of Florida while the school was being investigated for various rule violations. He had been banished to various minor professional sports leagues during those fifteen years, until Paterno gave him a chance. "Galen's a good coach and a great teacher," he told reporters. When they pressed him on the violations at Florida, violations Hall consistently denied, Paterno replied, "He got screwed." Paterno also gave his son Jay added responsibilities and hired the same graduate assistant who had told him about Sandusky in 2001, Mike McQueary.

For his part, Paterno seemed optimistic. He admitted to Pat Jordan of the *New York Times Magazine* that he had not coached at his best during the previous few years, but that he was recommitted. If the team kept losing in 2004, he promised, "I'll say something's missing." Well, the team kept losing. The defense played well all year, but the offense was all but helpless. Penn State lost at Wisconsin, at Minnesota, and at home against Purdue. After a humiliating 6–4 homecoming loss to Iowa, Paterno told the fans to blame him, not the players or coaches. There was no objection to that; so many furious emails poured into Penn State that President Spanier asked Paterno to answer some of them. "What's email?" Paterno responded.

There were other, more personal challenges. In late September, Paterno's son-in-law Chris Hort, husband of Mary Kay, was seriously injured in a cycling accident; for a short while it appeared he would not survive. He recovered. In November, Paterno's son Scott lost his congressional race to incumbent Tim Holden by twenty points.

Joe's reaction: "He got licked, and he shoulda got licked—the guy he was running against was one of the better congressmen we've had." The family found the constant attacks on Joe difficult to handle. "I couldn't read [the newspapers]," said his oldest child, Diana.

Before Penn State played Northwestern, Paterno tried to relieve the tension by reminding his players that this was just a game: "We're playing football in the fall. The leaves are out. Everything is great. It's such a beautiful day, and you're young. Let's go out and play a football game, have some fun, and forget about what the media is saying." Penn State lost again, 14–7. "[It's] indisputable that Paterno can no longer put together a team that can contend or, for that matter, be competitive," Mike Wilbon wrote in the *Washington Post*. That theme was repeated in newspapers, on talk radio shows, and in Internet chat rooms all over America. There was no need for question marks, no space left for doubt. Joe Paterno was done.

And then something peculiar happened. Penn State defensive star Tamba Hali described it as "that whole 'To be or not to be' thing."

PATERNO NEVER HESITATED TO GO deep into his love of literature in his darkest moments. He built much of his own life around the *Aeneid*. He read and reread various classics when he wanted inspiration. Every team he ever coached heard him recite from Robert Browning's poem about the Renaissance painter Andrea del Sarto: "Ah, but a man's reach should exceed his grasp, / Or what's a heaven for?"

The week in 2004 that Penn State played Indiana—after losing six games in a row, convincing the last holdout that Paterno's time had come and gone—Paterno invoked what he considered the greatest words ever written about taking a stand and deciding whether it is better to live or to die. That week, he gathered together his players and, mostly from memory, recited Hamlet's soliloquy with a fury that outshone anything they had come to know about him:

To be, or not to be: that is the question:
Whether 'tis nobler in the mind to suffer
The slings and arrows of outrageous fortune,
Or to take arms against a sea of troubles,
And by opposing end them?

The players, many of them, would say they had no idea what he was talking about. But they were captivated, if not by the words then by the passion of the legendary coach who spoke them. "I remember the 'Sea of wars,' " Tamba Hali said. "I remember when Joe read that to us, it made sense. . . . Are you going to fold up your tent, or are you going to fight the battle, fight through the tough times?"

Penn State quarterback Michael Robinson said it this way: "There aren't many coaches who can get you fired up reading Shakespeare. But it wasn't so much the words he was using. It was the way he said it. You could tell it was from deep in his heart. He was telling us, this was it. This was our time."

That week, Penn State led Indiana by 6 points with time running out. But Indiana was driving, and then quarterback Matt LoVecchio threw a pass over the middle to receiver Travis Haney, who was pulled down at the Penn State 1-yard line. There were two minutes left. All Indiana had to do was punch the ball in from the 1-yard line, and the Nittany Lions certainly would lose their seventh game in a row.

On first down, Indiana's Chris Taylor ran up the middle, but Penn State tackle Ed Johnson pushed through, grabbed him by the leg, and did not let go.

To be, or not to be: that is the question.

On second down, Taylor again ran up the middle, and this time Penn State's sophomore linebacker Paul Posluszny stepped in front, held his ground, and stopped Taylor cold. Dan Connor, a freshman, grabbed Taylor from behind and would not let go. Taylor lost a yard.

Whether 'tis nobler in the mind to suffer the slings and arrows of outrageous fortune . . .

On third down, LoVecchio sprinted right, an option play, but there was no option. Linebacker Derek Wake had pushed his blocker upfield and reached out an arm to slow down LoVecchio. Safety Calvin Lowry raced toward the ball—"Go to the ball!" Paterno had yelled countless times—and pulled LoVecchio to the ground 2 yards shy of the goal line.

Or to take arms against a sea of troubles . . .

On fourth down, Taylor ran up the middle one more time. This time there was a small opening, and he was able to get up to full speed. Four Penn State defenders converged. Taylor fell to the ground about six inches short of the touchdown.

And by opposing end them.

The Penn State celebration was intense, perhaps the most joyous victory celebration for Penn State football in a decade, which might have seemed odd since they needed a near-miracle to beat a not very good Indiana football team. But Paterno heard Shakespeare and he saw glory.

"Guys," he told them afterward in the locker room, "I'm telling you. Next year, we're going to be playing for the national championship." If anyone outside that locker room had heard those words, the only possible response would have been laughter. Inside, though, there were cheers. "After Indiana," Tamba Hali said, "we believed."

GRAHAM SPANIER WAS NOT A typical university president. His father had escaped to South Africa from Nazi Germany in 1936, when he was just fifteen years old, just two years before Kristallnacht and the beginning of the Holocaust. Graham was born in South Africa after the war. He moved with his family to Chicago when he was just a boy, and it was there that he began his life as a tireless overachiever. He worked four jobs at once, earned enough college credits in high school to skip his freshman year of college, and became the first member of his family to graduate from college.

He was a dynamic and curious personality. He craved attention. He performed magic tricks at parties. He played washboard regularly in a State College band called the Deacons of Dixieland. (His band biography read, "In his spare time he serves as President of Penn State University.") He dressed in a gorilla costume when he became chancellor at the University of Nebraska–Lincoln, and when he was Penn State's president he sometimes dressed as the school's mascot. He had run with the bulls in Pamplona, and he had his pilot's license, flying whenever the opportunity arose. He would wander around campus before classes began to help students move into their dorm rooms.

He was also secretive—he fought against the release of any Penn State records, even those that seemed harmless—and numerous people who worked for him said that he was meddlesome and pushy and too concerned about getting credit. Many Penn State employees would wake up to find an email President Spanier had sent in the middle of the night, often with a picky point or a detailed request that did not seem worthy of 3 A.M. typing.

For a long time, the relationship between Paterno and Spanier was cordial but not much more. They were different types. Paterno did not seem interested in the opinions of people outside his circle; Spanier was a political animal who cared deeply about everyone's opinion. Paterno was a believer in dignity and etiquette; whenever one of his sons wore dirty shoes or a wrinkled shirt, he raged, "Do you see the CEOs of companies dressing like that?" Spanier enjoyed being unconventional, being viewed as quirky and offbeat and even a bit goofy.

For a long time, they respected each other's turf. Paterno appreciated that Spanier had a strong record of recruiting women and minority candidates into academia, and he admired Spanier's great ambitions for the university. Spanier believed in Paterno's vision of college athletics and was aware that no person had ever raised more money for the school. The two didn't have to be close friends; they worked together. That is, until 2004.

That's when Spanier reportedly came to believe what everybody else believed: that Joe Paterno could no longer succeed as a coach. He never publicly lost faith; he gave Paterno a four-year extension in May 2004. But people close to both men said that the grim 2004 season was too much for Spanier. Some were calling him the puppet of a football coach who could no longer do the job. They were saying he was not the most powerful man at the school. He set up a meeting at Paterno's home.

PATERNO'S NOTES LEADING UP TO this meeting are fascinating. They suggest that he finally realized that it was time for him to step down. First, he had some small demands. He wanted veto power on his replacement. He sketched out a plan if the next coach came from his own staff; defensive coordinator Tom Bradley was the leading candidate. If the next coach was hired from another school, he wanted guarantees that many of the current coaches would be retained. He made a list of coaches from across the country who might fit in as the next head coach. He offered to stay on and help in a fund-raising capacity.

But the more notes he wrote, the more his reluctance to leave became apparent. He believed, especially after the Indiana game, that the tide had turned and the team was coming around. "We have momentum," he wrote to himself. "We have enthusiasm on the squad." He remembered that several people on the Penn State Board of Trustees wanted him gone way back in 1988, and look at what he'd accomplished since then: he helped get Penn State into the Big Ten; he led another undefeated team; he continued to graduate players and win games and raise money.

Paterno wrote, "You guys relax. Bad days are behind us now."

He scribbled down a Teddy Roosevelt quote: "Youth is a disease, but it can be cured."

The notes grew more defiant: "Are we going to be influenced by ripped-up game tickets? Is money our goal regardless?"

"I have a staff and a squad that (with two or three more players) can win a national championship next year," he wrote to himself.

And finally this: "There have always been anti-Paterno people (media, etc.). They said we can't throw the ball . . . [and] in 1994 we had the best offense in the history of the Big Ten. This is the world we live in. I understand it. I can operate in that. Problem is: Can you?"

"You," in this case, was Graham Spanier.

Joe Paterno had decided he was going to stay.

THEY SAT AROUND THE KITCHEN table, the same table where the family had talked through the years. Paterno and Spanier were joined by Tim Curley, Vice President Gary Schultz, and former Penn State football captain and chairman of the board of trustees Steve Garban. Paterno and Spanier had different ideas about what was going to happen. Spanier expected this to be a talk about who would replace Joe Paterno. Paterno expected this to be a talk about how he was going to lead the team to glory in 2005.

The talk was strained but good-natured for a while. Paterno told Spanier that the team was just a couple of plays away from being very good. He explained that the defense was already good enough to make them a national championship contender (Penn State was the only team in the country to not allow more than 21 points in a game) and that he had some exciting ideas about how to make the offense good again. Spanier responded with a bit of skepticism, but nothing too threatening. And then, Paterno recalled, Spanier cleared his throat and said that he was going to recommend to the board that 2005 be Paterno's last year as coach.

At the end of his life, Paterno said, as if asking for forgiveness, "I have a temper. I shouldn't have said what I said, but I was very angry. I had thought he came over to talk. But he already had made up his mind what he was going to do."

Paterno put both hands on the table, looked Graham Spanier in the eye, and growled, "You take care of your playground, and I'll take care of mine."

Spanier looked at him with surprise. Paterno went on. Before the meeting, he had written notes to himself that seem to be for use in case the argument got hot:

> *I am NOT going to resign.*
>
> *I am 77, but not old, and the arena is where I thrive.*
>
> *Loyalty—Commitment to Education—more than wins + losses.*
>
> *I've raised millions of dollars at this very table for the University.*
>
> *Realizing that graduation rate, etc., are what Penn State athletics are all about.*
>
> *I can rally the alumni. People in the country. We are special. We are Penn State.*

All this and other scribbles were written in pencil. In blue pen, at the bottom of the yellow graph paper, he wrote what appears to be his final bid: "If I fail (7–4, 8–4), I retire."

Paterno was not going to surrender. He was not going to allow Spanier or anyone else to make him step down. "Dad basically dared Spanier to try and fire him," Scott Paterno recalled. "And Spanier backed down. But he obviously wasn't happy about it." The next year, after things turned around for Penn State football, Paterno told the story in public about how he had rebuffed the president. "That was another mistake," Paterno admitted.

Over the next few years, Spanier and Paterno clashed, and the board of trustees began to move away from Paterno. At the end, the very end, Paterno would look to the board and look again, but he could not find a friend.

But that was at the end. First, there would be one more Paterno miracle.

Paterno leads his team onto the field *(Jason Sipes/Altoona Mirror)*

Winning

Paterno often admitted that his feelings about winning were contradictory and conflicted. He said that winning wasn't the most important thing. The quest was what mattered. The journey was what mattered. Transcendence was what mattered. He longed for opponents to play their best game because only then could his own team reach its highest standard. He looked for talented football players who wanted to be a part of something larger, and he worked his whole career to create that something. He cherished those players who played football with intensity but lived with an even deeper and greater passion. When he looked in the mirror, he liked seeing an

Ivy League–educated man who listened to Puccini, read Shakespeare, pondered poetry, devised disarming football strategies, and believed that winning and losing football games was a frenzied and heart-pumping but ultimately meaningless element of a life spent teaching.

Ah, but Joe Paterno loved to win.

"Yes, I know, I preach a lot about being willing to lose, that there can be valor in losing to a better opponent," Paterno wrote in his autobiography. "Yes, I know it seems contradictory, inconsistent, maybe even hypocritical. I'm sorry about that. The world is a more complicated and ambiguous place than I wish it were."

After the meeting with Spanier, after the "To be or not to be" goal-line stand, after the five toughest years of his coaching life, Joe Paterno rededicated himself to winning. He was seventy-eight years old, written off, but he believed that he could still lead Penn State to victory without cheating, without compromising on academics, without resorting to shortcuts.

But there would be concessions. There had to be concessions. The media requests, some of which had already been weeded out, would be cut off almost entirely. The speaking engagements, the appearances, the dinners with sponsors that had become rarities were stopped entirely. The radio show, which was done live with callers, became a few minutes of talking into broadcaster Steve Jones's tape recorder sometime during the week. The engagement with the board of trustees and other power brokers at the school would be reduced to a minimum. Paterno would concentrate on coaching football. "Let me coach my football team!" he screamed repeatedly at Guido D'Elia. Everything else—everything that didn't directly involve the football team and its success—faded into the distant background.

Paterno attacked the recruiting process with an energy he had not shown in years. There were two players he desperately wanted: a wonderful athlete from a suburb of Pittsburgh named Justin King, and Derrick Williams, a wide receiver almost unanimously viewed as the top high school prospect in America. Paterno personally went to King's home, went to see his cousin play basketball, tried to impress upon King that Penn State football still meant something special. With King, Paterno had a slight advantage because King's stepfather, Terry Smith, had played at Penn State for him.

Derrick Williams was trickier. He was from Greenbelt, Maryland, which did not put him in the usual sphere of Penn State recruiting dominance. Every major college team in America wanted him. The odds of his choosing Penn State, which had suffered four losing seasons in five years and was coached by an aging legend who had lost much of his fan base, seemed the longest of long shots. But Paterno saw something in Williams that others didn't see. He saw a young man who longed for a deep challenge and the possibility of greatness.

He wrote in one of his handwritten letters to Williams:

Derrick, we are one or two "big play" skill people away from a team that can compete for the national championship in 2005. . . .

Everybody on our staff believes you are the wide receiver who can immediately fill that need. . . .

Derrick, ordinarily I don't recruit in the spring, but this year—but this year—the first day we are allowed on the road I'm going to be in Eleanor Roosevelt High School. I want to make sure you know how much we want you and how important you are in our future plans.

Before I retire, I want to have one more great team that can win a National Championship. We have been fortunate enough to have Undefeated-Untied National Championship Contenders in four different decades.

The rest did not need to be said. Paterno wanted Williams to know, to believe that he could play the starring role in bringing Penn State back to glory. Yes, of course, he could go to thriving programs at Oklahoma or Ohio State or Florida and be a part of something there. But at Penn State, he could achieve unimaginable heights. Williams bought in. "Penn State is missing a piece of the puzzle," he told reporters after choosing to go to State College. "Maybe it's cocky or whatever, but I think I'm that piece."

This kind of recruiting was unusual for Paterno. Throughout his career he had told high school players that he wanted them to come to Penn State, but the football team would be fine if they did not come. Always he had emphasized the team over the individual and insisted that no one was irreplaceable. Always he had insisted that winning was secondary to the life and academic lessons of college. He did not back away from those words, but he had to get Derrick Williams and Justin King. "I wouldn't care if we didn't get anybody but those two kids," he said on his radio show.

Paterno sent a couple of coaches, including his son and quarterback coach Jay, to Austin to watch how Texas coached their offense around star quarterback Vince Young. Joe helped redesign the offense; he wanted it built around a gifted but unproven senior quarterback named Michael Robinson. The man who had always believed that defense wins championships wanted an offense as new and electrifying as any in America.

It worked. Penn State scored more than 40 points in back-to-back weeks against Cincinnati and Central Michigan. They pulled off a spectacular comeback against Northwestern—the winning touchdown a spectacular pass from Robinson to Williams—then smashed Minnesota 44–14. It was astonishing. Williams was almost impossible for defenses to cover, and Paterno said they had to find more ways to get him the ball. (Paterno, who for so long had been against freshmen even playing, called Williams the most talented freshman he'd ever coached.) Justin King was a defensive player, but Paterno used him a bit on offense as well. Two other freshmen receivers who were not as highly recruited, Deon Butler and Jordan Norwood, played major roles. When Penn State upset sixth-ranked Ohio State, people began to accept that this young Penn State team was very good.

Penn State lost a breathtakingly close game to Michigan, another game with an officiating controversy. Late in the game, with Penn State leading, Michigan coach Lloyd Carr was able to get the referees to put a few seconds back on the clock, time the officials determined had run off incorrectly. That time was the difference. Michigan quarterback Chad Henne dropped back with six seconds left and threw an incomplete pass. But, because of the extra time, one second remained. In that one second, Henne threw a 10-yard touchdown pass to Mario Manningham that won the game. Paterno was so distraught and angry after the loss he did not allow his players to talk to the media.

"I just wanna get them on the bus, get to the airport and go home, so we can start thinking about next week instead of having them moan about what happened," Paterno told reporters. He would always believe that his team got cheated at Michigan. He felt so strongly about what he saw as a pattern of controversy at Michigan—and about what he viewed as an old boys' network in the conference—that, privately, he talked again about getting Penn State out of the Big Ten.

But this team was too good to falter after the loss. The Nittany Lions obliterated Illinois 63–10 the next week. They beat Purdue, Wisconsin, and Michigan State in succession and with relative ease to win the Big Ten and earn a place in the Orange Bowl. (The Rose Bowl, where the Big Ten champion usually went, was reserved that year for the national championship game.) Suddenly the press about Penn State and Paterno gushed. Reporters called him the miracle man. They admonished themselves for ever doubting him. "If nothing else," Harvey Araton wrote in the *New York Times*, "Paterno's resurgent season should shut people up long enough to allow him to retire on his own terms." Araton did not have to point out that the *Times* was among the loudest in the crowd trying to push Paterno out.

Penn State played Florida State in the Orange Bowl, which meant that Paterno would face Bobby Bowden, the man who had passed him on the all-time victories list. At the start of the game, Bowden had 359 victories, Paterno 353. It was at the Orange Bowl that Paterno revealed the contentious meeting he'd had with Spanier and how he emerged victorious. "[Spanier and other officials] didn't quite understand where I was coming from or what it took to get a football program going," he told the *Pittsburgh Post-Gazette*. "I said, 'Relax. Get off my backside.' "

"When Joe told everyone how he had told off the president, that was terrible," one Penn State official said. "It was beneath him. He could have just stayed quiet about it and let the season speak for itself. But I guess he was so angry that President Spanier tried to force him out that he wanted to get in the final word. It was close to insubordination, really. And after that, Joe lost a lot of support around the school."

Penn State beat Florida State 26–23 in triple overtime, and the miracle season was complete. "Nobody believed in us," Tamba Hali told reporters after the game, and for once that "no respect" cliché that so many teams relied on rang true.

"I would watch Coach Paterno," said Adam Taliaferro, who was in law school at the time, "and I would see how passionately he believed the team was going to start winning again. And I knew that nobody outside the program believed in him. Nobody. . . . But they just didn't know the strength of Coach. They didn't understand how deeply he believed."

I asked Taliaferro if he really believed the team would turn around during those hard years. He hesitated for a moment. "It was looking pretty rough. But I was at practice every day. I saw the way he was coaching. . . . You don't underestimate Joe Paterno. I learned that when I was in the hospital. He was such strength for me. That's how he is as a coach. Yes, I thought he would win again . . . if they would give him the chance."

PATERNO'S TEAMS NEVER AGAIN SUFFERED a losing record after that. They won another Big Ten title in 2008 and were again only seconds away from an undefeated season. But that did not mean that things went smoothly. Penn State fans expected more than just winning seasons and near glory; Paterno himself had taught them to expect more. "Ah, maybe we got a bit spoiled up here," he would say.

His refusal to step down as coach evolved from questionable to controversial to outrageous and finally to unalterable fact. In 2006, at age seventy-nine, he was beaten up physically. He had to leave the sideline against Ohio State because of what he called a nasty stomach flu. At Wisconsin, he broke his leg when Wisconsin's DeAndre Levy and Penn State's Andrew Quarless inadvertently ran him over on the sideline. There were those who thought this might be the thing that would finally convince him he was too old to coach. He sat out the next week's game against Temple, but he was in the press box coaching a week later against Michigan State. He turned eighty barely a month after that.

His hearing began to go, leading to painfully awkward exchanges in the few press conferences he held. In 2010, at eighty-three, he had an allergic reaction to medication, and he looked so worn down that many observers were convinced he was near death. They were not wrong; even family members wondered if he would recover. At the bowl game that year, there were rumors that Paterno had been rushed to the hospital. This time the rumors were not true.

Still he coached.

He more than coached. Behind the scenes, he was as feisty as ever. He fought battles; many he lost. At the end, when it fit the narrative, there would be much talk about how Paterno ran State College and Penn State like an unopposed dictator. The truth was different. Paterno was powerful enough to fight off the president of the university and powerful enough to win some other fights. But he lost as many as he won. He did not want a new baseball stadium built adjacent to Beaver Stadium. He thought it a waste of money—"I think some Big Ten schools are going to drop baseball," he griped to friends—and, perhaps closer to home, the stadium would cut deeply into prime parking spaces for football games. He fought against it furiously, using whatever political power he had. The stadium was built anyway. He strongly opposed the Big Ten Network, an all-sports television network the conference wanted to launch to make money for the schools. He thought it was misguided and sold the league short. The Big Ten Network launched anyway.

"I know people think I run things around here, but I'm really just a guy with a big mouth," Paterno would say. "I have a lot of opinions. The only ones who have to listen to them are my players and my family. And even my family doesn't listen to them all the time."

There was one behind-the-scenes battle Paterno fought with ferocity. And this one, unlike the others, he decided he could not lose.

VICKY TRIPONEY BECAME THE VICE president for student affairs at Penn State in 2003. She would become one of the most quoted people of 2011, when, in the aftermath of the Jerry Sandusky scandal, she told the *Wall Street Journal* and others that Paterno had fought her relentlessly over football player discipline. She released some interoffice emails to and from athletic director Tim Curley and president Graham Spanier that strongly suggested Paterno wanted favorable treatment for his players. In one of the emails she submitted to the *Journal* she had written, "The Coach is insistent he knows best how to discipline his players . . . and their status as a student when they commit violations of our standards should *NOT* be our concern."

"Ex–Penn State Official Saw Paterno's 'Dark Side' " was the *USA Today* headline. Triponey's describing Paterno's "dark side" was galvanizing for a media hungry to find corruption in Paterno's past. Paterno's lawyer Wick Sollers put out a standard denial, calling her allegations "out of context, misleading and filled with inaccuracies." Scott Paterno said, "We can't swing at every pitch in the dirt."

Her story played for weeks and months, and stories and chapters written after Paterno's death continued to be built around her quotes. One close friend of Paterno wondered, "Don't reporters know how to use Google?" If they had, they would have found that Triponey's time at Penn State was not without controversy, including well-publicized clashes with student government, the campus radio station, and fraternities.

Paterno had numerous letters in his files from parents complaining about how their sons had been treated by the Office of Judicial

Affairs. He believed that Triponey and the Office of Judicial Affairs targeted his football players. Maybe this was the skewed view of a football coach; maybe it was the truth. Paterno believed it until the day he died.

The decisive battle between Paterno and Triponey was over a fight in April 2007 that involved several football players. The team's safety Anthony Scirrotto was reportedly walking with his girlfriend when they got into an argument with three young men, who were also students at Penn State. The girlfriend may have kicked one of them, and she was pushed down. Scirrotto stepped up and was hit in the face. He would admit to following the men to their apartment complex and calling his roommate for support. One text message led to another, each sounding more serious than the last, and in time at least seventeen football players showed up at the apartment complex.

Several of the football players forced their way into the apartment and found the men who hit Scirrotto. Punches were thrown, a table was overturned, a bar stool was thrown and may have been used to hit someone. Beyond this, the stories diverge. The story that would be reported in the newspapers and on television was of an out-of-control scene where one man was knocked unconscious with a bottle and then pummeled; another claimed to be punched and kicked in the face repeatedly. The football players involved said this was wildly exaggerated. The police arrested six Penn State players and charged them with a total of twenty-seven offenses, nine of them felonies.

Paterno believed that Judicial Affairs, and Triponey in particular, had no business getting involved in something already being handled by the police. He believed even more strongly that Triponey would not give his players a fair hearing. He did not condone the fight, but, as is clear in his notes, he agreed with his players that the details had been overblown. He never believed the fight had been excessively violent or that anyone was hit with a bottle. Two of the men in the apartment had gone to the hospital but had been immediately released, so there were no long-lasting injuries. (One victim told ESPN that he suffered headaches for weeks afterward.) There was underage drinking going on in the apartment before the players even got there. He thought it an unfortunate incident that merited harsh punishment, but he also believed that because it was a fight involving football players, it was his responsibility as coach to handle the school discipline. He wrote in his notes:

In my time at Penn State, no University official has ever tried to destroy a football season and a football team over a fight—especially involving a party organized by underage drinkers.

- *No guns.*
- *No Drugs.*
- *Nobody seriously hurt.*
- *No robbery.*
- *No Sexual Harassment.*

If somebody knocked somebody out with a beer bottle and/or a bar stool, and if somebody punched an unconscious person I WANT TO KNOW and I will handle them appropriately. They will be gone. . . . But I want to know. I don't want to guess. The problem is people assume the worst. I won't do that.

BASED ON THE EMAILS SHE released, Triponey believed that Paterno would be too lax in his punishment of players; she insisted that such punishment was the purview of Judicial Affairs. Paterno believed Triponey wanted to make headlines punishing football players. Maybe one was right and the other wrong. Maybe there was something to both of their arguments. "It's not a fight I want—it would be a Pyrrhic victory," Paterno wrote in a note to himself. "But if I fight, I cannot afford to lose." He announced that every member of the team would perform ten hours of community service and spend two hours cleaning up the stadium on Sundays after home games. And then, in quick succession:

- Four players had their charges dropped, leaving Anthony Scirrotto and Chris Baker.
- Scirrotto had five of his charges dismissed and pled to a lower charge on the sixth; the judge said there was no evidence to suggest he had assaulted anyone or tried to incite his teammates.
- Baker allegedly got into another fight in October and was thrown off the team the following summer.

In the middle of it all, Vicky Triponey announced her resignation. Four years later, after the Sandusky revelations, she came forward with the emails accusing Paterno of favoritism and meddling. At the time, nobody would publicly stand up for Paterno, but one player who was involved in the fight said this on the condition that he would stay anonymous: "If it was up to that woman, they would have thrown me out of school and let me rot. That's how she was. They only cared about me on Saturdays. Some of them didn't even care about me then. But now I'm a father, and I have a child, and I have a good job. I owe that to Joe Paterno. He wasn't perfect. But he believed in me. When nobody else did, he believed in me."

THE FINAL ACT

Prince Richard: He'll get no satisfaction out of me.
Prince Geoffrey: My, you chivalric fool, as if the way one fell down mattered.
Prince Richard: When the fall is all there is, it matters.

—*THE LION IN WINTER*

{ *Aria* }

Joe Paterno, Guido D'Elia, Scott Paterno,
   and Dan McGinn
In Joe Paterno's kitchen
November 9, 2011 (reconstructed from interviews)

Dan McGinn (crisis manager): Okay, I'm going to read the statement out loud here, so all of us can hear it. We've been over this a lot, so let's go from the beginning to the end. Okay, here we go.

    I am absolutely devastated by the developments in this case. I grieve for the children and their families and I pray for their comfort and relief.

    I have come to work every day for the last sixty-one years with one clear goal in mind: To serve the best interests of this university and the young men who have been entrusted to my care. I have the same goal today.

    That's why I decided to announce my retirement effective at the end of the season. At this moment, the Board of Trustees should not spend a single moment discussing my status. They have far more important matters to address. I want to make this as easy for them as I possibly can.

This is a tragedy. It is one of the great sorrows of my life. With the benefit of hindsight, I wish I had done more. My goals now are to keep my commitment to my players and staff and finish the season with dignity and determination. And then I will spend the rest of my life doing everything I can to help this University.

Okay, thoughts?

Scott Paterno: I think it's the best we can do.

Guido D'Elia: I'm still a little worried about the part about Joe saying with the benefit of hindsight he wished he would have done more.

Joe Paterno: Guido . . .

Guido: I just think that people are going to misquote that. They're going to try to use it as an admission of guilt.

Joe: Guido, it's how I feel. I do wish I had done more. I thought I did what I was supposed to do, but you look at it now, everything that's happened—I do wish.

Scott: I don't think it's an admission of guilt. I think we're making it clear that if Dad had known what really happened, he would have done more. But he didn't know, and he's just saying he wished he had known.

Dan: I think, under the circumstances, this is probably the best we can do.

Joe: There's one thing that bothers me about this statement.

(Everybody looks at him.)

Joe: This part here that says, "I have come to work every day for the last sixty-one years with one clear goal in mind."

(Everybody continues to look at him.)

Joe: Well, I didn't come to work every day for sixty-one years. I was sick a couple of days, and there were other things, like when David got hurt. I don't know if I'd say that's completely honest.

Fall

Joe Paterno began the last football preseason of his life feeling great. Anyway, that's what he told himself. During the previous two seasons he had been ill and he looked gaunt; now he had the strength to walk again, and he walked all over State College. People spotted him miles from his home. "You need a ride, Joe?" they would shout through the car window, and he would wave his hand, smile, and keep walking, as he had as a young man, focusing on the road ahead. He was eighty-four years old, but he announced to anyone who would listen that he had not felt this good in years. And he had a good feeling about his team.

Later he would tell friends and family that he knew, even then, that this would be his last year as a coach. There were a few quiet signs of this, including the simple fact that he allowed me to write a book about him. But he mostly kept such thoughts to himself. First, it was nobody's business. Second, the last thing in the world Paterno wanted was one of those "We'll Miss You, Joe" celebrations that he called a "living funeral." Third, and perhaps most important, he wanted the freedom to change his mind. He would joke with reporters, using a line from Tennessee Williams: "I knew no one was immortal, but I thought I was the exception."

He entertained reporters with stories and jokes for more than an hour at the Big Ten Media Days in Chicago. This was Paterno as he had not been with reporters in a long time: at ease and engaging. A year earlier, the Media Days were notable only because Paterno was recovering from a virus and an allergic reaction to medicine, and he looked so near death that newspapers and magazines across the nation began writing his obituary in anticipation of the inevitable. They were not so far off: few people knew that a couple of weeks earlier, when the allergic reaction first struck, Paterno was in such bad shape that last rites were performed. A couple of family members felt certain he would not survive the month. "I thought Joe would live forever," his son Scott said. "But when I saw him in 2010, and I thought he was going to die, I came to grips with his humanity."

Paterno recovered, and his vitality slowly returned. He coached through 2010, and as the 2011 season was about to begin he was as feisty and sarcastic as ever. After going through a short question-and-answer session with the media in a ballroom, he stepped down from the podium, winked at Guido D'Elia, and said, "I didn't give them nothing." Later, as he sat at a table with about a dozen writers, he told marvelous stories. "That was the best I'd seen him in a long, long time," recalled Dick Weiss of the New York *Daily News*, who had been writing about Paterno for years.

At the Big Ten luncheon, Michigan State quarterback and Chicago native Kirk Cousins gave a stirring speech about how playing football was a privilege, and that with privilege comes responsibility to "work hard in the classroom . . . to give our all for fans . . . to represent the names on the front of our jerseys . . . to provide a true example of what it means to be a young man." It was as if the speech had been written by Joe Paterno himself. "It has been a privilege to go to places like Happy Valley," Cousins said, "and play a team coached by a man who embodies what it means to have a calling in life, and who proved you can have success with integrity."

Paterno stood and applauded with everyone else. A few minutes later, while the lunch was going on, Paterno walked over to Cousins.

They spoke for a minute, then Paterno headed for the exit. "Time to go back," he told Guido.

"But the luncheon . . ."

"Time to go," Paterno repeated. "We've got work to do."

THE LAST MONTHS OF JOE Paterno's life were so crowded with devastating events—injury, scandal, getting fired, cancer, and finally death, all in blinding succession—that it would be easy to miss the ripples and small surprises also taking place. Paterno was called to testify in front of the grand jury in January 2011 about his former coach Jerry Sandusky. According to his family and friends, he did not spend a lot of time thinking about what he would say. However, many of those friends and family, particularly Scott Paterno and Guido D'Elia, saw storm clouds ahead. Scott recalled interrogating his father about Sandusky, asking question after question about what he had known and what he had done. He also went through Joe's files, folder by folder, in an effort to find anything he could about Sandusky. He came away convinced that the only thing Joe knew about Sandusky's alleged crimes—or remembered knowing—was the vague conversation he had with Mike McQueary. Scott made himself his father's lawyer, and they met in Harrisburg, where the grand jury was sitting.

Paterno was on the stand for exactly seven minutes; his testimony filled less than two pages. He was not a target of the investigation. He told the grand jury that an upset Mike McQueary had visited him at home on a Saturday morning and told him in ill-defined terms about an incident involving Sandusky and a young boy in the showers of the Penn State football building. He concluded it was of a sexual nature, though he could be no more specific than that, and he told McQueary that he had done the right thing by bringing it to his attention. He did not remember exactly when he had called Athletic Director Tim Curley, but he remembered calling soon after to report the incident. He said had never heard another rumor about Sandusky, but admitted that things could have been said in his presence that he had forgotten. He had the utmost confidence in Curley to get to the bottom of things. As best anyone could tell, for Paterno that was the end of it.

When the story of Sandusky's being investigated broke in the Harrisburg *Patriot-News* in March, Scott Paterno and Guido D'Elia urged Joe to go public with what he knew. They did not know the depths of the Sandusky story, but they suspected that if it was bad—and they were hearing rumors that it was very bad—Paterno would be in the line of fire. And by the time the story broke, they thought, it could be too late.

"We begged Joe to just say publicly what he knew," D'Elia said. "He wouldn't do it. He wouldn't throw Tim or anybody else under the bus. He kept saying, 'Just let it play out.' In his mind, he had done what he was supposed to do, and he had told the truth about it, and that was that. That's how he was. Do what you think is right, tell the truth, you'll be fine.

"We were so desperate at one point, we thought about going around him to Sue, just to get her permission to release something in the summer, just to preempt anything. If we had done that, if we had gotten out what Joe knew and what he did before the presentment came out, it could have been different. It really could have been different."

ON THE THIRD DAY OF fall practice, inside the Holuba Hall practice facility, Paterno was looking the other way when a fast little receiver named Devon Smith ran a 20-yard out pattern, caught the ball, and slammed into him.

Smith checked to see if Paterno was all right, and was assured in no uncertain terms that it wasn't his fault and he better get his butt back into the huddle. Paterno got himself up. He wanted to shake it off, as he had always shaken off injuries. But he quickly realized his injury was serious. He had cracked his pelvis and hurt his arm.

Still, two days later he was back at practice. "I feel great except I'm in a lot of pain," he told the media, his best effort at a joke. The pain prevented him from walking—for weeks he had to be driven around practices in a golf cart—and the lack of walking prevented him from feeling like himself. He was mad at himself. "I was feeling so good," he moaned. He would never feel that good again.

The 2011 season was an odd one even before the tragic ending. Although the team kept winning, there was intense and persistent criticism of Paterno and his unwillingness to retire. There was something surreal about that. Coaches who win football games do not usually have people calling for them to step down, and after nine games Penn State was 8-1, their only loss to an Alabama team that would win the national championship. They were undefeated in the Big Ten. Paterno's players were still graduating at a high rate; in December (ironically at the same time that Penn State's interim president would suggest that the school had become a "football factory"), Penn State won the Academic Bowl for scholastic excellence among the best football programs in the nation.

Still, the calls for Paterno to step down were widespread and fierce. It was true that Paterno seemed out of sorts. He coached from the press box because of his injury, and he hated it; he did not even have time to go down and speak to his team at halftime. He was less available and less forthcoming than ever. Reporters who had long felt slighted by his testiness and secrecy pushed back.

Though the team kept winning, the ugliness of the games left no one feeling satisfied. Penn State needed a late defensive stand to beat Temple by 4. They beat Indiana by 6 in a deathly boring game that was tied 3–3 at the half. They held on to beat Purdue by 5, and they beat Illinois only when a last-second game-tying field goal attempt clanked against the upright and fell back. There was controversy when Paterno refused to make a decision about which quarterback would start or play the most, and there was general fatigue surrounding the football program. "It probably shouldn't be this way," one Penn State reporter told me. "But I think everybody just wants something to change. It's been the same here for so long that Joe's sick of us, we're sick of him; it would be nice to just move on to something new."

When Penn State beat Illinois on October 29, 2011, it was Paterno's 409th victory as a coach. He already had the record for Division I-A, so this wasn't exactly noteworthy. But he had passed Grambling's Eddie Robinson for the top spot on the Division I list for victories. It wasn't an official record, but it gave Penn State the opportunity to celebrate Paterno one more time. President Graham Spanier and Athletic Director Tim Curley showed up to give him a plaque. Paterno sounded tired. The reporters' questions sounded tired too. It wasn't much of a celebration.

Nobody knew it then, but that was the last game Joe Paterno would coach.

SCOTT PATERNO WAS THE FIRST in the family to understand that the Pennsylvania grand jury presentment that indicted Jerry Sandusky could end his father's career. This wasn't surprising; Scott tended to be the most realistic—or cynical, depending on who you asked—in the family. He had run for Congress and lost and along the way tasted the allure and nastiness of public life. He had worked as a lawyer and as a lobbyist. He would sometimes tell people, "Hey, don't kid yourself, I'm the asshole of the family." When Scott read the presentment, he called his father and said, "Dad, you have to face the possibility that you will never coach another game."

Joe thought his son was making too much of it. But he had not yet read the presentment. Scott had been getting word for weeks through his sources that the indictment was coming down, and that it was unimaginable. But even going over in his mind what might be the worst-case scenario didn't prepare him for the twenty-three-page firebomb. It told a hideous story of a famous former coach, philanthropist, and community leader who used his access to troubled youth and Penn State football resources to commit unthinkable crimes against children. As Scott struggled through the details—eight victims, charges of inappropriate touching, oral sex, sodomy—he grew angrier and angrier. He had known Sandusky for much of his life. He had showered in those athletic showers as a boy, with Sandusky undoubtedly in the same room. How was this possible? And the angrier he became, the more he understood that his own anger would be multiplied by the explosive reaction of millions of Americans who had never heard of Jerry Sandusky.

Those millions, most of them, *had* heard of Joe Paterno.

"Dad," he asked his father again, "did you know anything about Sandusky?"

"Other than the thing Mike told me, no," Joe answered.

"Nothing? No rumors? The coaches never talked about it?"

"No. I don't listen to rumors. Nothing."

"Dad, this is really important. If there is anything you heard . . ."

"I didn't hear anything, why are you badgering me? What do I know about Jerry Sandusky? I've got Nebraska to think about, I can't worry about this." Nebraska was the next game.

"I had to do everything I could to not cry right then," Scott recalled.

JAY PATERNO WAS ON THE road recruiting when he got the call from Scott. He asked, "How bad is it?" Scott said, "It's worse than anything." Jay sat in his car in an Ohio gas station and stared blankly into the darkness.

Still, Jay and others in the family clung to some hope that people would realize Joe had been fooled like everyone else. After all, Joe was not a target of the investigation. Two other Penn State officials, Curley and Schultz, had been indicted on counts of perjury and failure to report. Shortly after the presentment came out, there was a story in the online edition of the Harrisburg *Patriot-News* with the headline "Paterno Praised for Acting Appropriately in Reporting Jerry Sandusky Sex Abuse Suspicions." Multiple sources told reporter

Sara Ganim that "the deputy state prosecutor handling the case said that Paterno did the right thing and handled himself appropriately in 2002 [later changed to 2001] and during the three-year investigation."

This, in the end, was what the family believed: That Joe Paterno had been told a vague story about a former football coach he didn't like or trust. Then, following the law and university policy and his own guiding light, he had reported what he was told to Tim Curley. This was what he was required to do, and, knowing the circumstances, they believed this was what he should have done. He had not been charged with lying to the grand jury. (When he was fired, the Pennsylvania attorney general's director of communication Nils Frederiksen talked to ABC.com and called Paterno "a cooperating witness, an individual who testified and provided truthful information . . . who has not been charged.") If Jerry Sandusky was guilty, then hundreds of people had been fooled: child care professionals, law enforcement officials, coworkers at his charity, parents, judges, close friends of Sandusky, and many others. Those closest to Paterno believed that when he went public with what he knew and what he did, most people would understand he was fooled like everyone else. Joe Paterno believed the same thing.

Of course, there were those among the Paternos and their closest friends who wished Joe had followed up with more vigor after reporting to Curley and made sure there was a resolution. Penn State's official response—not to call the police and merely to ban Sandusky from bringing children on campus—was sickeningly inadequate if McQueary had seen and described a rape. Many of the people who had come to admire Joe Paterno believed that, no matter his own legal role, he should have made sure the incident was reported to the police.

"But, to be honest, that's just not how Joe was in the last years," said one of the people in his inner circle. "He was not vigilant like he used to be. I think a younger Joe would have said to Tim after a few days, 'Hey, what's going on with that Sandusky thing? You guys get to the bottom of that? Let's make sure that's taken care of.' But he didn't understand it. And he just wasn't as involved as he used to be."

As reported, interoffice emails suggest Paterno had been told more about Sandusky than he recalled and had followed up, at least unofficially, with Athletic Director Tim Curley. When some of the emails were released, there was a strong backlash against Paterno; many would believe he was involved in a Penn State cover-up. Paterno did not deny his own ineffectiveness—he spoke about it with deep regret—but he strongly denied any ill intent.

On the Saturday that the grand jury presentment went public, Graham Spanier came to the house, sat at the kitchen table, and read to Paterno the statement he was going to release. Paterno told him the statement would do more harm than good. "I just didn't like it. It struck me as a mistake." Spanier released it anyway.

> *The allegations about a former coach are troubling, and it is appropriate that they be investigated thoroughly. Protecting children requires the utmost vigilance.*
>
> *With regards to the other presentments, I wish to say that Tim Curley and Gary Schultz have my unconditional support. I have known and worked daily with Tim and Gary for more than 16 years. I have complete confidence in how they have handled the allegations about a former University employee.*
>
> *Tim Curley and Gary Schultz operate at the highest levels of honesty, integrity and compassion. I am confident the record will show that these charges are groundless and that they have conducted themselves professionally and appropriately.*

Paterno was right. The statement, particularly the part about "unconditional support" for Curley and Schultz, would set off a media already motivated to wonder what the heck was going on in Happy Valley.

● ● ●

ON SUNDAY, GUIDO D'ELIA RETURNED from an out-of-town trip and went to the Paternos' home. Like Scott, like millions, D'Elia had felt overwhelming rage when reading the presentment, and he had come to the conclusion that Joe would probably lose his job. Those feelings were confirmed when he learned that the university had cut off communication with the Paternos. There would be much back-and-forth later about who stopped talking first, who would not return whose phone calls, but in interviews almost every member of the Paternos' immediate family said that they tried to start a dialogue with the university trustees and were rebuffed. Sue Paterno said she called a couple. Mary Kay said she called three. And so on. Nobody responded. D'Elia saw the break as a terrible sign. The media intensity was slowly building to a boil. "And when that happens," D'Elia said, "there has to be a scapegoat."

The Paternos decided to release a statement. It revealed their state of mind at the time: what Joe knew, when he knew it, what he tried to do about it. It was substantially the statement that several of Paterno's advisors, including D'Elia, had wanted him to release back when the story first broke. D'Elia deduced that it was probably too late now.

> *If true, the nature and amount of charges made are very shocking to me and all Penn Staters. While I did what I was supposed to with the one charge brought to my attention, like anyone else involved I can't help but be deeply saddened these matters are alleged to have occurred.*
>
> *As my grand jury testimony stated, I was informed in 2002 by an assistant coach that he had witnessed an incident in the shower of our locker room facility. It was obvious that the witness was distraught over what he saw, but he at no time related to me the very specific actions contained in the Grand Jury report.*
>
> *Regardless, it was clear that the witness saw something inappropriate involving Mr. Sandusky. As coach Sandusky was retired from our coaching staff at that time, I referred the matter to university administrators.*

I understand that people are upset and angry, but let's be fair and let the legal process unfold. In the meantime, I would ask all Penn Staters to continue to trust in what that name represents, continue to pursue their lives every day with high ideals and not let these events shake their beliefs nor who they are.

Sue and I have devoted our lives to helping young people reach their potential. The fact that someone we thought we knew might have harmed young people to this extent is deeply troubling. If this is true, we were all fooled along with scores of professionals trained in such things, and we grieve for the victims and their families. They are in our prayers.

D'Elia had hoped people would pay special attention to the sentence "If this is true, we were all fooled along with scores of professionals." Sandusky had worked closely with child care professionals for most of his life. They had approved him for numerous adoptions and approved him many, many times to be a foster parent. "They were fooled, and that's their business," said Paterno. "What chance did I have?"

But D'Elia's fears were confirmed: it was too late. Sunday was the day that television cameras began to surround the Paterno home on McKee Street.

ON MONDAY, THE FAMILY TRIED to convince Paterno to read the presentment. He objected that he already knew what was in there, but they told him there was no room left for illusion. Guido D'Elia would remember telling him, "You realize that the people out there think you knew about this? They think you had to know because you know about everything."

"That's their opinion!" Paterno shouted. "I'm not omniscient!"

"They think you are!" D'Elia roared back.

Later, D'Elia described watching Paterno read the presentment: "It was like watching his innocence get blown away. What did he know about perverted things like that? When he asked Scott, 'What is sodomy, anyway?' I thought my heart was going to break."

The attorney general of Pennsylvania, Linda Kelly, had been in office for only a few months. Her predecessor, Tom Corbett, had initiated the grand jury investigation of Sandusky more than two years earlier. He was now governor and would play a substantial role in what was to follow. On Monday, though, Kelly held a press conference to discuss the Sandusky indictment. When Paterno's name came up, she was clear about his meeting his legal responsibility: "Mr. Paterno has been interviewed by investigators. You can see that he has testified in the grand jury that he reported this to individuals in the administration—being Mr. Curley and Mr. Schultz—as far as what occurred that night. He's been cooperative with the investigators in this case. He's not regarded as a target at this point."

However, the question had shifted: it was no longer about Paterno's meeting his legal responsibility; it was, as one Paterno family member bitterly called it, "the Joe Paterno morality clause." Had Paterno done enough *beyond* the law? Had he used what so many people saw as his immense power to stop Jerry Sandusky? Linda Kelly basically talked around the question: "I would have to say that all of us standing up here are law enforcement officials, and that we deal with evidence. . . . Those of us that have been in the law for a while know that there is a difference between moral and legal guilt. Right now, those of us up here right now are concerned with legal guilt."

This wasn't entirely true. One of the people on the podium with Kelly was Police Commissioner Frank Noonan. After the press conference ended, Noonan made his way out to the reporters. He had something to say: "Somebody has to question about what I would consider the moral requirements for a human being that knows of sexual things that are taking place with a child. . . . I think you have the moral responsibility, anyone. Not whether you're a football coach or a university president or the guy sweeping the building. I think you have a moral responsibility to call us."

The story was charging toward Paterno at warp speed. Even if

Noonan had not said anything at all, the question of whether Joe Paterno lived up to his moral responsibility would have been asked again and again, in offices and bars and churches across America. It would have been argued ceaselessly because he was Joe Paterno, the all-time winning coach, architect of The Grand Experiment, and he had been celebrated for almost a half century as a man of integrity. "Paterno was always the lead—what did he know and when did he know it," *USA Today* columnist Christine Brennan said at a media panel in late November on the Penn State campus. Mark Viera of the *New York Times* agreed. "We understood that the story was Paterno," he said later.

So, yes, the shift toward Paterno was inevitable. However, Noonan's statement did give a certain authority to the questioners. "Official Says Paterno Failed Moral Test" was a typical headline. And it would cast a shadow on everything Paterno said. When he said the 1998 incident had nothing to do with Sandusky's retirement in 1999, many didn't believe him. When he said McQueary was vague about what he said in 2001, many didn't believe him, even after McQueary concurred under oath. When he said he did not know about Sandusky's alleged crimes and that if he had understood he certainly would have done more to stop him, many did not believe that either.

On Monday, Paterno coached practice while the media swarmed his home. He had a regularly scheduled Tuesday press conference, and when he got home he prepared what he would say. He intended to use that press conference to explain what he did and when he did it.

On Monday night, Penn State sent out a press release to the media stating that Paterno would answer questions only about football. Paterno said they never talked about it with him.

Scott Paterno told his mother, "I think you need to brace yourself. They could fire Dad."

"Scotty, that will kill him," she replied.

• • •

JOURNALISTS BEGAN TO LINE UP outside the football stadium three hours before the press conference on Tuesday morning. It was a beautiful November day. On one side of the stadium, students rested and studied in the tent village they called "Paternoville," waiting for front-row seats to one of the biggest games of the year. The Nebraska game was huge, but that was just football. Around the corner from Paternoville, journalists were camping out for front-row seats to the biggest press conference the school had ever had.

Back at the house on McKee Street, the family prepped Paterno for the press conference. It was not going well. He had never developed the talent for being concise. He had never needed to. His whole life he had rambled. This was a charming quality when people were asking him about, say, Al Davis, and he started to talk about all the people who had grown up in Brooklyn. In this case, though, his ramblings made him sound unsure. Even in the short time he had spent before the grand jury, he had rambled. Here is his answer when asked if "fondling" was the right term to describe what McQueary had told him:

> *Well, I don't know what you would call it. Obviously, he was doing something with the youngster. It was a sexual nature. I'm not sure exactly what it was. I didn't push Mike to describe exactly what it was because he was very upset. Obviously, I was in a little bit of a dilemma since Mr. Sandusky was not working for me anymore. So I told—I didn't go any further than that except I knew Mike was upset and I knew some kind of inappropriate action was being taken by Jerry Sandusky with the youngster.*

One simple question led to all sorts of twists and turns of thought; there was a hint in there about his feelings toward Sandusky as a former employee, a bit about how McQueary hadn't really gone into any detail, a suggestion that Paterno didn't really know what had happened. Each of these could lead to a dozen other questions. And each of those questions, given the way Paterno rambled, could lead to dozens more.

Family and friends play-acted as reporters and fired questions at him: Did you know about 1998? What did McQueary tell you? Why didn't you go to the police? Why didn't you follow up? Paterno answered, got upset, answered again, rambled a bit more.

There was talk of having Paterno just read a statement, and one was crafted. It was never read.

The reporters who knew Paterno best understood that this press conference was going to be a fiasco of the highest order. With his hearing problems, his age, his crankiness, and his susceptibility to talking around his answers, along with the blood-in-the-water media frenzy that was building, they knew this press conference would make things much worse for him. "It will be a living funeral," one reporter predicted, echoing words Paterno had used through the years.

About an hour before the scheduled time, a representative of the university called Guido D'Elia and said the press conference had been canceled by order of the president. Later, a rumor surfaced that the university was going to have its own press conference.

"That's it," D'Elia told Paterno family members. "They're going to take Joe out."

STANDING IN FRONT OF BEAVER Stadium, Penn State's sports information director, Jeff Nelson, made the brief announcement that the press conference had been canceled. He refused to take questions. But there were hundreds and hundreds of journalists who had stories to write, reports to file, hours to fill. For a time, the reporters stayed out in front of the stadium and interviewed each other. Some walked over to Paternoville to get some thoughts from the students. Many went to McKee Street to stand in front of Joe Paterno's house.

McKee is a quiet, tree-lined street just off campus. The Paternos' house is the last house on the left; it backs up into Sunset Park. For the next few days, the parking lot of Sunset Park was crowded with satellite trucks. Media people stood across the street, on a neighbor's lawn, and pointed their cameras and their notepads at the front door of Joe Paterno's house. It looked more like a movie set than reality. Mary Kay remembered being nervous pulling the car into the garage for fear that she might clip the side and gain a national reputation as a bad driver. Other family members remembered looking out the window and seeing their neighbor raking autumn leaves in between the legs of camera tripods.

With the press conference canceled, the crowd around the house grew exponentially, and there was a new aggressiveness in the air. At one point, Scott accompanied Joe to the car to drive to practice. After Joe left, Scott was blasted with questions and, in the madness, tried to respond as best he could. It was another turning point. The scene had become unmanageable. The Paternos had always handled things in a small-town way. They entertained recruits and boosters at their home, with Sue making the food, Mary Kay and Diana washing the dishes, Scott and David eating the leftovers. They were never comfortable with the millions of dollars they made and gave much of it back to the school. They had lived their lives as though in a Norman Rockwell painting. But now Guido and Jay and Mary Kay looked outside, saw Scott drowning, and they knew: This wasn't a small-town issue anymore. The big city had roared in. They needed an expert. "It was time for a Hail Mary," Guido said. Scott agreed.

That night they called consultant Dan McGinn, whose job, in his own words, is "to help our clients solve their most complex problems." He had worked with Coca-Cola, Texaco, the London Stock Exchange, and General Motors. "I know why you're calling," were the first words out of McGinn's mouth.

JOE PATERNO WANTED TO TALK. He wanted to rush out into the crowd of reporters and have an impromptu question-and-answer session. He wanted to hold a press conference on his back patio. He did not like being silenced, and he was beginning to feel that he was being scapegoated. He was beginning to feel that some of the people who had wanted him fired years earlier now saw their chance. The story had gotten away from them. Now people were writing and saying that he didn't do anything when he was told that a child had been raped. People were writing and saying that it was ridiculous to call Tim Curley Paterno's boss. "He was the king of the whole state; he had no boss," one reporter said on television. People were writing and saying that Paterno certainly knew—he had to know—about Sandusky's crimes and that he had covered them up to protect his own legacy and his good friend Sandusky instead of protecting children.

When Dan McGinn arrived at the Paterno home, the Paterno family and friends were almost physically holding Joe back from giving a press conference right then and there. McGinn made a couple of quick assessments: First, Paterno was in no shape to speak to the media; with the atmosphere this toxic, anything he said would make their situation much worse. Second, Paterno was going to have to retire; the damage had been too great.

This is when McGinn learned just how far Paterno's influence and reputation had fallen. He asked D'Elia for the name of one person on the Penn State Board of Trustees, just one, whom they could reach out to, to negotiate a gracious ending. D'Elia shook his head.

"One person on the board, that's all we need," McGinn said.

D'Elia shook his head again. "It began in 2004," he whispered, referring to Paterno's clash with Spanier. "The board started to turn. We don't have anybody on the board now."

That's when McGinn realized that this was going to be the worst day of Joe Paterno's professional life. The family released the statement in which Paterno attempted to retire at the end of the season, but within an hour the news stories were reporting that the board might not give him the chance.

For the last time, Joe Paterno went to the Penn State football offices to coach his team in practice. He cried, the coaches cried, many of the players cried. Jay brought his son, Joey, to practice, something he almost never did. Joey idolized his grandfather. "I wanted him to always have that memory," Jay explained. At one point, Jay was standing in a place where he could see a silhouette of his father against

Mount Nittany, and in the distance also see his son, and he felt a stinging in his eyes, a mix of pain and pride and a futile wish for time to stop.

Jay still believed that his father would be allowed to finish the season. He thought his father had earned that—at least that. Jay was playing tennis that night when his cell phone rang. His wife told him to call home. Joe Paterno had been fired.

FRAN GANTER, WHO HAD PLAYED for Paterno at Penn State and coached with him for more than thirty years, showed up at the Paterno house just before 10 P.M. Wednesday night with an envelope. Later Ganter would tell friends he did not know what was inside.

Paterno opened the envelope; inside was a sheet of Penn State stationary with just a name, John Surma, and a phone number. Surma was the CEO of U.S. Steel and the vice chairman of the Penn State Board of Trustees. Paterno picked up the phone and called the number.

"This is Joe Paterno."

"This is John Surma. The board of trustees have terminated you effective immediately."

Paterno hung up the phone before he could hear anything else.

A minute later, Sue called the number. "After sixty-one years," she said, her voice cracking, "he deserved better." And then she hung up.

There have been accounts—and certainly will be others—of what happened inside that board of trustees meeting. Graham Spanier was forced out. There was a suggestion that Paterno's statement, particularly where he directed that "the Board of Trustees should not spend a single moment discussing my status," was seen as insubordination. There were reports that, when there seemed to be some hesitation or loss of will, Governor Tom Corbett reminded the board, "Remember the children." Board members spent the next few months justifying their reasons and recasting the firing as something less contentious.

As ESPN's Don Van Natta reported, "He was simply relieved of his coaching duties but was allowed to continue on as an emeritus professor and would be paid his full salary under his contract, the trustees said."

Joe Paterno was fired. Why and how the board made its decision is not my story to tell.

The campus was overrun with emotion. A riot broke out, several students were videotaped overturning a television truck, more than thirty-five people were arrested, and there was at least $200,000 worth of damage. Penn State students would be mocked for, as one news site put it, "rioting for a child-molester enabler." Students gathered in front of Paterno's house, and Joe and Sue came out for a few moments, he in a gray sweatshirt, she in a red bathrobe. His short speech to the students was quintessential Paterno, filled with raw emotion and winding roads:

> *I want to say hello to all these great students who I love. You guys are great, all of you—when I say "guys," you know what I mean, you know I mean girls too. Hey, look, get a good night's sleep, all right? Study, all right? We've still got things to do. I'm out of it, maybe now. That phone call put me out of it. We'll go from here, okay? Good luck, everybody. Thanks. Thank you! And one thing: Thanks. And pray a little for those victims. We are Penn State.*

Elsewhere on campus, a group of students standing around the statue of Paterno cried silently.

"Why are you crying?" I asked one young woman.

"Because everybody lost," she said.

AT 6 A.M. THURSDAY MORNING, Jay Paterno went to his father's house. He had not slept, and his eyes were red and swollen. The night before, he went through various phases of anger and outrage and disbelief. He told his son that his grandfather had been fired. Joey had a question: "When this is over, will we still be Penn State fans?"

"I don't know," Jay answered, and that is when he started crying, and he did not stop until he pulled himself together and went to his father's house. He could not get over the unfairness of it all. If Sandusky was guilty, everybody was fooled. The way he saw it, his father had followed university policy; he had done what he thought was right; he had heard about an incident and reported it. How could they fire him for this? How could they believe he knew about evils that nobody else seemed to know about?

Like the Penn State players, Jay always called his father "Joe" when they were on the field or in a game. But this was a private moment. "Dad," he asked, "what do you think I should do?"

"Is there even a question what you should do?" Joe replied. "You have to coach the kids. That's not even a question."

Tom Bradley, Paterno's longtime assistant coach and now the interim head coach, held a press conference. He stuck tightly to his script, calling Joe "Coach Paterno," referring four times to the "ongoing investigation," and saying, "That's up to the administration" three times. Bradley was a Pittsburgh guy who had played for Paterno, coached for Paterno, and liked saying that Paterno yelled at him more than anybody, even Sue. Only once did he go off script to say, "Coach Paterno will go down in history as one of the greatest men. Maybe most of you know him as a great football coach. I've had the privilege and honor to spend time with him. He's had such a dynamic impact on so many, so many, and I'll say it again, so many people and players' lives. It's with great respect that I speak of him, and I'm proud to say that I worked for him."

If Bradley had said such words even one week earlier, no one would have blinked. People had said things like this about Paterno countless times through the years. But this was not the week before; now people wondered how anyone could say anything good about Joe Paterno. As I was writing this book, the line between the Time Before and the Time After became clear: Before November 5, 2011, it was very difficult to find anyone willing to say a truly bad word about Joe Paterno. After November 5, it was far more difficult to find anyone willing to say a good word.

ON THURSDAY AFTERNOON, PATERNO MET with his coaches at his house. He sobbed uncontrollably. This was his bad day. Later, one of his former captains, Brandon Short, and his wife, Mahreen, stopped by the house. When Brandon asked, "How are you doing, Coach?" Paterno answered, "I'm okay," but the last syllable was shaky, muffled by crying, and then he broke down and said, "I don't know what I'm going to do with myself." Nobody knew how to handle such emotion. Joe had always been the strong one, had always seemed invulnerable. Jay claimed that the only two times he had seen his father cry were when Joe's mother died and when Adam Taliaferro was hurt on the football field. On Thursday, though, he cried continually.

"My name," he told Jay, "I have spent my whole life trying to make that name mean something. And now it's gone."

When Friday morning came, though, Joe was different. The crying was over. Nobody would ever see him cry again. Nobody would see him discouraged again. "It was like a transformation," Mary Kay said. "He had one bad day. But after that, he was positive."

"You know what?" Joe said. "I'm not going to feel sorry for myself. Are you kidding? I've lived a great life. Healthy children. Healthy grandchildren. Loving wife. I look around the world and see people who have real problems, serious problems. I'm the luckiest guy."

The stories swirled on television and radio, the Internet and newspapers, each getting progressively darker. A couple of people from Paterno's past, including Vicky Triponey, emerged to air their grievances. The press gave them a big stage. Anything resembling a Paterno defense was attacked mercilessly. When Franco Harris publicly defended his old coach, a Pittsburgh casino—a *casino*—put its relationship with Harris on hold. There was talk of canceling the rest of the Penn State football season. Paterno stayed silent. He watched the Nebraska game on television. Penn State lost 17–14.

A few days later, it was announced that Paterno had lung cancer. He had not felt well for a few weeks, but he would not have gone to see the doctor had he still been coaching. When the doctor gave him the diagnosis, Paterno felt confident he would beat it. In their press release, the family described it as "treatable." They always did hope for the best.

"We had been through so much," Sue Paterno recalled. "And I always thought, in the end, we would win."

Paterno walks off the field before a game against Notre Dame *(Jason Sipes/Altoona Mirror)*

Finale

There were good days and bad the last month and a half of Joe Paterno's life. Most of them were bad. Outside, the cancer diagnosis was seen as something unreal. If Paterno's life had been a novel, an editor would have insisted there be some time placed between Paterno's firing and the discovery of the cancer that would end his life. But it happened all at once in real life. And while the cancer diagnosis was seen by the outside world as merely another surreal part of a surreal story, it was from Paterno's perspective all that mattered. The chemotherapy and radiation wrecked him. When he got out of bed one evening and tried to go to the bathroom without turning on the light, he fell and broke his pelvis. He was in pain except when medicated.

Every now and then he seemed like his old self. He loved the television show *M*A*S*H*. The show had gone off the air in 1983, but he was too busy to watch it then. Now he watched the show every chance he could, and he talked about it often. "Alan Alda is an Italian kid from Brooklyn, I think," he would say. Alda was actually an Irish Italian kid (nine years younger than Paterno) from the Bronx. But close enough.

He tried to be spirited. The family threw an eighty-fifth birthday party for him just before Christmas, and for that one day he seemed younger, not older. He told stories; he laughed at jokes. Friends called, former players showed up, and he came to life. Paterno did not party often, but when he did he was usually the most enthusiastic person in the room.

Most days, though, he felt tired. The treatments were hard on him. He refused to be somber. In many ways, he reverted back to the young man who sent cheery letters home from Korea. He talked about getting better, traveling with Sue, maybe writing down a few of his thoughts for a book. He talked about writing a book of poetry. "My poems will rhyme," he promised. But as the days went on, it grew harder and harder for him to build up his energy even for such thought. Outside his home, outside State College, it was open season on Paterno. The Big Ten Conference took his name off their football trophy. Jim Boeheim, the Syracuse basketball coach whose team had once been banned from tournament play by the NCAA for recruiting violations, told reporters, "I'm not Joe Paterno," when child molesting allegations were made against his longtime assistant coach. Former Oklahoma coach Barry Switzer insisted that Paterno and his staff had to know about Sandusky. (An outraged Galen Hall called Switzer to say that he had been Switzer's assistant coach for years and didn't have any idea of some of the private stuff Switzer had been doing.) *Sports Illustrated* put a photo of a downtrodden Paterno on the cover under the headline "The Failure and Shame of Penn State." As Guido

D'Elia had predicted, dozens and dozens used Paterno's own words — misquoted, even — to assert that he should have done more.

Was Joe Paterno bitter? It is impossible, of course, to know his deepest thoughts. Again and again his formers players would call to check up on him and find, instead, that Paterno said: "Ah, don't worry about me. How is your family?" When he was told about someone on television or in the newspaper charging Paterno with grave sins, he would say: "Ah, the truth will come out." He had his dark moments, certainly, when he wondered how old friends could turn so suddenly on him and how people at Penn State, the school he had loved and championed for most of his life, could believe such terrible things about him. But by all accounts, he would not allow those dark moments to torment him. He read. He watched television. He talked with family and friends and former players. He talked about how the love people expressed for him overpowered the condemnation, fair and unfair.

"[The criticism] really doesn't matter," said Paterno in our last conversation. "It really doesn't. I know what I tried to do. Maybe everybody will see that in time. Maybe they won't. Maybe they will judge me by what I tried to do. Maybe they won't. What difference does it make? I just hope there's justice for the victims."

He was spent. After we talked, I called my wife to say that Joe Paterno would not live much longer. When she asked me what made me say that, I told her that Paterno had said, "If I make it through this, I think I'd like to travel to Italy again."

"So?" my wife asked.

"He said 'if.' And Joe Paterno is not an 'if' kind of person."

THE WEEK BEFORE PATERNO DIED, he did an interview with Sally Jenkins of the *Washington Post*, the only interview he would grant except for the conversations we had for this book. He and his team thought Jenkins was a good and brave journalist and that she would be fair. They had dinner with her at the round table in the kitchen.

Her story ran in the *Post* on a Sunday, and the family agreed it was fair. By then, Paterno was back in the hospital.

By Wednesday, most of the family suspected that Joe would never come out of the hospital. Sue, who had seen her oldest son, David, come back from near death, was the last holdout. She still hoped for a miracle. But reality was harsher this time. Too many organs were failing. By Saturday, everyone knew that it was a matter of hours. He was not in pain, but he was also unable to speak. People tried to read his eyes and his face as they came to say their goodbyes. Guido D'Elia leaned in close and told him, "We'll keep that stadium filled. We'll get the right players. We'll graduate them." At that point, Mary Kay said, "Look! His lips moved. He said 'Thank you.' "

"No, he didn't, Mary Kay," Guido said, smiling though there were tears in his eyes. "I worked with this man for forty years, and he never once said thank you."

They lined up, one by one, to share a final moment: his children, his wife, some of the players who were closest to him. Jay, who idolized his father probably more than anyone, wrote some football plays on a pad. There was I-Right 643, the pass to Gregg Garrity that had won the 1982 championship. There was Slot Left 62Z, a pass to Bobby Engram that won the game at Michigan in 1994. Jay leaned in close to his father and said, in his strongest coach's voice, "Remember how you always told us that you have to keep something back, something in your back pocket, something you will use when you need it most? Well, if you held anything back in your life, now's the time. Use it now! Use it now!"

On Sunday morning, January 22, 2012, Jay again leaned in close to his father. This time he whispered, "You've done all you can do." Moments later Joe Paterno died. The obituary in the *New York Times* led with a paragraph stating that he had won more games than any other major college coach, became the face of Penn State and a symbol of integrity, and had been fired during a child sexual abuse scandal. Joe Paterno was eighty-five when he died. People lined up for three days to walk by his casket. They lined the streets of State College as his hearse passed through. At the memorial, his son Jay led the gathering in a reading of Joe's favorite prayer, the Lord's Prayer:

> *Our Father who art in heaven,*
> *Hallowed be thy name.*
> *Thy Kingdom come,*
> *Thy will be done*
> *On earth as it is in heaven.*
> *Give us this day our daily bread.*
> *And forgive us our trespasses*
> *As we forgive those who trespass against us;*
> *And lead us not into temptation,*
> *But deliver us from evil.*
> *For thine is the kingdom,*
> *And the power, and the glory,*
> *Forever and ever.*
> *Amen.*

Joe Paterno would end every game by gathering the players and reciting the Lord's Prayer. He loved it—not so much for religious reasons but for the words. Look. The Lord's Prayer uses the words "us" and "we" and "our." It doesn't use the word "I" or "me" or "mine." Paterno understood. It's a team prayer.

Joe Paterno gets carried off the field after winning his first national championship
(*Penn State University Archives, Pennsylvania State University Libraries*)

{ *Encore* }

When Diana, Joe Paterno's oldest child, was getting her master's degree in business, she wrote a paper about how to motivate people without offering monetary rewards. She called to interview her father. He told her that he found he had to treat everyone differently. Some of his players responded to screaming; some did not. Some responded to praise; some did not.

"How did you know which was which?" she asked.

"I wasn't always right," he answered. "Sometimes I missed the mark. Sometimes I thought they could handle it when they couldn't. But I think I was right most of the time."

Diana laughed when thinking about this. Her father was hard on her. He expected her to do well, to stand up for herself, to do the right thing even when it was hard. The expectations were always there. She was not allowed to wear jeans, and straight A's were expected. As she said, "Dad could be very intimidating." But she also remembered him growling, pretending to be a monster, and chasing her and the other kids around the house. She remembered him reading to her at night. And, of course, she remembered the dinner table conversations.

Shortly after Joe died, Sue gave Diana a letter Diana had written to her father in 1981, the year she turned eighteen and headed off to college, shortly after a friend's father had passed away.

Dear Dad,

Going to Chrissy's father's viewing tonight made me realize how much my own father, you, means to me. I never really get the chance to tell you how much I love you. I owe everything I am to you and Mom—all my values and knowledge. You've taught me so much about life—the importance of being yourself and doing what you feel is right, because in the end you have to live with yourself. You've also shown me how much honesty means, and treating everyone equally, never being snobby and accepting people for what they are while respecting their beliefs.

You've taught me so many other things too, not just by word of mouth, mostly by example! I will always admire and respect your integrity and selflessness. I can only pray to be half the person you are.

I think I've finally realized the meaning of growing up. It's learning to accept and respect yourself and to always do what you know is right ("To thine own self be true!"). I think I have a pretty good idea of who and what I am.

Your little girl always.

"Since he died," said Diana, "I have thought a lot, 'What would Dad do?' I thought about his character, the whole thing, the board of trustees, the way it ended. People talk about revenge or getting back at people or whatever. That's not what Dad would have wanted. He would have wanted the truth to come out. That's all."

———

JOHN SKORUPAN PLAYED FOOTBALL AT Penn State and graduated in 1973. He became a salesman, and in his daily life he would think often about how Paterno had always told his players that they needed to play every down believing that they would make the big play that would turn the game around. Of course, most of the time they would not make that play or even have the chance to. But every so often, Paterno told them, the opportunity will arrive: the ball will come your way, your opponent will make a slight mistake, your anticipation will perfectly meet the moment. And the only way to make it work is to be ready for it. "There will be opportunities that will change your life," he remembered Paterno saying. "You need to be ready."

———

JIM BRADLEY—THE BROTHER OF TOM Bradley, who had replaced Jerry Sandusky as Paterno's top defensive assistant coach, and had become the interim coach after Paterno was pushed out—also played for Paterno. He became an orthopedic physician in Pittsburgh after he finished playing at Penn State. He remembered the time he crashed into Paterno during practice. Paterno had a knack even as a young man for getting in the way in practice.

"I thought I killed him right there and then," Bradley said. "Amazingly, he springs up and says, 'I didn't hurt you, did I?' "

———

TIM JANOCKO WAS A RESERVE player in the 1970s, and when he graduated he became a high school coach. One day, late in Paterno's life, Janocko showed up at Paterno's office early for a gathering of the Pennsylvania Scholastic Football Coaches Association. Even in his fifties, Janocko was still living on Paterno time.

He arrived early enough that Paterno could give him a tour of the offices. When Janocko was playing, Paterno once asked him, "Have you ever heard about the guy who didn't get ulcers but was a carrier?" This was the sort of thing Paterno said to players. Now, though, Paterno stopped and said, "Janocko, I'm proud of what you've done with your life. You're helping kids."

"I'm fifty-two," Janocko would say, "and I teared up. It meant that much to me."

———

THE CHILD VICTIMS OF JERRY SANDUSKY—their names replaced by numbers as they grew older and told their stories—would see Joe Paterno as the man who should have saved them. Many could have stepped forward, of course: Sandusky was surrounded by people who were supposed to be experts at spotting and preventing child abuse. He was the most recognizable of figures in State College, almost as unmistakable as Paterno. Over the years, many people could have understood Sandusky's crimes and stepped forward to stop him.

But it is Paterno who stands out. Some would call him all-powerful. Some would say he was a past-his-prime coach clinging to his job. Some would argue that he led a cover-up to protect his legacy; others that he was simply one in a faltering chain of command.

But in the end he did not stop Jerry Sandusky. "Find the truth," he told me. This, in the storm, is the closest thing I could find.

———

MARY KAY PATERNO NEVER LIKED it when people called her father a saint, but she was never entirely sure why it bothered her so much. She thought maybe it was because it wasn't true; she knew her father to be opinionated and cranky and tough to be around sometimes. But she thought there was something bigger involved in her reaction.

At the end, when people who did not know her father charged him with horrible crimes and sins, she thought she understood. To call someone a saint or a fiend is to reduce him to cardboard, to turn his life's decisions into mere computer code, to invest him with super-human powers—in other words, to make him unlike real people.

One of her favorite photographs was of her father sitting on a park bench outside the Creamery in State College, eating an ice cream cone. He loved ice cream. He would chomp on pretzels when he worked. He sang off-key. He often dragged an old chair out to his back porch and would roll up his pants and design game plans in the sun.

"He always tried," she said. "That's what I take from him most."

———

HIS AMAZING MEMORY: THAT'S WHAT so many of them thought about after they graduated. Jim Litterelle graduated from Penn State in 1967, so Paterno was still an assistant coach under Rip Engle when he recruited Litterelle. Still, Litterelle remembered the scene of Joe at the dining-room table, talking to his mother and father, laughing.

About twenty-five years later, Paterno was speaking at a luncheon, and there was a line of people waiting to get his autograph. As he looked up he saw Litterelle.

"Hi, Jim!" he shouted. "I still remember the cheesecake your mom served Rip and me when we came to your home to recruit you."

———

TED SEBASTIANELLI WENT INTO THE National Guard after he graduated from Penn State in 1969, and fifteen years later he visited Paterno. They talked about Ted's sister Lisa and a Penn State cheer-leader who also happened to be named Sebastianelli. Paterno asked if they were related. "No," Ted said. "My sister is older than her."

"She," Paterno said sharply. "Older than she."

Sebastianelli was embarrassed to have bungled the language in front of his old coach. But a year later, he was watching a Penn State game on television, and he heard the color commentator Pat Haden, a Rhodes scholar, admit that Paterno had corrected his English in their pregame meeting. And Sebastianelli felt better.

"To this day," he said, "whether I'm reading, writing, speaking, or listening, it's as if I have a little voice in my head asking me, 'Is that word used correctly?' "

———

TAMBA HALI, WHO WOULD GO on to be an NFL star, remembered Paterno yelling at him, "You are the dumbest player to ever play for me." He remembered it as one of the cruelest things anyone had ever said to him. But more than a decade later he found the story hilarious, a story he liked to tell again and again.

Ron Pavlechko would become a high school coach and athletic director in State College, and he recalled Paterno screaming, "Pavlechko, keep up that effort and you'll never be anything but a journeyman!"

"I have always relied on that comment for fuel," Pavlechko said. "I have relied on it every day for my entire life. I did not want to be a journeyman."

Matt Millen, who became an NFL star, a team general manager, and a television personality, would never forget the day in 1979 when Paterno stripped him of his captaincy and told him, "Millen, you're never going to amount to anything." It took Millen a while to come to grips with some of the hard moments. Years later, he was at Penn State with his own children, chasing them around, trying to keep them in line. "And I look over at Joe," Millen said. "And he was laughing his head off."

———

SCOTT HETTINGER WAS NOT A highly recruited player; it took him four years to score his first touchdown. In his excitement, he left the ball on the ground and celebrated with his teammates. After the game, Paterno came over to Hettinger, who prepared himself for the coach's congratulations. Instead Paterno shrieked, "Hettinger, next time, hand the ball to the official. Act like you've been there before."

When Hettinger served in the navy, when he became an insurance salesman, when he was with his family, he thought about that. Act with grace. Always. Years later, when his mother passed away, he found a shoebox. Inside were dozens of little notes Joe and Sue Paterno had sent his family.

———

KEITH KARPINSKI WAS ONE OF many fine linebackers to play at Penn State. For thirty years, if you were young and wanted to be a linebacker, there was a good chance you wanted to play at Penn State. Karpinski did. His father, Carl, saw it differently. He saw other coaches from other schools aggressively recruiting his son. Paterno was nowhere to be found. "You call Paterno," Carl told Karpinski's high school coach, "and tell him if he wants my son to play for him he should come to the house for dinner."

Paterno came for dinner. There were more than thirty people at the table, including the mayor of Hamtramck, Michigan, Karpinski's hometown. At one point, Paterno saw Carl sitting off by himself in a lounge chair. "Hey Carl," he said, "you look like Archie Bunker sitting there in your chair." Archie Bunker, a character in the television show *All in the Family*, was famous for his ethnic insensitivities and general bigotry.

"Hey, watch your mouth, you dumb dago," Carl Karpinski said, doing his best Archie Bunker impression.

Keith was mortified. He rushed over to stop his father from saying any more, but there were Joe and Carl acting out scenes from *All in the Family*, calling each other all sorts of names, laughing. Karpinski went to Penn State, where he was a star on the football field, and he played briefly in the NFL. He became a school principal.

———

PATERNO WAS FAMOUSLY BAD WITH names. Well, players' names. Parents' names, wives' names, kids' names: those he never forgot. But players' names—even when he was talking to the media he would sometimes call players by their numbers.

When Rob Luedeke was a senior at Penn State, he started at center. Before the game against Rutgers in 1990, while Luedeke was stretching, Paterno walked by and said, "Hey, Bob, the guys tell me it's your birthday. What can I do for you on your birthday?"

Luedeke responded, "Joe, I've been here for five years now. You could call me Rob."

Everybody broke up laughing. Paterno replied in that famous squeal, "Ah, Luedeke, you're a wisecracker."

Luedeke became a district manager for Abbott Laboratories. "I live Joe's lessons every day."

———

DAVID PATERNO WAS ALWAYS WORKING, even as a young boy. Joe wanted it that way. David shined shoes and cut grass. He found a snow-blower at a garage sale and borrowed forty dollars from his father to buy it. (He paid the money back by shoveling the Paterno driveway for free in perpetuity.) And so on.

After his father died, he realized that he worked all those jobs because his father had taught him that a person was not meant to sit around; a person was meant to do. That was Sue's lesson too, of course. But there was an unspoken charge in the way Joe Paterno lived his life: that you had a duty to help people, to share your gifts with them, to leave things better than you found them.

David loved to climb and he loved to run. This was true before his near-tragic trampoline accident, but it was true afterward as well. He felt at his best in motion. And every now and again he would challenge his father to a race.

"I don't think I ever beat him," he said.

———

WHEN KEITH CONLIN WAS TEN, Paterno came to the house to recruit his older brother, Chris. This was in Glenside, Pennsylvania, a bedroom community of Philadelphia, and Keith saw an opportunity. He asked Paterno for fifteen autographs. He might have mentioned that he wanted one for every kid in his class. He might not have mentioned that he hoped to sell the autographs to those kids.

In any case, Paterno smiled and signed the autographs. But on the fifteenth, he looked into Keith's eyes and said, "Okay, this is the last one I'm signing. But in a few years I'm going to want your autograph." Keith smiled and nodded.

In 1991, Paterno showed up at the Conlin home again. And this time he looked at the eighteen-year-old Keith, who was now six-foot-seven and close to three hundred pounds, and said, "I'm here for your autograph." Keith Conlin signed with Penn State and became a dominant offensive lineman for the 1994 team that Paterno would always believe was as good an offense as there ever was in college football. Conlin got his master's in health education from Penn State and become a businessman in State College.

CHRISTIAN MARRONE HURT HIS KNEE severely, and not for the first time, during spring practice his sophomore year. Paterno sat him down and said, "Chris, we're not going to let you play football anymore. We could probably get this knee fixed enough for you to play, but then the same thing will happen, and the next time it happens you might not be able to walk. You're twenty years old, and you have a whole other life waiting for you. I want you in particular to think about going to law school. I know you want to try other alternatives, but I'm telling you, you can't play anymore."

Marrone looked up at Paterno with tears in his eyes.

Paterno continued, "Now, this doesn't mean you get a free pass. I want you to be part of our coaching staff. You will be a part of this team, and you will work your rear end off. But I want you to focus on school. You have the ability to do other things in life. And I promised your parents that I would do everything I can to help you do those things."

Marrone hated coaching, but he did it. Then he got his master's degree at the University of Pennsylvania and went to law school at Temple, all under Paterno's watchful eye.

Marrone had another story, though, one he liked even more. When he was a freshman and still had big ambitions to become a football star, he was sitting with the other freshmen on Christmas Eve. It was 1994, and they were in California getting ready for the Rose Bowl.

Christmas Eve was also the time when the grades came in, and the other freshmen were nervous. They had all heard about the way Paterno raged at freshmen about their grades. Marrone, however, felt good. He had made Dean's List. And so—he was still embarrassed to say this years later—he got a bit of perverse pleasure watching Paterno unload on his teammates. He listened to Paterno scream at these kids about how they were cheating themselves and their families and their team by not working harder in school. Marrone was sitting next to Jim Nelson, who was frantic because his grades were not good. He was right to be worried. "Nelson!" Paterno shrieked. "You're a slacker. A nobody. A nothing. You will never play football at Penn State with these grades." This went on for a little while. When Paterno was finished, he turned to Marrone, who waited for the praise.

"And you, Marrone!" Paterno screamed. "You made Dean's List. Big deal. You think that's something? You think you're going anywhere with the effort you put in? If you want to do something with your life, you've got to do a lot better than that."

Nelson graduated, played seven years in the NFL, and started several businesses. Marrone worked his way up to special assistant to the U.S. secretary of defense. "It was yet another lesson: Never be complacent," Marrone would say. "You can always do better."

———

SCOTT PATERNO, THE YOUNGEST SON, had a similar thing happen to him when he was in his first year at Dickinson Law School at Penn

State. Up to that point, Scott had seen himself as the screwup of the family, a view he was pretty sure he shared with his father. He had been sent to boarding school to straighten up, and he fooled around in college way too much. But at law school, he decided to apply himself, and at the end of the first semester, he was seventh in his class. Seventh! He was thrilled, and he could not wait to call home to tell his father. "I call him up, 'Hey, I'm seventh in my class,'" Scott recalled. There was a silence on the other end of the phone.

"Do you know what he said to me? He said, 'Six people are smarter than you, and you're okay with that?' That's it. Not 'Good job.' No, it was 'There are six people ahead of you, and you're calling me like you won? You're in seventh. You didn't win.'"

———

WE WERE SITTING AT JOE PATERNO'S table—me and him, alone—and he asked me to stop questioning for a moment. This was a couple of weeks after he had been fired, when the madness was at its height. He had just been through a dreadful coughing fit, and his face was still red from the effort. He asked me: "So, what do you think of all this?"

I told him that it was crazy, but that was not what he was asking.

"What do you think of all this?" he asked me again.

I had not intended to include this in the book. It was a personal moment between writer and subject. But as the story has played out, I decided it was important. I told him that I thought he should have done more when he was told about Jerry Sandusky showering with a boy. I had heard what he had said about not understanding the severity, not knowing much about child molestation, not having Sandusky as an employee. But, I said, "You are Joe Paterno. Right or wrong, people expect more from you."

He nodded. He did not try to defend or deflect. He simply said, "I wish I had done more," again, and then he descended into another coughing fit.

———

BRANDON PARMER WAS A WALK-ON at Penn State with a specialty for long-snapping back to punters. He was, in other words, a player Paterno had no reason to pay attention to. But one day, when Parmer was a freshman, Paterno was watching special teams practice when he suddenly barked out, "Hey! Where is that red-headed kid from Cincinnati? Get him in there!"

Parmer was from Columbus, not Cincinnati. His hair was blond, not red. But he went in there. He would start for three years, long enough for Paterno to learn his name. One day, Parmer went into Paterno's office to ask for a scholarship. He pleaded his case by saying that if he blew a long snap, it could cost the university millions of dollars, perhaps by costing them a major bowl bid. Paterno gave him the scholarship. And from that day forward, Paterno had it in his mind that Brandon Parmer should go to law school. He did, and he became a tax analyst in Columbus.

"Very few players understand the *why* behind Coach's methods," Parmer said. "Coach Paterno's lessons made very little sense until after graduation and, with the benefit of hindsight, when we are thrust into the real world."

———

IN THE EARLY YEARS, PATERNO relied on his passion and forcefulness to impose his will on his younger players. But by the end, much of that was no longer necessary. He was a legend. He had won all those big games, coached all those great players. When John Bronson was a freshman, he was in awe of Paterno. Bronson was from Kent, Washington, one of the rare players who traveled across the country to play for Paterno, and it was all for this moment.

"Here! Here! And here!" Paterno shouted. As he said each "here" he pointed, first to his head, then to his heart, then to his legs.

"Here!" he said again, pointing again to his head. "Here!" he said again, and he banged on his chest so hard that his glasses fell off. He did not even reach down for them. "And here!" he said again, and he pointed to his legs. "You got that, Bronson?" And he went on: If you don't have it in the head and you don't have in the heart, you can't have it in the legs. It all goes together. Mental. Spiritual. Physical. That's how it works on the football field, Paterno said. And that's how it works in life too. You have to think. You have to believe. And only then can you do.

Bronson knew, even then, that this was the lesson he would remember. He would be a starter at Penn State, graduate, play for a little while in the NFL, and then become a multifaceted businessman in Phoenix. "His words have been in my head every day, guiding me through my life."

———

CHRIS HARRELL WAS A GOOD player at Penn State. He was a cornerback and safety, and he could hit and cover and do everything else. When he was a sophomore, he went to talk to Joe Paterno about his future. He remembered the conversation like so:

> *Harrell:* Coach, I'd like to play in the NFL. What do you think my chances are?
> *Paterno:* I think you will be a governor or a senator before it's all said and done. That's how much I believe in your future. And I will do what I can to be at your first fund-raiser.
> *Harrell:* But what about my future in the NFL?
> *Paterno:* Chris, the scope of your future is much bigger than football. I believe you could run an entire state. There will come a point in life where you will have to choose what's more important: three new cars or a house with a three-car garage.

Harrell left the office furious. He believed the old man was trying to keep him down. He felt sure Paterno did not see his full potential.

A few months later, Harrell broke two vertebrae in his neck; he had to miss the entire 2004 season. He played, and played pretty well, in 2005, but he had a different outlook on life by then.

Harrell became a technology risk consultant at a big Washington firm. He would call it one step closer to public office. "There's no question I would be poor, disgruntled, and discouraged, if I had not had Joe's words to rely on."

———

KEVIN BLANCHARD TURNED DOWN SEVERAL scholarship offers and moved across the country from Texas to walk on for Joe Paterno. He would never forget the first time he met Paterno; he and his family had come to Penn State in the springtime on an unofficial visit. Paterno walked over to talk to them: "I would invite you to the house for dinner, but since this is an unofficial visit, the NCAA won't allow it."

Then he turned to Blanchard, who stood six-foot-six and weighed about 280 pounds. Paterno pulled out his index finger and began jabbing Blanchard in the chest as he explained what would be expected. Blanchard wrote it down from memory, and it reads like slam poetry:

> *If you come to Penn State*
> *JAB!*
> *You have to go to class*
> *JAB!*
> *And if you don't go to class*
> *JAB!*
> *I'm going to call you in my office*
> *JAB!*
> *Where I have a bat*
> *JAB!*
> *That I'll use*
> *JAB!*
> *To hit you over the head!*
> *JAB!*

And if that doesn't work
JAB!
I'm going to call your mother.
JAB!

Blanchard made the Dean's List in 2011. When Paterno died, he served as an honor guard for his coach's viewing.

———

SOMETIMES GUIDO D'ELIA WOULD WONDER if he could have done more for his old friend. "I'm not sad about Joe himself. I'm really not. Nobody can touch him now. He got to do exactly what he wanted to do his whole life. He spent his retirement coaching, if you think about it. And that's all he wanted to do."

"So why are you sad?" I asked him.

D'Elia looked at me, then slammed his fist on the table. "It wasn't a fraud. It was real."

He continued, "You know what Joe told me before he died? He said that he wasn't worried about his legacy. He said that in time, people would see that he tried to do the right things. He said that in time, people would be able to step back and see his accomplishments as well as his mistakes and judge him for the whole life."

"Do you believe that?" I asked.

"I don't know. I hope so. The only thing I do know for sure is that this is the end, my friend. There will never be another one like him."

———

SCOTT PATERNO REMEMBERED ONE MORE story. He was with his mother and father in a State College restaurant shortly after the Iraq War had begun. They were planning Scott's wedding. While they were eating and discussing logistics, three Muslim women walked in. They were wearing hijab, and Scott noticed a drop in volume in the restaurant as they sat down. There was a lot of tension in America then. The Paternos continued their conversation for a short while, but Joe kept looking over at the table of women. Finally, Joe said, "Excuse me for a moment." He walked over to the women, sat down at the table, and began a conversation with them, asking them where they were from, how they liked State College, what they were studying, and so on.

It was, Scott said, the smallest thing. But that might be the biggest lesson he learned from his father, the same lesson hundreds of football players learned: *Take care of the little things. The big things will take care of themselves.*

———

DON ABBEY KNEW JOE PATERNO in ways others did not. They were, over the years, coach and player, enemies for a long time, and finally, fitfully, friends. They were not alike, or at least Abbey did not see the similarities for many years. At one point, the lowest point, Abbey felt on the brink of destruction. He was an alcoholic. He could not see a life worth living. In large part, he blamed Joe Paterno.

Then Don Abbey became a billionaire. He was sitting at the head of a glorious dining-room table in his mansion overlooking Pasadena, and all around him were vases and paintings and rugs and imported stone and wood and the kinds of opulent things that both look and are obscenely expensive, things that substantiate a life powerfully lived. "Unlike Joe," he said, "I like spending money." Don Abbey was a billionaire, and for him this was the point. He won. When the problems of his job or his life felt too heavy, he retreated to his home a few miles above the city and soaked in the grandeur of what he had built. "I don't come down," he replied when I asked him how he handled the tough times. "It's through isolation. You just don't need to deal with all those people."

His fascination with Paterno had many flavors: hate, disgust, contempt, grudging respect, and then, finally, most surprising of all, fondness. Hundreds of men who played for him talked about going through these various Stages of Paterno, but it seems likely none of them reached the extremes that Abbey had. He was in Paterno's first recruiting class. He was Penn State's leading scorer on Paterno's first good team, in 1967. He was at the heart of things when Paterno became Paterno, when Penn State always won, when Vietnam raged and students protested and Nixon picked Texas and so many people chose Joe Paterno as their hero. To Abbey, Paterno most certainly was not a hero. Abbey thought Paterno was a bully and a tyrant.

"I kind of think, in retrospect, it's like what Nietzsche said: 'That which does not kill us makes us stronger.' Well, Joe made me really strong because he tried to kill me, and he damn near succeeded. And I don't think he did that to make me a better guy. I think he did that because I was difficult to coach, and he'd run out of ideas."

Abbey was one of the few who did not go to Penn State after being dazzled by the recruiting charms of Joe Paterno. Quite the opposite. His mother, unlike almost every other mother of a Penn State player, could not stand Paterno. The Abbeys had made their money in the granite business, and when Paterno sat at the table in their home he reminded Don's mother of those Italians who did the stonecutting in the business.

"I never wore jeans because jeans are what the stonecutters wore," Abbey said. "And we never ate pasta because pasta's what the stonecutters ate. So Joe, I think, reflected some of that to my mother. . . . She didn't like him. She still doesn't like him."

Abbey went to Penn State anyway, not because he liked Paterno ("I didn't really have an opinion of Joe"), but because he did not want to play at Boston College and "get educated by the nuns, being the white Anglo-Saxon Protestant that I am." When he left for college, his mother warned, "You're going to have trouble with that coach."

"Always listen to your mother," Abbey advised.

———

THEY CLASHED REPEATEDLY. PATERNO HAD a thing about players wearing socks all the time. Well, Abbey didn't wear socks. He came from prep school, where kids never wore socks. The two went round and round about that. It sounds simple and pointless, but they both remembered those socks. Of course, they went round and round about everything.

"In retrospect," Paterno said, "I probably could have been a better coach for Don. He was headstrong, and I was headstrong. I was just starting out, and I felt like I needed to prove myself all the time. I'm sure I could have done a better job with a lot of guys, and particularly Abbey."

When Abbey was a sophomore, he scored three touchdowns and kicked four extra points in a big win at Boston College. This was near his hometown, so reporters surrounded him. Paterno did not like it. He did not like stars. He did not like young players getting too much attention. He did not like Abbey's attitude. He was not comfortable or confident yet in his job; this win made his career record seven wins and seven losses.

Here is a paragraph in the *Daily Collegian*'s story of the game:

It didn't seem like Abbey could have done too much wrong, but Paterno saw it differently. "He's a young kid, he's got speed, but he makes too many mistakes." He then quipped to the Boston press, "If it weren't for Massachusetts, we might make him first string."

Abbey would remember Paterno walking up to the reporters and saying, "Why don't you get away from Abbey and talk to a real football player like Ted Kwalick." Abbey's father was standing behind Paterno at that moment and tried to pick a fight with him. It was tense. Abbey said that after the Boston College game, he didn't get the ball anymore. He was told to block for star running backs like Charlie Pittman, Franco Harris, and Lydell Mitchell. "I was going to quit. Twice. I thought, 'I don't need this shit, I'll go to Princeton.' I would have been an Ivy League guy. I'd probably have gotten into the leveraged buyouts of the 1970s and just be getting out of jail now for rigging something. So I guess my life has changed."

Abbey became a ferocious blocker. Penn State won every game his junior and senior seasons. But he and Paterno never got along. Paterno threw him off the team for a game in his senior year. Abbey went to Joe's house and watched that game on television with Sue.

When Abbey left Penn State, he told himself he was never coming back. And for twenty-five years he did not. He went through terrible lows. He had a drinking problem. He had trouble finding his way in business. He felt pain from his playing days, and from his college career not being what he had hoped. "We hit on Tuesdays back then. He was maniacal. I remember I was thinking about going into the Marine Corps because I was getting sick of Joe. I had gone down to see the Marine recruiters, and they knew who I was, so they wanted to go to practice.

"Joe let them on the field because he didn't feel like the Marine Corps wanted to steal anything he was doing. So afterward, we go down to Herlocher's—which was the only bar in town that served Heineken, by the way—and these were all former drill instructors. One of them was from Parris Island, and he says, 'You know, Don, if we did half of the stuff that Joe just did to you, we'd be court-martialed.' And this is the marines. That's how vicious Joe was.

"The coaches would walk around with wiffle-ball bats and hit you in the head if you lifted your head on a block. . . . And then Joe had this thing that someone invented that was this long steel pipe that had kind of a tripod on the end. And you would stand right under the tripod, and they would take this metal perpendicular pipe and put a punching bag on it. And they had a spring connected to it, stretch it, and they would hit a button and this thing would come down and you had to block it. They first had two springs on it, and it knocked out the first two guys, so they had to take one of the springs off. Who comes up with this? The Marquis de Sade?

"I wasn't going back. I didn't have any good memories from that time."

After a long while something changed. Abbey began to get his life together, began to build his business, and he started to think that blaming Joe Paterno was not beneficial. "In all fairness to Joe, I brought a lot of this stuff on myself. Because I didn't care." He found himself back at Penn State one day in the early 1990s, and he and Joe met. Paterno told him, "You know, Don, if only you'd come four or five years later, things might have had a different outcome." Abbey saw that as something close to an apology.

Then Paterno reached out to Abbey, tried to do whatever he could to help his business. Abbey wasn't wealthy then. "There wasn't anything I could do for him [in return]. I hadn't been there for twenty years. He had no dog in the hunt. Yet he was willing, for whatever reason, internally, he was willing to get out there and try to help me get my business going using his reputation." Paterno introduced Abbey to the businesspeople he knew. He wrote letters on Abbey's behalf. He tried to open as many doors as he could.

"Joe's management style was inappropriate. But his desires were very appropriate. . . . I think he has always had, to this day, if you can get him to focus, a real concern for the welfare of his players. Coat and tie. Be on time. Go to class or you don't play. He really did that stuff."

"Did you forgive him?" I asked.

"It wasn't for me to forgive," Abbey answered. "I just thought I understood him better."

———

JERRY SANDUSKY WAS A GRADUATE assistant coach on Abbey's first team. When the scandal blew up, Abbey felt many emotions. He had not been happy that Paterno kept coaching in those final years. "You know, he's got a horrific ego. I'm not judging that. Great guys have horrific egos. General Patton was not a mild-mannered guy. Larry Ellison [CEO of Oracle] is not a mild-mannered guy. The Microsoft guy [Bill Gates], he's trying to change the world, and you just don't do that on a little ego.

"You look at Joe, and Joe was a very interesting guy, and I don't understand it because I came from the exact opposite thing. Joe had no liking for money. Joe lived in that austere house, and I know how much money he was making with Pepsi and Nike and Burger King. He was doing really, really well. . . . He didn't care about money, and he didn't care about fame, and he didn't care about the damned wins record. He didn't care about any of those things."

"So, if it wasn't money, and it wasn't fame, and it wasn't the wins, then . . ."

"To me, his ego was driving him because it was all about Joe Paterno. He just got buzzed at those press conferences; he loved telling [reporters] to piss off. . . . I just think he liked being the boss. He liked being in charge. That drug of being in charge was what drove him. . . . He defined himself by what he did. I can talk about that because I define myself the same way."

Abbey wondered just how much Paterno knew about Sandusky. He could not help but wonder. There were so many stories buzzing around, and one contradicted another. I asked Abbey what it all came down to, and this is what he said: "You have to throw all your personal observations and opinions out of the discussion to really understand or appreciate what Joe did. Could he have done it a different way? Yes. But that wasn't in his DNA, so he couldn't have done it a different way. So the result is, he got this phenomenal won-lost record, and he's got this phenomenal graduation rate, and he's got a lot of guys that went through his system that have become extremely successful. And that's his accomplishment. That's what made him great. Not a bad decision, if it was a bad decision, at seventy-five. Not the fact that he stayed too long.

"Joe has all these human flaws that I love to talk about because I have a bunch too. . . . But still you've got to look at the scales, and balance accomplishments versus the negatives. And boy, the accomplishments, no matter how he did them, overwhelm the negatives. And if that's not the definition of a positive, productive life, I don't know what is."

—

IN THE END, JOE PATERNO will not have one legacy. No one does. Perhaps a life is too large to measure by its best day, or its worst. Maybe Don Abbey is right; maybe you measure life with a scale, good on one side and bad on the other. Then again, maybe life is measured by what is left behind. Paterno's teams won 409 games, a record; five times his teams went undefeated; twenty-four times they won their bowl games. His teams graduated between 80 and 90 percent of their players, and there was almost no gap between the graduation rates of white and black players. Paterno gave millions of his own dollars to build the Penn State library, the spiritual center, the Paterno Fellows Program for Liberal Arts, and he raised many millions more for charities and every aspect of campus life. He also died less than two months after he was pushed out of his job for what a Penn State board member called a "lack of leadership."

Maybe a life is best measured by what people remember; with Paterno, the players and his family mostly remembered the words he shouted at them, again and again, autumn after autumn:

Take care of the little things, and the big things will take care of themselves. Always run to the ball. Hope for your opponent to play well. If you want to be a good person, hang out with good people. Winning is a habit, but losing is also a habit. On your way down, think about getting up. You have to believe you're destined to do great things. Publicity is like poison: it can only hurt you if you swallow it. The will to win is important, but the will to prepare is vital. You cannot be afraid to lose. A man's reach should exceed his grasp. If you're not early, you're not on time. You have to find a way to make big plays. You either get better or you get worse, but you never stay the same. If you keep hustling something good will happen. Don't do anything that would embarrass yourself, your family, or your team. The team that makes fewer mistakes wins.

Maybe the last of these sentences is the truest. Maybe the team that makes fewer mistakes wins.

—

"SO TELL ME SOMETHING, GIUSEPPE, how are you going to get my whole life into one book?" Paterno asked me on our last visit.

"I have no idea," I told him. "It's a big life."

"Yeah, it's not bad," Joe Paterno said. "Not bad at all."

A Note on Sources

The vast majority of material in this book was obtained through several hundred interviews and email exchanges, along with access to Joe Paterno's personal files and letters, granted by Paterno and his family. In cases where previously reported information was used, I have tried to acknowledge the sources directly. When quotes were given in a public setting, such as a press conference, and were reported in more than one publication, I was more general (for example, "Paterno told reporters").

I wish to express special gratitude to all the Paterno family— especially Joe and Sue Paterno—for their openness. Every member of Joe Paterno's immediate family was generous, both in their participation and their patience, but I would particularly like to thank Mary Kay Hort, Jay Paterno, and Scott and Heather Paterno. In addition, I thank the Paterno Library, the Nixon Library, the Brown University archives, Guido D'Elia, Penn State's sports information director, Jeff Nelson, Dan McGinn, Mara Vandik, Paul Levine, John Schulian, Bill Blatty, Rich Scarcella, David Jones, Tom Donchez and the many people involved with the documentary *The Joe We Know*, and the good people at the Mid-Continent Public Library in Kansas City. I also want to make special mention of Don Abbey; the long interview he gave me in his home was thoroughly enlightening.

A selected bibliography follows, but I would like to make note of three books that were particularly helpful. First there was Joe Paterno's autobiography, *Paterno: By the Book*, written with Bernard Asbell. Second was the well-researched *No Ordinary Joe* by Michael O'Brien. And finally there was Lou Prato's *Penn State Football Encyclopedia*. No one knows more about Penn State football than Lou Prato, and he was kind and helpful throughout.

Selected Bibliography

Asbell, Bernard, and Joe Paterno. *Paterno: By the Book*. Random House, 1989.

Bergstein, Mickey. *Living Among Lions*. Trafford Publishing, 2007.

———. *Penn State Sports Stories and More*. RB Books, 1998.

Centre Daily Times Staff. *40 Years of the Joe Paterno Era at Penn State*. Canada Hockey LLC, 2006.

Denlinger, Ken. *For the Glory*. St. Martin's Griffin, 1994.

Fitzpatrick, Frank. *The Lion in Autumn*. Gotham Books, 2005.

———. *Pride of the Lions*. Triumph Books, 2011.

Hagdu, David. *The Ten-Cent Plague*. Farrar, Strauss & Giroux, 2008.

Halvonik, Steve and John Cappelletti. *Cappelletti: Penn State's Iron Horse*. Ethic Sports, 1998.

Hyman, Jordan and Ken Rappaport. *Playing for JoePa*. Sports Publishing LLC, 2007.

Hyman, Mervin D. and Gordon S. White. *Joe Paterno: Football My Way*. Collier Books, 1978.

Kriegel, Mark. *Namath: A Biography*. Viking, 2004.

Maraniss, David. *When Pride Still Mattered*. Simon & Schuster, 1999.

Missanelli, M. G. *The Perfect Season*. The Pennslvania State University Press, 2007.

Monti, Ralph. *I Remember Brooklyn*. Birch Lane Press, 1991.

Moore, Lenny and Jeffrey Jay Ellish. *All Things Being Equal: The Autobiography of Lenny Moore*. Sports Publishing LLC, 2005.

Newcombe, Jack. *Six Days to Saturday*. Farrar, Strauss & Giroux, 1974.

O'Brien, Michael. *No Ordinary Joe*. Rutledge Hill Press, 1998.

Paterno, George. *Joe Paterno: The Coach from Byzantium*. Sports Publishing LLC, 2001.

Pencek, Matthew and David Pencek. *The Great Book of Penn State Sports Lists*. Running Press, 2011.

Peterson, James A. and Dennis Booher. *Joe Paterno: In Search of Excellence*. Leisure Press, 1983.

Pittman, Charlie and Tony Pittman. *Playing for Paterno: A Father's and Son's Recollections of Playing for JoePa*. Triumph Books, 2007.

Prato, Lou. *The Penn State Football Encyclopedia*. Sports Publishing Inc., 1998.

Prato, Lou and Scott Brown. *What It Means to Be a Nittany Lion*. Triumph Books, 2006.

Riley, Ridge. *Road to Number One: A Personal Chronicle of Penn State Football*. Doubleday, 1977.

Rudel, Neil and Cory Giger. *They Know Joe*. Altoona Mirror, 2010.

Sandusky, Jerry and Kip Richeal. *Touched: The Jerry Sandusky Story*. Sports Publishing Inc., 2000.

Werley, Kenneth. *Joe Paterno, Penn State and College Football—What You Never Knew*. University of New Haven Press, 2001.

Acknowledgments

This book was the most challenging and emotional project of my life. Because of this, I am determined to keep these acknowledgments short; if I try to thank everyone who helped and guided me, I will double the word count. I hope I have personally thanked everyone who helped me, inspired me, and stood up for me while I was working on this book. If I have not, I promise I will soon. I will never forget your friendship.

I must begin by thanking Joe Paterno. He did not want me to write a book about him, but he was unfailingly kind and generous to me, even after the worst had happened. The only thing he ever asked of me, even at the end, was "Write the truth." I have done my best to live up to that mission. I thank the entire Paterno family, beginning with Sue Paterno, for their guidance, patience, and honesty. Diana, Mary Kay, David, Jay, and Scott, along with their spouses and children and close friends, gave of themselves for this book, even as their own lives were thrown into turmoil, and I will never have enough words of gratitude for them.

I want to thank the hundreds of players, friends, coworkers, fans, critics, and rivals who took the time to communicate their feelings about Joe Paterno. Many of their names are included in the book, but unfortunately at least as many of their names are not. Joe Paterno lived a big life. There are two other books, at least, on the cutting-room floor.

Too many friends helped for me to list them all, so I will name five: Mike Vaccaro, for pushing me through the darkest hours;

Tommy Tomlinson and Alix Felsing, for always being there for us; Michael Schur, for a frank conversation in a bizarre hotel lobby that I clung to often; and Bill James, who was my steadying influence in the storm. I must also take a moment to thank a hero of mine, David Maraniss, whom I did not know before I started this project, but whose wisdom guided me more often than I can say.

No acknowledgments section would be complete without a nod to the agent, and I am lucky enough to have the best one in the world, Sloan Harris at ICM. I do not have words strong enough to thank my editor, Jonathan Karp, who never wavered. From Simon & Schuster, I also want to thank assistant editor Nick Greene, whose blunt suggestions were of great help, along with art director Jackie Seow, marketing specialist Nina Pajak, associate publisher Richard Rhorer, publicists Anne Tate and Kelly Welsh, copy editor Judith Hoover, designer Joy O'Meara, production editor Jonathan Evans, production manager John Wahler, assistant managing editor Gina DiMascia and managing editor Irene Kheradi. I would also like to thank Terry McDonnell and the wonderful people at *Sports Illustrated* for their support, as well as Larry Burke and Steve Madden at my exciting new project, *Sports on Earth*.

I was fortunate to have Matt Brown as my research assistant, fact-checker, sounding board, and Penn State history buff. I could not have done this book without him. Someday, after Matt writes his fifth bestseller, his role in this book will make for a great trivia question.

Finally, I thank my family: first my parents, Frances and Steven Posnanski, who instilled in me everything that is good, and also my brothers and my in-laws. This book affected all of them. Then there are the three most important people in my life. I'm one of the lucky ones; my wife, Margo, is also my best editor and my best friend. Our daughters, Elizabeth and Katie, were so patient and supportive and did their homework throughout, often without complaining. Every now and again, though, they would ask, "Is the book written yet?" We had promised them a puppy when I finished writing. Well, girls, the book is written.

Index